THERE ARE
NO DEAD HERE

THERE ARE
NO DEAD HERE

A STORY OF
MURDER
AND DENIAL
IN COLOMBIA

MARIA
MCFARLAND
SÁNCHEZ-MORENO

NATION
BOOKS

New York

Nation Books
116 East 16th Street, 8th Floor New York, NY 10003
http://www.publicaffairsbooks.com/nation-books
@NationBooks

Printed in the United States of America

First Edition: February 2018

Published by Nation Books, an imprint of Perseus Books Group, LLC, a subsidiary of Hachette Book Group, Inc.

Nation Books is a co-publishing venture of the Nation Institute and Perseus Books.

The Hachette Speakers Bureau provides a wide range of authors for speaking events. To find out more, go to www.hachettespeakersbureau.com or call (866) 376-6591.

The publisher is not responsible for websites (or their content) that are not owned by the publisher.

Print book interior design by Cindy Young at Sagecraft Book Design.

Library of Congress Cataloging-in-Publication Data has been applied for.
ISBN: 978-1-56858–579-6 (hardcover); ISBN: 978-1-56858–580-2 (ebook)

LSC-C

10 9 8 7 6 5 4 3 2 1

For those who refuse to be silenced.

And for Seamus,
with love and hope.

Contents

PROLOGUE:
LAND OF SMOKE AND MIRRORS

"IF THIS COUNTRY KNEW THE whole truth, it would fall apart," Rodrigo Zapata announces, smirking at me. We are uncomfortably perched on a couple of battered plastic chairs next to a grimy desk in the stifling visitors' room in Itagüí prison, on the outskirts of the Colombian city of Medellín. This is the very same city that, while in the grip of co-caine kingpin Pablo Escobar more than two decades earlier, was known as the "murder capital of the world," on account of its astronomical rate of killings. When we meet, it is June 2014, and news coverage of Me-dellín is more likely to fawn over the city's world-class metro and librar-ies than to focus on the brutal realities on which its gleaming infrastructure rests. But if anyone knows about those realities, it's Zapata.

A soft, large man in his forties, in new sneakers, jeans, and a fresh blue-and-white-checked shirt on which he has affixed a small pin with the image of a Catholic saint, Zapata looks nothing like what you'd expect in a hardened criminal charged with multiple murders. A for-mer senior member of the country's vicious cocaine-running paramili-tary groups, Zapata had worked for one of their top commanders, Vicente Castaño—a man said to be so cold-hearted that he had his own brother assassinated.

Starting in the late 1990s, the paramilitaries carried out a bloody expansion campaign throughout much of Colombia. Fueled by an end-less stream of drug profits, they committed gruesome massacres in the name of defending the country from the brutal Marxist guerrillas of the Revolutionary Armed Forces of Colombia, or FARC (Fuerzas Armadas Revolucionarias de Colombia). They killed trade unionists, human rights activists, journalists, schoolteachers, and judges. They gouged out the eyes of their victims, tore off their limbs, and raped them in front of their families.

Nobody, it seemed, was trying to stop them: vast sectors of the gov-ernment and military secretly supported them. The United States, more interested in the appearance of success in its "war on drugs" than in stopping the carnage in a country that few in the United States understood, largely ignored them even as it poured billions of dollars into Colombia's military. Those who did dare to stand up to the para-militaries almost always ended up dead.

Swatting at the gnats hovering around us, Zapata tells me that he was mainly a financial adviser to Castaño, helping him with ac-quisitions for his farms and handling some of the group's "political" work, though he doesn't really explain what that means. He would later be convicted of leading a paramilitary unit operating along the Pacific coast of Colombia—one of the nation's poorest areas. The paramilitary onslaught in the region had forced thousands of Afro-Colombians and indigenous persons along the coast to flee their farms; in several cases, their land ended up fraudulently registered in the name of the paramilitaries' cronies. Even though the groups have supposedly disarmed, many of the original owners are still too terrified to return.

But things are starting to change. Over the past few years, some of the truth about the paramilitaries' relationships with senior members of Colombia's military forces and government has started to trickle out. My sources have described Zapata as a key player in handling those relationships. So I'm hoping that he will tell me more than what is already publicly known.

He doesn't. Sitting in front of me, Zapata is friendly, chatty, and far from frightening. He speaks with a child's glee at a new toy, and through his grin I catch a glimpse of tiny front teeth. Combined with his saucer-shaped eyes, they give him an almost cartoonish appearance, like an oversized toddler or teddy bear. Could this guy really be as bad as people say?

But few things in Colombia are what they appear to be.

THE FIRST TIME I traveled to Bogotá, Colombia's mountainous capital, a hailstorm hit the city. It was November 2004, and as my colleagues and I weaved our way through traffic from the airport to our hotel, clumps of ice the size of golf balls pounded the car's windshield. A gray haze enveloped us, obscuring the mix of run-down old homes, modern red brick buildings, and tall mountains that give the city its contours.

The hail surprised me. Having grown up in neighboring Peru in the 1980s and early 1990s, I thought I would be able to predict certain things about Colombia, including the weather. Rain was common in the mountain cities that I knew in Peru, but I had never seen hail. It was only the first time my expectations were shattered during that and countless other visits to Colombia over the next six years, when I covered the country as an investigator for the international organization Human Rights Watch.

Like the Peru of my childhood, Colombia had for years been ravaged by a brutal internal war between left-wing guerrillas (in Colombia
the most prominent were the FARC) and government forces. Even the
wealthier classes in the major cities were affected by the war: it was
hard for them to travel on highways or visit their country homes, because of the risk of kidnapping by the FARC. But, as in Peru, it was the
country's poorest and most vulnerable—indigenous people, peasants,
Afro-Colombians—who, trapped between the warring factions, bore
the brunt of the violence.

Of course, I knew going into Colombia that things would be different. In Peru, the war had been ideological, fought between the
government and the Shining Path guerrillas, who adhered to an extreme interpretation of Maoism that was similar to that of the Khmer
Rouge in Cambodia. In Colombia, the war between the government
and the FARC certainly had ideological roots, but after forty years it
had become much murkier, in part because of the explosion of the
drug war, which in the 1980s and early 1990s pitted the Medellín and
Cali cocaine cartels against each other and the Colombian government. Under the leadership of Pablo Escobar, the Medellín cartel
had carried out a bloodbath: bombings, assassinations, and kidnappings were in the news every day, and thousands were killed every
year in Medellín alone.

A joint US-Colombian operation had led to Pablo Escobar's killing
on the roof of one of his safe houses in 1993, but former Escobar associates linked to the country's shadowy right-wing paramilitary groups
had picked up the reins of a cocaine business far too profitable to drop.
These groups portrayed themselves as heroes trying to defend the
country from the FARC. Instead, they operated like a massive mafia,
seizing peasants' land for themselves or their associates, taking over
key drug-trafficking corridors, and killing anyone who got in their way.

By the time I started working on Colombia in 2004, the violence
had forced more than 3 million people—nearly a tenth of the country's
population—to flee their homes. Hundreds of thousands of Colombians had been killed, and thousands more were being held hostage or
had been forcibly "disappeared." Massacres had become so common
that nobody could say for sure how many had taken place over the
previous decade or two, as no one was counting. Guerrillas had recruited hundreds of children to serve in their ranks and laid

antipersonnel landmines around rural communities, regularly maiming civilians to protect their turf. The paramilitaries were enforcing their control in towns and cities through torture, threats, and murder, and hardly anyone was ever prosecuted or even investigated for these crimes.

I knew many of the facts—the numbers, historical events, and names—but nothing could prepare me for what I would encounter in the reality of the mother who told me about how paramilitaries had suffocated her seven-year-old daughter with a plastic bag, or another who described how she had attempted suicide after losing a leg—and her ability to work in the fields—to a guerrilla landmine. They would not prepare me for the courage of an activist in Villavicencio, Meta, who insisted on helping me meet with people to talk about the threats against them, even though every single one of her colleagues had been assassinated only a few years earlier. They would not prepare me for the news that the FARC had shot her as she traveled by boat down a nearby river—though, thankfully, she survived. They would not prepare me for the effervescence of a young politician in Medellín who, full of smiles, and without pausing, told me a long story about how paramilitaries were trying to take over local city councils. Nor would they prepare me for his murder in broad daylight by those same paramilitaries two years later.

Colombia is a country of extremes. There are extremes of weather, ranging from hail and sharp cold to tropical heat; and of terrain, with mountains, beaches, and rainforest within only hours of each other, and sometimes jumbled together. Fabulously luxurious homes and exclusive tourist resorts sit within miles of slums overflowing with people who live in crushing poverty. Joyful carnival celebrations and a rich heritage of music and dancing coexist with daily stories of tragedy and indescribable pain.

The suffering was on a scale that, as a relatively inexperienced activist in my twenties, I had not imagined. It often seemed as though everyone I met—cashiers at grocery stores, taxi drivers, newspaper editors, doctors—had a story; everyone had been touched by the war in one way or another. So many of the people I interviewed had witnessed or survived massacres and the destruction of entire towns, rapes, bombings, or the killing or disappearance of their parents, spouses, or children. And the nightmare was ongoing.

But behind some of these grim stories, there were also more subtle lessons, about right and wrong, about truth, and about hope. Many Colombians display a daily honesty, courage, and nobility in the face of grave danger that I still find hard to explain. Perhaps the best way to account for it is that in such a difficult place, sometimes integrity is the only solid thing to hold onto. At the same time, it is hard to match the capacity for cruelty, ruthlessness, and deception of some of the people I met.

All this is not to say that Colombians are themselves unusually good or bad people. But the circumstances in which they have found themselves are exceptional. So many Colombians have spent their lives in constant fear of death, of losing their families and homes, of being kidnapped. They have also lived knowing that, if they made certain choices—to take the bribe, join the local gang, or simply look away from their neighbors' and leaders' crimes—they could not only protect themselves and their families but also, perhaps, acquire wealth and power beyond their wildest dreams.

I am lucky never to have faced such stark choices. And who is to say what any of us would do in a similar situation? Living in a world shaped by these desires, opportunities, and fears, perhaps it is no surprise that some people grow as twisted and knotty as seaside trees battered by powerful, unpredictable winds. What is more surprising is that so many do not, and that, incredibly, a few go on to engage in acts of tremendous, if largely forgotten, heroism.

This book tells the stories of three such people—a prosecutor, a human rights activist, and a journalist—who, since the late 1990s, have made extraordinary sacrifices to expose the truth about the brutality and corruption that were engulfing their country long after the end of the government's war against Pablo Escobar, and to fight for a more just and humane society.

IN SOME WAYS, Zapata is right about the impact the full truth would have on Colombia: the country's success story is built on the quicksand of lies and half-truths. Getting to the bottom of it will require that Colombians begin to weave a new understanding of themselves, their society, and their leaders. To many, including the people whose stories I tell here, that fight is well worth it.

PART I

DEATH
MEDELLÍN, COLOMBIA, 1996–1998

Chapter 1

The Prophet

"Bloody events have been taking place in the Municipality of Ituango," Jesús María Valle began his letter to Álvaro Uribe, then governor of the Colombian state of Antioquia, as Valle's sister and receptionist, Nelly, punched the words into his worn Olivetti typewriter. "Numerous people have been murdered and disappeared, with no action being taken by the army, police, or attorney general's office to defend the population."

Valle had been growing increasingly alarmed about the situation in Ituango, a remote rural municipality in the north of Antioquia, where he had spent his early childhood working the land alongside his father. The now well-known lawyer and activist had never lost sight of his humble Ituango roots, and he had represented the region as a councilman for over a decade.

On many weekends, after five busy days of teaching law school classes, making court appearances, giving speeches, and drafting endless letters and briefs, Valle would slip out of his suit and tie and hop on a bus or drive the 120 miles on dirt mountain roads from bustling Medellín to Ituango. He would roam through the region's small towns, chatting with people who had lived there since he was small, or offering little treats to the children playing in the paths between houses.

Recently, his constituents, mostly impoverished peasants, had been telling him stories of groups of armed men in military camouflage, whom they called "paramilitaries," brazenly walking through their land, threatening them, and even killing people. The paramilitaries claimed to be fighting Colombia's left-wing guerrilla groups, but from what Valle was hearing, their victims were usually just ordinary community members whom the paramilitaries accused of having aided the guerrillas in some way, such as shopkeepers who might have sold food to them.

Valle had heard that the paramilitaries were working closely with the military and police in Ituango. In fact, several dozen of them were said to be based right outside the perimeter of Ituango's municipal capital, very close to where the Girardot Battalion, part of the Fourth Brigade of the army, was headquartered.

An especially violent attack happened on June 11, 1996, when about two dozen paramilitary troops descended in a couple of large trucks on the tiny Ituango town of La Granja and killed a string of locals—a construction worker, a mentally disabled farmworker, a housewife, and the coordinator of a technical training center. Valle heard about the massacre soon afterward, as La Granja was his birthplace and he was close to many of its people. He soon learned that the day before the massacre, the Girardot Battalion had inexplicably ordered most of its units operating in the area to relocate, giving the paramilitaries free rein. Thousands began to flee the region in fear.

Now, Valle was sounding all the alarm bells. He had little hope that Governor Uribe or the military would reply: for years he had been hearing stories and seeing evidence indicating that sectors of Colombia's military were colluding with the paramilitary groups. And Valle didn't trust Uribe. A young, stiff, fiercely intelligent lawyer from an affluent Antioquia family, Uribe sold himself as a progressive but seemed to have a single-minded fixation on pursuit of the guerrillas that translated into unquestioning support for the military. Valle feared that some of the policies Uribe backed—such as arming civilians—would allow for covert assistance to the paramilitaries.

Still, Valle knew that the only hope for Ituango's population was for the authorities to step in and protect them. He had to do everything he could to make that happen. That included creating a paper trail showing that the authorities were on notice of the bloodshed, which might make it harder for them to ignore their obligations.

Like other letters Valle sent to officials that year and the next, his November 20, 1996, missive to Uribe was a plea for help: "The anguish being experienced by the people—especially women, children, and the elderly—force me to request, very respectfully, your immediate intervention to protect the lives of the defenseless civilian population."

MOST COLOMBIANS PAID little attention to what was happening in Ituango—a mountainous region that, like much of rural Colombia, is still barely connected to the rest of the country by roads. Some parts of Ituango are entirely inaccessible except by boat and footpaths, or on muleback. Most of its residents were peasants who didn't have telephones in their homes. Some didn't even have electricity. Many never finished high school. Some were members of the Catío or Embera indigenous tribes. Few people moved there from elsewhere, and people from Ituango usually did not venture far from home.

But to Valle, Ituango was special: it was the region where, fifty-three years earlier, he had been born. It was where he had spent his early childhood, surrounded by green, orchid-dotted slopes and farms, as one of eleven siblings in a family that worked the land. The robust lawyer, with a broad, easy smile, strong brows, and a full head of dark hair, often spoke proudly to his friends of his rural heritage. And decades after having left Ituango, he retained a gentle, almost sweet accent that set him apart from others in the city. To him, Ituango was home. It was also the place where life, for a few years at least, had been peaceful.

Not that Colombia has ever known much peace: in just the one hundred years after it declared its independence from Spain in 1810, the country had lived through six civil wars, as well as multiple conflicts involving its neighbors. It was a starkly divided country—not only politically, between traditional Liberal and Conservative forces—but also, and more importantly, socially and geographically. For most of its history, the country's overwhelmingly poor peasant population had been scattered across different regions, each group with its own customs, economy, and power brokers. The Andes mountain chain that sliced the country's halves was at a low enough altitude to support vibrant agriculture, but it made travel and communication between communities difficult. The same was true for the rainforest covering much of the country's south and east, as well as the marshlands spread out along parts of the Caribbean and Pacific coasts. Meanwhile, the political class that governed the country from the mountainous capital of Bogotá consisted largely of city elites who, in many cases, had built their wealth as large landowners and industrialists, and had historically shown little interest in the plight of small landholders, peasants, and laborers, or in the country's varied indigenous and Afro-Colombian populations. These unresolved divisions, along with the exclusion of large majorities from power, set the stage for renewed brutality in the mid-1900s.

War took its first steps toward Valle on April 9, 1948, when he was five years old. Around noon that day, Jorge Eliecer Gaitán and a couple of his colleagues ambled out of his Bogotá office on their way to lunch. It had been an eventful couple of days for the charismatic politician, who was actively participating in the Pan-American Conference, which had brought together the United States and most of the countries in the region. These were the early days of the Cold War, and US officials had high hopes of using the conference to consolidate regional alliances, including through the establishment of the Organization of American States, nipping in the bud the Soviet influence in the Americas. Gaitán was not a communist, but he had earned wide acclaim with his calls for land reform and a reduction in the yawning gulf between the nation's rich and poor. A member of Colombia's Liberal Party, he was viewed with suspicion by his own party members, as he was an outsider to the political establishment that had ruled the country—through the Liberals or Conservatives—practically since its inception. But with popular support, he was gaining increasing prominence and power within the party, and he seemed on track to run for president that year.

As soon as the three men stepped out of the office building, an unknown assailant intercepted them, shooting Gaitán once in the head and twice in the back. Police quickly grabbed a man they identified as the killer, while Gaitán was rushed off to a clinic. The leader, beyond saving, died shortly afterward.

Colombians would never know what motivated the assassin, or whether others were involved in the murder. On the streets, rage and speculation as to the role of the political establishment in the killing swiftly mounted, and within minutes after his arrest, a mob had seized the suspected murderer from police custody. His lifeless, mutilated corpse was later found on a plaza, on the way to the presidential palace. Gaitán's murder unleashed El Bogotazo, several hours of intense rioting, looting, and burning of public buildings that left several hundred,

possibly even thousands, dead and many others injured. In the aftermath of the murder, Liberals and Conservatives in Bogotá engaged in
an intense scramble for power, tensions mounting to the point that on
November 9, 1949, the president of Colombia, Maríano Ospina Pérez,
a Conservative, declared a state of siege and shut down the Congress.
In elections that December, another Conservative, Laureano Gómez,
known for his radical right-wing views, won the presidency unopposed
after the Liberal candidate withdrew out of concern for his own security. Gómez kept the state of siege in place.

Outside the capital, these events opened the door to nine years of
uncontrolled carnage, a period now known simply as "La Violencia,"
The Violence. In town after town, particularly in rural Colombia,
members of the Liberal and Conservative parties shot, throttled, and
stabbed each other, devising ever more sophisticated and grisly ways of
murdering their neighbors. There were few ideological differences between the two political parties—the Conservatives traditionally believed in a stronger role for the Catholic Church in the state, and a
more centralized government, and the Liberals were for decentraliza-
tion and separation between church and state. But bodies piled up as
political differences became the cover for personal feuds, score settling,
and land disputes.

A WORLD AWAY from the high politics of Bogotá, in rural Antioquia,
La Violencia quickly spread. When Valle was still a small child, his
family, at the insistence of his mother, had traveled for several days on
muleback to move from Ituango to Medellín. A Medellín native who
valued a good education, his mother had wanted her children to be
able to attend school and have the other advantages of city life. But his
father, a peasant from Ituango who had always worked the land, found
it impossible to make a living in Medellín. Soon, he jumped at a job as
a caretaker for someone else's land in Puerto Berrío, on the eastern
fringes of Antioquia, while Valle and his mother and siblings stayed in
Medellín. Every week, they would go to the train station in neighboring Envigado to pick up the bundles of food that Valle's father shipped
to them.

His father's timing could not have been worse. In the early 1950s,
Puerto Berrío was a major hub for La Violencia: between 1949 and
mid-1953, official records suggest, Puerto Berrío lost 6 percent of its

population to inter-party killings, with nearly five hundred deaths in 1952 alone.

One day, a family friend called Valle's mother to tell her that armed men had slowly tortured and killed a man they knew, the caretaker for a farm near the one where her husband was working: first they peeled off pieces of his skin, then they sliced off his ears, and then his nose, before finally murdering him. In a letter, Valle's father urged his wife not to visit, assuring her that everything would be okay. But fearing for her husband's life, she boarded a train to Puerto Berrío, accompanied only by the seven- or eight-year-old Valle. She gave her son strict instructions: "If we run into any armed men, on the train or anywhere, don't speak. Pretend you're a mute child."

They got to the farm where Valle's father was working by around 6 p.m. without incident. But two hours later, two hundred armed Liberals came to their door and demanded to be fed. Valle's Conservative parents feigned support for their cause and, by candlelight, cooked up chickens and served the men fresh juice from the farm. Valle's young mother charmed them with her stories and singing, while his father chatted amiably with the men about their weapons. Both of them braced for an attack. Some of the men tried talking to Valle, but, following his mother's orders, he stared silently, pretending to be mute.

The men finally left, well past midnight, and the family immediately fled Puerto Berrío, never to return. Two days later, Valle's father heard that the armed men had been back at the farm looking for him, saying that the only reason they hadn't killed him before was that his wife and child were there.

With their father now unemployed, Valle's family struggled to get by alongside the city's *desplazados*, the thousands of rural people who were increasingly flocking to poor neighborhoods in Medellín, Bogotá, Cartagena, and other major cities, forced to flee their homes and land, often losing all they had to La Violencia. Most were barely able to scrape by in these urban environments, where they were not welcome in any case. As an eight-year-old, Valle went to school, but he spent much of his free time working, running errands for a small grocery store in their neighborhood in exchange for rice, beans, or other items he could take home.

Within a couple of years, Valle was back in Ituango, where his father was running a ranch for a local landowner. The family's plan had been to keep the kids in Medellín, but Valle had started skipping school and ignoring his homework. When he wasn't working, he sat in the park and read—poring over anything he could get his hands on, from comic books and adventure stories to bits and pieces of the newspaper. His sister Magdalena later said she thought Valle simply didn't find the classes in school challenging enough, and he was so excited about learning to read that he just plowed ahead on his own. But his lack of interest in school angered his mother, who decided to send him to his father. Valle spent the next year of his life doing hard physical labor—waking up at the crack of dawn, herding cattle, planting and picking beans and fruit. The year left a deep mark on him, both because it was so difficult and because it helped to cement his strong bond with Ituango.

When he finally got back to Medellín in 1955 or 1956, things were a little easier financially for the family, as his older brother Octavio was now working and helping to support the family. Valle, who no longer had to work, was better able to focus on school, and he began to excel academically. During his junior year of high school, when he learned how to play chess, he became obsessed with the game, once again ignoring his schoolwork. But his mother made him give up chess, and Valle went on to finish school with top grades. He was a leader among his classmates. While he tended to be reserved and did not have a lot of friends, he had strong views about right and wrong that his fellow students admired, and that would eventually lead him to law school and a career of activism.

LA VIOLENCIA FINALLY ended in 1957, when the Liberals and Conservatives made a pact to establish a system of joint government known as the National Front. By then, more than 200,000 people out of a population of around 12 million had died.

The end of La Violencia offered a brief respite from the carnage of the previous decade, though a number of individuals and groups involved in the slaughter continued operating as "bandits" in rural regions. It also, however, contained the seeds of the next war, which started up just a few years later, with the rise of several left-wing guerrilla groups that took up arms against the government. The Revolutionary Armed Forces of Colombia, or FARC, one of the most prominent of these groups, had its roots in smaller groups affiliated with the Communist Party, which even before La Violencia had been protesting what they viewed as the unjust appropriation of land by wealthy landowners, oppressive public policies on land, and the exploitation of workers by business. During La Violencia, some of them had armed themselves and formed what they called "self-defense groups"; at the end of La Violencia, they refused to lay down their arms, instead asserting control of municipalities in several parts of Colombia, which the government then labeled "independent republics." In May 1964, the Conservative government of Colombian president Guillermo León Valencia, said to be under pressure from the United States to stamp out any revolutionary activity in the country—launched a military assault on the republics, beginning with one in the area known as Marquetalia in the mountainous state of Tolima, not far from Bogotá. More than 1,000 (and possibly as many as 16,000, according to the FARC) Colombian troops, which were being advised by the United States, descended upon the area, backed by airplanes that dropped bombs and, according to several accounts, used napalm. Over the next months, the army seized the area. But several members of the armed group there, led by Pedro Antonio Marín (later better known by his aliases, "Manuel Marulanda" or "Tirofijo" [Sureshot]), escaped, and in 1966 they formally established the FARC.

By the mid-1980s, the FARC had become active around the country, "taxing" (that is, extorting funds from) individuals and businesses, kidnapping citizens, and killing those who didn't comply with their orders. Other groups, such as the National Liberation Army (Ejército de Liberación Nacional, or ELN) and the M-19 guerrillas, which were popular among urban, middle-class youth, were also active. The Colombian security forces responded savagely, arresting large numbers of people, often on flimsy evidence, and in some cases executing and torturing people whom they viewed as guerrilla sympathizers.

Meanwhile, shadowy groups commonly known as paramilitaries began to crop up—seemingly spontaneously—in different parts of the country. While also describing themselves as "self-defense" groups organized to protect their communities from guerrillas, the paramilitaries were hard to distinguish from death squads for the military, or private armies for wealthy landowners and drug lords.

When Colombia's government tried to negotiate a peace deal with the FARC in 1985, a political party known as the Patriotic Union

(Unión Patriótica, or UP) formed to be a democratic, civilian arm of the guerrillas, roughly equivalent to Sinn Fein in Northern Ireland. But no sooner had the party been established than paramilitaries or other assassins linked to the security forces began to systematically murder UP politicians. Over the course of the next few years, they would kill two presidential candidates, scores of mayors, city council members, and members of Congress, and thousands of party members.

BY THE MID-1980S, Valle had become a respected lawyer in Medellín, a professor of ethics, and a founding member of the Permanent Human Rights Committee of Antioquia, an all-volunteer collection of lawyers, doctors, academics, and others who were troubled by the social injustices around them. Valle had tried his hand at politics, serving as a state assemblyman for the Conservative Party, but he had grown disgusted at the corruption he observed and quit. The human rights community, with its focus on pushing for social change peacefully, on the basis of universal principles rather than ideology, was a better fit for him. But it was a challenging time for human rights activists: as Valle soon learned, UP members were far from being the paramilitaries' only targets. In those years, anyone who was viewed as close to the political left, or as threatening to the interests of the military or business establishment—including labor union or community leaders, as well as social activists—was courting death.

On August 25, 1987, Valle's dear friend Héctor Abad, a renowned physician, university professor, and advocate for public health services for the poor, decided to end his workday by attending a wake for Luis Felipe Vélez. Vélez, the president of the local teacher's union, had been assassinated by shooters in a Mazda sedan as he had entered his office that morning. Abad was then serving as the president of the human rights committee, and he knew he might be next.

Several days earlier, another doctor and university professor, Senator Pedro Luis Valencia of the UP, had also been killed. Abad organized a march to protest Valencia's murder, and in an op-ed he wrote that paramilitaries were behind the killings. On August 24, a radio station contacted Abad—who was also running to become the mayoral candidate for the Liberal Party—to tell him that his name had appeared on an anonymous list of people to be killed—the list called him a "medic to guerrillas, false democrat, dangerous. . . . Useful idiot of the Communist Party." But the news, the following day, of Vélez's killing had enraged Abad, and when, that evening, a woman he had never seen before came to his office and urged him to attend the wake, he agreed. Doctor Leonardo Betancur, another committee member and a favorite student of Abad's, went with him.

As they greeted other mourners at the entrance to the union offices—the same spot where the union leader had been shot—a pair of young men leapt off a motorcycle at the door. Before anyone could react, one of them gunned down Abad, shooting him first in the chest, then several times in the head, and then the neck and chest again. The other chased Leonardo Betancur into the union building, killing him as well.

In those days, the members of the Permanent Human Rights Committee didn't know who the paramilitaries were, exactly. As Carlos Gaviria, another cofounder of the committee in Antioquia and—decades later—a justice on Colombia's Constitutional Court, recalled, "We knew that around the military there was an extreme right-wing group that did a sort of 'cleansing' job, in the sense that they viewed anyone who disagreed [with them] as a representative of the left. Héctor [Abad] was a liberal doctrinarian, someone incapable of having a weapon[,] . . . yet [to the extreme right], anyone who disagrees is the enemy and must be destroyed."

Abad's death was only the beginning. In December, Abad's successor as president of the committee, Luis Fernando Vélez, was kidnapped, tortured, and also murdered. Another senior committee member, Carlos Gónima, was shot to death in February 1988.

The killings sparked a large exodus from the committee. Some of those who quit, such as Carlos Gaviria, left the country under threat. Others simply resigned. "There was a huge and widespread fear, because in that environment, the committee was being portrayed as a communist stronghold," Gaviria later said.

But Valle, then forty-four years old, refused to leave. He was grieving—that was evident to his family, from his stony silence—but he was also unwilling to be cowed. The group decided not to name a new president, so they wouldn't have a visible head to be targeted, but in practice, Valle took on the committee's leadership. Along with a few remaining members—mostly women who volunteered their time, including a lawyer, María Victoria Fallon; an insurance agent, Patricia

Jesús María Valle receiving a document honoring him at an Antioquia Bar Association event, 1993. © Jairo León Cano.

Fuenmayor; and Beatriz Jaramillo, a teacher whose family Valle had helped when Jaramillo's cousin, Luis Fernando Lalinde, had been forcibly "disappeared" a few years earlier—Valle brought the group back to life. He poured himself into causes large and small, from fighting for justice for the police murder of nine children in the neighborhood of Villatina in 1992, to organizing protests over forced evictions of displaced persons in the most miserable parts of Medellín, to providing free legal representation to low-income persons he believed were wrongfully accused. And while he was sympathetic to many of the concerns of the political left, he was fiercely independent, refusing to join any political organization.

In Valle's view, the mission of a lawyer should be to serve the poor. Even though he could have made large sums of money as a defense attorney, he spent much of his time on his activism and working for the people of Ituango. He lived extremely frugally—that was why he had never bothered to update or replace the manual typewriter in his office, or to install a security camera outside its door, even when there were threats against him. He gave most of his money to his family, buying a house where he lived with many of his siblings, and, once his parents retired, a plot of land near Medellín, where they could grow some of their own food and raise animals, more for fun than out of need. He had a habit of giving money and things away—once in a while, decorative items around the house would disappear. His sister Magdalena would ask Valle about them and he would explain: "Oh, so-and-so was here and really admired it, and she's very poor, while you have lots of things, so I gave it to her." Another time, he organized and paid for festivities in Ituango to celebrate International Women's Day, arranging for several women professionals to travel from Medellín to Ituango to give Ituango's women classes on their rights.

Valle's colleague and friend Beatriz Jaramillo was struck by one incident in particular around 1997, when he called her at 5:30 a.m. to tell her that they needed to go to Blanquizal, a squatter community on the outskirts of Medellín, because the city government was about to evict its residents to make way for a highway construction project. They had to protect those people, he told her. Once in Blanquizal, he called the community together to talk about the problem. Seated on a modest little bed in one of the houses, "he spoke to them so beautifully, making them feel important, telling them that they were Colombia, that they had rights," she recalled. Repeatedly, he asked them "not to respond to violence with violence." Eventually, the police and the bulldozers arrived and started to demolish the precarious little houses. It was tragic, Jaramillo recalled, to see how they loaded the municipal garbage bins with the pieces of wood the residents had used to cobble together their homes, "knowing that the wood was the fruit of enormous efforts to get some way to protect themselves from the elements at night." Meanwhile, Valle, Jaramillo, and fellow committee member Patricia Fuenmayor accompanied the residents and organized a quick census of the population, so that Valle could later help them find some kind of solution to their housing situation. At one point, a young pregnant woman, with a toddler in her arms, came out of one of the few houses in the community that was built out of bricks. She started to cry, wondering what she would do now. As the bulldozer approached, Valle sat in front of the house: if they wanted to bulldoze the house, they'd have to drive over him. The police chief overseeing the demolition ordered the bulldozer to retreat, and the house was temporarily left alone. Over time, Valle would represent the entire community in

Jesús María Valle at a party for children in the El Cucaracho
shelter, with displaced persons from the community of La Playita,
Medellín, 1992. © Patricia Fuenmayor, Grupo Interdisciplinario de
Derechos Humanos.

proceedings against the city, and he ultimately succeeded in getting
them resettled in good housing elsewhere in town. It wasn't the first
time he had done something like that: in the early 1990s, Valle, Fuenmayor, and other committee members spent years working with the
residents of another community, La Playita, who had also been evicted
by the city. They organized sit-ins, and Valle filed suit; together they
built up so much pressure that they got the city to build a whole new
neighborhood from scratch for the displaced residents.

Although Valle could be passionate when it mattered, his general
demeanor was calm and optimistic. "A positive mental attitude" was
one of his mottos—it was the only way, he said, to deal with adversity.
His sister Magdalena recalled that once, in the middle of the night,
when Valle was in law school, their mother had overheard him crying
out in pain. When she went to see what was wrong, she discovered
that his hand was badly swollen from an injury he had sustained playing soccer earlier that day. He had gone to the hospital for treatment,

but he had not told his family about it so as not to worry them, instead keeping the pain to himself.

Valle became known for his oratorical skills: "His language was that of a lawyer, but it was always charged with great feeling," remembered one of his friends. He told incisive jokes, and he enjoyed dancing, though he was not exactly the best dancer. On his long drives to Ituango, he would listen to cassette tapes of Argentine tango music, which had been popular for years in Medellín—ever since the famous tango performer Carlos Gardel had visited the city in the 1930s (Gardel later died in an airplane accident there).

COLOMBIA'S WAR DRAGGED on throughout the late 1980s and 1990s, though for a while it was overshadowed by another conflict, the parallel war on drugs between the Colombian state, backed by the United States, and the Medellin cartel, led by cocaine kingpin Pablo Escobar. The drug war littered Medellín's streets with bodies for years, until Escobar was killed in 1993. A few things seemed to change for the better: some of the guerrilla groups, including the M-19 and the Popular Liberation Army (Ejército Popular de Liberación, EPL), demobilized in the late 1980s as part of a peace process with the government. And in 1991, in part as a result of a student movement demanding political reforms to make the government more participatory and open, the country adopted a new, more progressive, constitution. Valle had been involved in some of the activism around the constitution, alongside his friends and fellow lawyers J. Guillermo Escobar and Iván Velásquez, and had even run for a seat on the constituent assembly. After the spate of killings of activists, leftist leaders, and others in the mid- to late 1980s, human rights groups knew they needed to watch their security, but for a while, it looked like the dark forces behind those assassinations might be taking a step back.

Then, in the mid-1990s, things started to take a turn for the worse once again. Valle started hearing reports that in remote rural regions, including in his beloved Ituango, groups of armed men were killing peasants. Unlike the anonymous killers of the mid-1980s, who committed targeted, high-profile killings, these groups of paramilitaries seemed like small armies. In Antioquia, they would often wear camouflage and introduce themselves as members of the Peasant Self-Defense Forces of Córdoba and Urabá (Autodefensas Campesinas de Córdoba y Urabá, or ACCU, in Western Antioquia). They seemed intent on committing very visible, gruesome killings, often of shopkeepers and bus drivers, whom they accused of assisting the guerrillas. But they were also seizing land, replacing local officials with their own people, and effectively asserting their control of entire regions. And nobody, it seemed, was stopping them.

URIBE RESPONDED TO Valle's November 20, 1996, letter by meeting with him and several colleagues on Monday, December 9. At the meeting, Valle once again described his concerns about the increasing violence by paramilitaries in Ituango, stressing that he had unquestionable evidence of collusion between the paramilitaries and members of the security forces in the region. Among other examples, he noted, when the heavily armed paramilitaries had passed by an army base in the municipal capital of Ituango on their way to the only road leading to La Granja, later coming out the same way, the army had done nothing to stop them. According to a witness, Uribe looked unsettled, got up from the meeting table, went into a neighboring office, and picked up the phone. They overheard him say that Valle was making "false" statements by claiming that there was collusion between the paramilitaries and the state, and that he probably should be sued for slander. Uribe then looked at Valle and asked whether he would be willing to repeat his statements the next day to General Alfonso Manosalva, the commander of the Fourth Brigade of the army, based in Medellín. Valle calmly agreed—he later told his friends that if he was sued for slander, it would be fine, because it would give him a chance to present his evidence in court. He then continued talking to the governor, stating that he knew where the paramilitaries had dug some mass graves to bury their victims. Uribe immediately made arrangements for Valle to travel by helicopter to Ituango with a number of officials, so that Valle could show them where the graves were. But on the morning of the following Saturday, the appointed day of the expedition, Valle received a call before 5 a.m.: the caller informed him that he would no longer be allowed to go on the helicopter—it was full, and there was no longer room for him. He considered driving, but quickly abandoned the idea: the trip would have taken seven hours by car, and by the time he got there, the committee would have left.

A few months after Valle had first written to Uribe about the para-militaries' activities in Ituango, another attack in the region offered further proof. The army reported that on July 7, 1997, FARC guerrillas had attacked one of the brightly painted rural buses known as *chivas* on one of the roads leading to Ituango, killing one Colombian soldier and injuring another. At the same time, media reported, several individu-als had been admitted to a nearby hospital for similar injuries, though the military denied that they were in any way related to the attack.

A few days later, Valle announced that the military was lying: the additional injured people were in fact paramilitaries who had been rid-ing in the bus with the military. Only the driver, Valle said, was a civil-ian, and in fact he was a well-known resident of the area—the military had forced him to drive them around. He was now seriously injured. "This proves the collusion [between the military and paramilitaries] that I've been reporting for nearly a year and which the Governor of Antioquia and the Commander of the Fourth Brigade have not wanted to believe," he said. "The civilian population," he added on a TV news program, "is defenseless." Since September 1996, he charged, more than 150 people in Ituango had been killed. These included most of the shopkeepers in the small towns—whom the paramilitaries accused of feeding the FARC. A paramilitary group was operating in the center of Ituango and the military and the police knew it.

Valle stressed that he was speaking out on the basis of solid infor-mation, and because he had no choice—he had gone to every govern-ment office he could think of to beg them to protect the civilian population, but he had received no answer. "I'm not motivated by ha-tred against the Governor or the commander of the Fourth Brigade . . . or because of political interests," he said. "I'm doing this because these are my people and I don't want them to keep suffering. I do it because too many of my people have died, unjustly, in the middle of the public plaza, while everyone remains silent. Because one has to tell the truth, whatever the cost."

Valle's explosive charges drew a quick retort from the bland-faced and droopy-eyed Fourth Brigade commander, Carlos Alberto Ospina, who drily snapped back that the allegation was simply false, because everyone in the vehicle belonged to the military.

Uribe backed Ospina: "The reports of doctor Jesús María Valle don't match those given by the Brigade or the Police. . . . As governor,

I have to support our security forces." A young army major filed a civil suit on behalf of the Fourth Brigade against Valle for libel.

A few days later, Uribe went further, accusing Valle of being "an enemy of the Armed Forces," recalled the lawyer María Victoria Fallon. According to one of Uribe's advisers, José Obdulio Gaviria, Uribe believed Valle's allegations were inappropriate because any such charges should be made before the inspector general's office and the military justice system; Valle, he said, was simply trying to discredit the armed forces. But given the history of assassinations of people perceived as being enemies of the military, Valle's friends viewed Uribe's statements as a veiled threat. Acquaintances began to avoid him, sometimes crossing the street out of fear of being seen with him.

Chapter 2

Early Warnings

Iván Velásquez didn't like to drive, so his wife, María Victoria, usually took the wheel. That Saturday in October 1997, she was driving Velásquez and their three kids on a day trip out of Medellín. Catalina, then seventeen; Víctor, fourteen; and Laura, nine, had piled into the back of the car, and the family had started to make its way along the Las Palmas highway, snaking up the tall mountains embracing Medellín.

Except during the rainy season, Medellín was nearly always sunny and warm, a messy, heavily trafficked, polluted city sitting in the bright green Aburrá Valley, which was dotted with shiny yellow *guayacán* trees and luxuriant bougainvillea vines. Butterflies and a large variety of birds—egrets and crakes, osprey and kestrels, warblers, various hummingbirds, cuckoo birds, and even macaws and occasional flocks of parakeets—regularly visited the city's many gardens and parks, which provided much-needed relief from the concrete jungle at Medellín's center. Today was another bright day, and Velásquez was enjoying being with his family again.

Velásquez had just started a new job as chief prosecutor for Antioquia and the neighboring states of Córdoba, Caldas, Risaralda, and Chocó. He had not, at first, been at all interested in the job. Regional prosecutors at the time were known as "prosecutors without a face," meaning that—for their own security—they operated anonymously; neither defendants nor witnesses knew their names. To Velásquez, the

27

idea of anonymous prosecutors seemed deeply unfair; defendants should be able to see those who were accusing them of crimes.

But he had been living far from his family, working eight hours away, in Bogotá, for over a year. María Victoria's job was in Medellín, and she didn't want to quit and have to hunt for new employment in a strange city. Velásquez would sometimes meet María Victoria and the kids in a relative's cottage halfway between Bogotá and Medellín for a weekend, and then, on Sunday afternoon, wave longingly through the window as Catalina, Víctor, and Laura settled into María Victoria's car to drive back to Medellín. When the kids were smaller, he had always been deeply involved in caring for them: preparing their food, taking them to school, playing with them. But more and more, Velásquez feared his kids were growing up without a father, and he worried about the harm the distance might do to his relationships with his children and wife. So when a colleague had suggested him for this position, he had agreed to consider it—and eventually accepted.

Velásquez's office had assigned him the bulletproof car they were in, saying he must use it for his own security: any number of people could want the chief prosecutor dead. Velásquez had agreed without thinking too much about it; security concerns were not new to him.

ONLY A FEW years earlier, Velásquez had been stuck between two warring factions during some of the worst violence Medellín had ever experienced. He was serving as inspector general for the city, charged with monitoring abuses by public officials, in the final years of the drug war that cocaine kingpin Pablo Escobar was waging against the Colombian government.

Even as Colombia's war between guerrillas and the government churned, during the 1970s and 1980s, Colombia had become the epicenter of the world's thriving cocaine business: enterprising black-market businessmen like Escobar, who had grown up in the Medellín suburb of Envigado, saw in marijuana, and then cocaine—derived from coca grown in neighboring Peru and Bolivia—an opportunity to reap profits beyond their wildest dreams. That opportunity lay in processing and shipping the drugs to US shores. By the early 1980s, Escobar, along with Gonzalo Rodríguez Gacha and the brothers Jorge Luis, Juan David, and Fabio Ochoa Vásquez, had formed a powerful narco-trafficking syndicate, commonly known as the Medellín cartel, which at its peak some sources estimated to have supplied as much as 80 percent of the global cocaine market, bringing in billions of dollars a year. When *Forbes* magazine published its first list of world billionaires in 1987, both Escobar and Jorge Luis Ochoa made the list. Escobar stayed on it for another seven years.

From the start, the cartel used savage means to achieve its goals: torturing and executing competitors or opponents, threatening or bribing officials to achieve its aims. Colombia's government was slow to take action against the drug business—in the 1970s and early 1980s there was even some debate, led by a prominent politician (and future president), Ernesto Samper, about legalizing drugs. Samper pointed out that the drug business was rapidly becoming too powerful for the state to control, and that they needed to find an alternate way of regulating it: "We are, at the end of the day, faced with a choice of either recognizing and redirecting the mafias, or having them . . . take us all down the wrong path."

Meanwhile, Escobar, who came from the middle class and aspired to a sort of legitimacy among the country's elites, had built up some popular support by pouring money into public works, including the construction of an entire neighborhood for low-income residents of Medellín, as well as multiple soccer fields across the city. While some of Medellín's traditional circles of power shunned the new-money drug lords, others quickly attached themselves to their wealth. Escobar became famous for his supermodel lovers and his extravagant spending on parties, cars, and the personal zoo full of wild animals that he kept on his lavish property, the Hacienda Nápoles. In 1982, he even won a seat as an alternate (a substitute, in the event the primary office holder could not perform his duties) to a member of the Colombian Congress.

But in the mid-1980s, the administration of Ronald Reagan in the United States, which was ramping up its own war on drugs, increased the pressure on Colombia's government to take legal action against the drug lord. President Belisario Betancur named Rodrigo Lara, a strong critic of the Medellín cartel, minister of justice, and the Colombian Congress began to debate an extradition treaty with US officials that would allow the government to send narco-traffickers like Escobar to the United States for trial. Then, in March 1984, in a joint operation, the Colombian national police and the US Drug Enforcement

Administration (DEA) raided Tranquilandia, a vast cocaine-processing complex hiding in the jungle plains of the eastern Colombian states of Caquetá and Meta, run by the Medellín cartel.

Escobar reacted furiously, unleashing a wave of terror in Medellín and in other cities that had escaped earlier bouts of large-scale violence in Colombia mostly unscathed. Within a month, assassins sent by the cartel had murdered Lara. Over the following years, murders—including assassinations of high-profile officials—would become commonplace. In 1986, assassins murdered Colonel Jaime Ramírez Gómez, the antinarcotics police chief who had led the raid on Tranquilandia. Escobar was believed to have ordered the 1989 assassination during a political rally of popular Liberal presidential candidate Luis Carlos Galán, an anticorruption crusader and critic of the cartels, who supported the extradition treaty with the United States. Shortly afterward, Escobar ordered the planting of a bomb on a domestic passenger airplane on which he believed Galán's replacement, César Gaviria, would be flying. Gaviria wasn't on board, and went on to become president. But more than one hundred people died when the jet exploded five minutes after taking off from Bogotá.

Hospitals in Medellín became dangerous places to go, as shooting victims who made it that far often had assassins on their heels—teenagers on motorcycles, gang members, or simply killers for hire. Many of the assassins would themselves die before ever becoming adults. Often, the sun would rise to find the city littered with human bodies, many of them never to be identified. Various criminal gangs and armed factions silently battled for control of the city and its profitable cocaine markets. With his seemingly limitless resources, Escobar gave public officials a choice between *plata o plomo*—silver or lead, meaning a bribe or death by a bullet. It became nearly impossible to tell who was with Escobar and who was against him. Meanwhile, the Colombian military and police engaged in their own acts of brutality, killing and "disappearing" young people believed to be Escobar's associates.

By 1991, when Velásquez became inspector general of Medellín, Escobar had agreed to a policy of "submission"—he turned himself in to the authorities, but on the condition that he would not be extradited to the United States and would stay at La Catedral, a "prison" he had built for himself on the top of a mountain with a view of all of Medellín. But the killings continued: the drug kingpin kept running his criminal operations from La Catedral, and at that point, he was conducting a war not only against the government, but also against the rival Cali cartel, run by the brothers Gilberto and Miguel Rodríguez Orejuela. And in his efforts to maintain ever tighter control over the cartel and its profits, he had alienated some of his closest associates.

AS INSPECTOR GENERAL, the thirty-six-year-old Velásquez took his job seriously, and in one of his early investigations uncovered a torture chamber that he believed was being used by members of an elite joint anti-kidnapping squad operated by the army and police known as UNASE (Unidad Anti-Secuestro y Extorsion, or Anti-Kidnapping and Extortion Unit). His work angered sectors of the public security forces, but at the same time, Velásquez had to constantly worry about an attack from Escobar's people: on one of his first days on the job, a former colleague had introduced him to two nicely dressed men who, claiming to be emissaries from Escobar, had offered him a suitcase full of tens of thousands of dollars, "in appreciation" for his work on behalf of the people of Medellín. Velásquez had rejected the money, insisting that his salary was paid by the government. But, concerned that Escobar would seek revenge, he had then visited the drug lord at La Catedral, to explain in person why he would not accept money from him. Fortunately, the sweaty Escobar, who was in the middle of a game of soccer when Velásquez arrived, had seemed to be in an amiable mood at the time. Far from being the scary, aggressive figure Velásquez had always imagined, Escobar acted surprisingly submissive, with his head bent down, staring at his feet as they moved pebbles around on the ground. Only occasionally did he look up at Velásquez, with an expression of something akin to shyness. Velásquez never was able to figure out why Escobar acted that way—it was not as though he had much power to intimidate the drug lord. Velásquez immediately explained what had happened with Escobar's envoys, and that he could not accept money. Escobar listened, and apologetically told him not to worry: it was too bad that there had been a mistake, but he wasn't seeking anything in exchange, he said. He simply wanted to recognize the good work Velásquez was doing. Velásquez repeated that he would not take money from anyone, as he was simply doing his job, and Escobar seemed to take it in stride. With that, Velásquez left, feeling a surge of relief: it looked like the drug lord was leaving him alone—at least for now.

Velásquez would go to La Catedral two more times. In early 1992, his boss in Bogotá, Carlos Gustavo Arrieta, the national inspector general, ordered him to conduct an inspection of the inside of the prison. There were concerns about the prison's security and the illegal activity possibly taking place inside. Few public officials had ventured inside La Catedral, but Velásquez got to meet Escobar again. He took photos of what he discovered was a luxurious, well-furnished house with a gym, kitchen, and several bedrooms. It was filled with expensive televisions, pool tables, and elegantly carved, heavy wooden furniture, all of which a prisoner was not supposed to have. There was even a large doll's house for Escobar's young daughter, Manuela, to play with when she visited. It would have been impossible for all that to get into La Catedral without National Prison Institute officials noticing. The photos were eventually made public, generating a national outcry over the government's permissiveness, but as far as Velásquez could tell, the government did little to change the status quo.

In July 1992, Velásquez received instructions to go to La Catedral again, though he was not told why. A few weeks earlier, Escobar had killed two of his associates, Fernando Galeano and Kiko Moncada, and had their bodies dismembered and incinerated on the grounds of La Catedral itself. That was the last straw for the government of César Gaviria, which then decided—according to official accounts—to transfer Escobar to another prison. But the operation was poorly coordinated. When Velásquez arrived outside the inner perimeter of the prison in the late afternoon, he encountered a stout but tough-looking army general, Gustavo Pardo Ariza, who was having an animated discussion with the young, polished vice minister of justice, Eduardo Mendoza, and the national prisons director, Colonel Hernando Navas. Mendoza and Navas, who had flown in from Bogotá, were arguing that they should go inside to explain the transfer to Escobar. Pardo Ariza opposed the idea, but upon their continued insistence, suggested that Velásquez join them. To Velásquez, it seemed odd that they disagreed: Why didn't Mendoza and Navas want witnesses to whatever they were going to say? Navas then said that he should go in alone. After much back and forth, Pardo eventually relented. Navas went in, and, after a while, Mendoza was called in as well. Velásquez waited outside for a couple of hours. At one point, a guard came up to the fence and sum-moned Velásquez: Navas and Mendoza wanted him to join them, he said. Velásquez was uneasy, but got ready to go in, when Pardo stopped him—things didn't look right. He instructed the guard to tell Escobar that nobody else was going in until he knew that Mendoza and Navas were safe. Well into the evening, they learned that Escobar was claim-ing he had taken Mendoza and Navas hostage. He was reportedly furi-ous: he believed the transfer was really an effort to extradite him.

Velásquez spent the rest of the night sitting on a small chair in a shack outside the prison, with only his suit to protect him from the dark mountain chill, as he and the army general waited for a break-through. At one point, he jumped when an airplane flew low overhead and all the lights went off in the prison. Finally, at dawn, as if in a dream, Velásquez glimpsed heavily armed soldiers materializing through the fog and trees, encircling La Catedral. He heard an explo-sion and shouts. Bullets whizzed by him, in both directions, and he ran out of the exposed shack to hide behind a tree. By 9 a.m., the news was out: special forces had seized the prison. Escobar was gone.

Meanwhile, María Victoria had spent the whole night without news from Velásquez. She had told the kids that everything was fine, but she was worried sick. Had he been killed? Abducted? The news reports about the seizure of the prison did not mention him. So when morning came, she dropped the kids off at school and drove to Envi-gado, the hometown of Escobar, to try to talk to Mayor Jorge Mesa, who was rumored to be close to the drug kingpin. By sheer force of will, she got Mesa's guards to let her in. Mesa was initially unfriendly, but eventually made a phone call. He then told her: "Your husband was a coward who didn't want to go in and talk to Escobar. I recommend that you hide your children immediately. You don't know who Pablo is when he's mad." Velásquez was alive, he said, but he reiterated that Escobar was angry, and their children would pay the price. Relieved to hear her husband was alive, María Victoria thanked him and rushed to the pay phone to call her sister, asking her to pick up the children from school right away and hide them.

While María Victoria was in Envigado, Velásquez had completed an inspection—required by his position—of what had happened at La Catedral after special forces entered, and had come back to Medellín. But he was almost immediately pulled into a meeting at the office of

María Victoria Velásquez, Medellín, 1980s.
© Iván and María Victoria Velásquez.

Juan Pablo Gómez Martínez, the governor of Antioquia. In the middle
of the meeting, a phone call came in from Escobar's brother, Roberto,
who was also known as "El Osito" (The Little Bear). The person with
whom Velásquez was meeting turned on the speaker-phone: El Osito
was railing against Velásquez, saying Pablo Escobar viewed Velásquez
as part of a plot against him. "He has to pay, he knew what was going
to happen," Velásquez later recalled El Osito saying. That night,
Velásquez appeared on local news shows, explaining what had happened from his perspective: he had been sent to La Catedral with no
information about what was going to happen, and had not been involved in any of the planning about the transfer. Some of Escobar's
associates later told him that the interview had saved his life—it had

corrected their impression that Velásquez had been planning to trick Escobar into being extradited to the United States.

The family was finally reunited that night. María Victoria later recalled that Velásquez was so stressed and tired that his hands were shaking as he lit one cigarette after another.

Escobar's escape marked the beginning of a long period of constant fear for Velásquez and his family, not only because of Escobar's threats, but also because of what Escobar's enemies might do. Now that Escobar was on the run, he had escalated his attacks on the government and his enemies in the drug world. At the same time, an elite Colombian police unit, the Bloque de Búsqueda, or Search Bloc, focused on finding Escobar; it worked closely with a US special forces team known as Centra Spike, which fed intelligence to the Colombians. There were also rumors of the involvement of a group of former associates of Escobar who had turned against him. Known as Los Pepes (for Persecuted by Pablo Escobar, or Perseguidos por Pablo Escobar), the group was said to be torturing, kidnapping, and killing Escobar's cronies, weakening his influence. A few of Escobar's associates had turned themselves in to the government through Velásquez's office, which they viewed as safe—unlike the police, who might call in Los Pepes. At one point, Velásquez even sent officials to accompany Escobar's family on a drive from the airport to their apartment in Medellín, as they feared an attack by Los Pepes. After all, "the fact that he was a killer did not mean that we had to tolerate other killers murdering his family," recalled Velásquez. But all these actions meant that the members of Los Pepes might view Velásquez himself as an enemy. For months, the Velásquez family lived with a heavy military guard. For the first, but not last, time, María Victoria started receiving threatening phone calls at work, though she kept them to herself so as not to upset her husband. They kept the kids in their apartment—not even letting them go to the door of the apartment complex, much less to the park or to friends' parties. Her parents tried to keep what was happening from her, but Catalina, who was then twelve, could sense the tension, and she had recurrent nightmares about something happening to her father.

The tense atmosphere came to an abrupt end on December 2, 1993, when the government announced that a squad from the Search Bloc had located Escobar in a Medellín house and shot him to death as he

tried to escape through the roof. US and Colombian officials cele-
brated the killing as a landmark success in the war on drugs, and many
people in Medellín breathed a sigh of relief: with Escobar's killing spree
over, maybe now they would enter a time of renewed peace.

For a while, as the slaughter slowed, that seemed to be the case. Few
people understood that Escobar's slaughter had planted the seeds for
yet another brand of terror.

BY THE TIME Velásquez came back to Medellín four years later, he
was forty-two years old. Tall and gaunt, with large brown eyes set in a
pale face, straight brown hair that crept over his ears, and a strong,
slightly curved nose above a thick mustache, he usually projected a
thoughtful calmness that only broke when he smiled or laughed, making his whole face light up. He could be very affectionate with his kids,
but that would have surprised most people, as he usually came across as
distant and formal with colleagues. His everyday attire was formal, too,
though simple, consisting mainly of suits and sweaters in solid grays or
earth tones; he didn't spend much time or money on his appearance.
Only his smoking habit hinted at the stress he sometimes felt.

Velásquez had left his job as inspector general of Medellín in 1994,
when a new national inspector general took over. For the next four
years he had served as a representative of the inspector general's office
before an administrative tribunal in Antioquia, and then, in Bogotá, as
an assistant justice for the Council of State, one of Colombia's four
high courts, which also focused on administrative matters. These jobs
kept Velásquez busy, so he had little time to stay on top of how the war
was evolving in Antioquia beyond what appeared in the news media.

It was only when he took over as chief prosecutor in 1997 that
Velásquez started to grasp the nature of the new threat facing the region: the newly organized, seemingly very well-funded paramilitary
groups that were swiftly taking over the countryside. They were especially active in two of the states he was covering: Córdoba and Antioquia. Certainly, paramilitaries had been killing activists for years, but
these groups seemed much larger, more brazen, and even more blood-
thirsty than the death squads of the past. His bosses in Bogotá, Attorney General Alfonso Gómez Méndez and Deputy Attorney General
Jaime Córdoba, had urged him to make investigating the paramilitaries a priority, but they had warned him that it would not be easy. Two

criminal investigators from his office had been killed, apparently by paramilitaries, earlier that year, and there were reports that paramilitaries had infiltrated the CTI (Cuerpo Técnico de Investigación, or Technical Investigation Team, a branch of the attorney general's office that conducted criminal investigations).

Worse yet, if Velásquez's old friend Jesús María Valle was to be believed, the military was actively backing the paramilitaries. In the preceding months, Velásquez had watched Valle embark on a one-man crusade to draw attention to what he viewed as complicity between the military and the paramilitaries.

VELÁSQUEZ HAD KNOWN Valle since the mid-1980s, when his law school thesis adviser, J. Guillermo Escobar, had invited him to join an informal group of lawyers calling themselves the Group for Prisoners' Human Rights. Velásquez had married and begun having children in his twenties, and had invested most of his energy in those years in working and supporting his family while María Victoria went to law school. But Velásquez had always had a quiet but deep passion for issues of social justice, so when J. Guillermo called, Velásquez jumped at the opportunity to join the group.

The group organized prison visits to talk to inmates, found them legal representation, and checked on their prison conditions. In doing so, they found one prison where inmates who "misbehaved" were locked up in a narrow, windowless corridor known as the "tunnel." There, they had to scurry, lest they get drenched in waste from other prisoners on the floors above, which poured down from openings in the ceiling. In another prison, inmates were punished by being locked up together in six-by-six-foot cells, ten prisoners to a cell, with no toilet and only a bottle they passed around to take care of their physical needs. Through letters, complaints, and public statements, the Group for Prisoners' Human Rights protested the conditions, and sometimes they managed to get institutions to change the rules.

Members of the group, including Valle and Velásquez, would regularly meet at each other's homes. Over cups of bitter coffee (or, in J. Guillermo's case, endless glasses of Coca-Cola), often smoking, they would stay long into the night talking about politics, law, and current events. It was a thrill to Velásquez: here was a community of people like him, who believed—all evidence to the contrary—that a more

Iván Velásquez and his daughter Laura, 1988 or 1989. © Iván and María Victoria Velásquez.

just society in Colombia was possible. Not only that, but they were doing something about it.

Velásquez enjoyed Valle's lively storytelling style and the expansive smile under his thick, dark brows. The two men had a lot in common beyond their idealism. Both Valle and Velásquez had grown up poor, the children of deeply Catholic, politically conservative parents, and both had worked their way through law school at the University of Antioquia, though a few years apart.

The two also had differences: by the time they met, Valle, as part of the Permanent Human Rights Committee of Antioquia, was an outspoken activist on behalf of various social justice causes in Medellín. By contrast, although Velásquez was friendly with several of the committee's members, and was deeply shaken by the murders of so many of its leaders in the mid-1980s, he never seriously considered joining it. In his mind, he was simply a lawyer who did what he could to improve the system—not an activist. Still, in 1989, Valle convinced Velásquez to replace him as head of the Antioquia Bar Association, and with that platform, Velásquez regularly organized groups of lawyers to raise issues of public concern with the authorities. When, in 1990, the Colombian government held elections for a constituent assembly—a group of people to draft a new constitution for Colombia—Velásquez, Valle, J. Guillermo Escobar, and a few other friends ran together for seats. Flyers promoting their candidacy described them as representing "the damaged justice system, the massacred youth, [and] those who have been tortured," and, most importantly, it said, "WE ARE HUMAN RIGHTS."

They did not get elected, but it was an exciting experience. Velásquez began thinking more about public service through government, which may have influenced his eventual decision to take the inspector general job in 1991. He had refused the job at first, but María Victoria had teased him relentlessly: "Ay mijo" ("Oh my boy"), she said in her sassy style, "aren't you the one who's always going on about people's rights? And now that you have a chance to do something about it, you say no? I guess it was all just talk after all . . . oh well." Valle had also encouraged him: Velásquez was perfect for the job, and it would make a world of difference to have someone trustworthy there. Eventually, Velásquez agreed: "I guess I'm stuck: either I look like a hypocrite, or I have to not only take the job, but also do something with it."

But as much as he liked and trusted Valle, when Velásquez returned to Medellín after two years away, he was not quite sure what to make of his friend's accusations about paramilitaries and their links to the military. He was particularly surprised and concerned by the tension between Valle and Governor Uribe, whom Velásquez knew a bit and had once even admired.

A SLIGHT MAN in his mid-thirties, with perfectly combed and parted hair and a Boy Scout's look about him, Álvaro Uribe seemed like a different kind of politician from those of Colombia's past: he had gained notoriety in 1985 when, along with his second cousin Mario Uribe, he had founded a dissident faction of the Liberal Party known as the "democratic sector" of liberalism in Antioquia, rebelling against the traditional patronage system by which the party was run in the state. In those days, it was common for politicians to dole out gifts, promise jobs, or serve alcohol at political events, to encourage voters to vote for them. Senior party officials, rather than voters, decided who would get to run for office or hold positions in government. Uribe, however, refused to engage in patronage; instead, he devoted himself to traveling widely within the state, talking directly to voters, and trying to understand their concerns and address their problems head-on. He developed a reputation as a workaholic. When he took over the governorship, the US embassy in Colombia described him in a cable as "a bright star in the Liberal Party firmament."

Like Valle and Velásquez, Uribe had studied law at the University of Antioquia, though Uribe was finishing his studies around the same time that Velásquez was starting his, in 1975. Uribe had been a good student when he attended in the early 1970s, but he had also become deeply involved in the school's politics, constantly speaking out against protests by an alphabet soup of leftist or anarchist student movements—JUPA, MOIR, IRI, GUB, as well as the ELN—whose protests often led to classes being canceled. María Victoria, Velásquez's wife, who was a student there in the late 1970s, recalled that for a time, there were people at the university "burning many cars, throwing stones, and things like that." "One day," she said, "they burned a car with a nun inside, and even though they tried to open the doors, they were unable to do so. After that, there was a general repudiation. But throughout that time it was more or less the same story: a lot of noise without much structure." A former classmate of Uribe's recalled thinking that, given what he viewed as Uribe's right-wing positions, it was strange that Uribe was attending the university. Uribe surrounded himself with a small group of students with similar views, and he routinely stood up in the middle of protests to object. It was a gutsy and unpopular thing to do, but it earned Uribe a reputation early on for speaking his mind, regardless of the consequences.

Uribe had grown up in relative comfort between Medellín and the small Antioquia town of Salgar a few hours away, where his family owned land. His father was extremely charismatic—a "snake charmer," as one of Uribe's friends put it—but also a demanding rancher who loved horses, parties, and women. Despite some accounts saying that the family was wealthy, people close to Uribe say that his father bought and sold a lot of land, and was a risk-taker, so his wealth fluctuated a great deal. This might explain Uribe's attendance at the University of Antioquia, a public school. Uribe's mother was said to have been a strong figure, deeply involved in the women's suffrage movement, who taught Uribe to recite poetry from Pablo Neruda, as well as speeches by Jorge Eliecer Gaitán and Simón Bolívar, and encouraged his political aspirations. His parents separated in 1964, when Uribe and his four younger siblings were small—by some accounts, the separation was traumatic for the children, especially because marriage break-ups were highly unusual and viewed as shameful in their conservative society. But Uribe seems to have remained close to both his parents, and several people close to him say that he inherited his father's authoritative temperament, if not the more jovial aspects of his character. Instead, the younger Uribe had acted, since he was very small, as a man with a mission. Friends, relatives, and former teachers remembered that even as a small child, Uribe wanted to be president of Colombia—not out of personal ambition, but because he was utterly committed to the country. One colleague recalled Uribe saying, in the mid-1980s, "I would like, at the end of my days, to look back upon my life and see that I have spent it in the service of the nation."

Immediately after finishing law school, Uribe landed a senior management job in Empresas Públicas de Medellín (Medellín Public Enterprises), the city's public utilities company. It was the first in a string of increasingly high-profile public positions he held, which included, in the early 1980s, serving as director of the national civil aviation agency charged with overseeing and regulating all civilian air travel in the country. He also served a brief stint as mayor of Medellín.

Despite his advantages, Uribe had also been scarred by Colombia's conflict. Years later, in his autobiography, he would recount a memory from childhood that mirrored Valle's own experience during La Violencia: One afternoon, when he was five or six, more than three hundred Liberal Party fighters arrived at his family's farm demanding food and refuge. "I remember watching as my mother . . . cooked meals for this gang of men," he wrote. "I remember watching as my father . . . talked with these outlaws with guns. And I remember yearning, at the purest, most primal level, to live in a Colombia where armed men would never invade our farm, where my family would all be safe, and where no one would ever have to lock herself inside her home, staring at the door in terror."

On June 14, 1983, Uribe's father, Alberto, was killed by the FARC on one of his ranches, Guacharacas, where Uribe recalls that the family employed forty workers and a butler. His father, Uribe later said, had resisted many extortion attempts by the FARC, and had become increasingly worried about security on the ranch. The day his father was killed, Uribe's brother Santiago and sister María Isabel were at the ranch with him and several of the workers when a group of FARC members showed up and attempted to kidnap him. He resisted, shooting at them, but the FARC shot him twice, killing him before running away. Santiago was wounded but managed to flee. In his autobiography, years later, Uribe would write eloquently about the terror that the FARC had inflicted on so many Colombians. But, he stressed, he did not believe in revenge. Instead, he wanted to wrest the country back from lawlessness. "The final stage of all this grief," Uribe wrote, "was not hatred but love: love for my country; love for my countrymen; and love, above all, for a future Colombia where fathers would not be torn away from their daughters and sons."

Velásquez's first impressions of Uribe were very positive. He liked Uribe's stance against corruption and patronage in the Liberal Party. Uribe was young and democratic, and he seemed like a different, more honest type of politician. María Victoria did not share Velásquez's admiration: "Uribe said he exited [liberalism] because of corruption. Iván believed him. He thought that that was a dignified, brave position, and that all political movements needed to have people like Uribe, that he was the model to follow." Many other Medellín residents seemed to agree with Velásquez. But something about Uribe always rubbed María Victoria the wrong way: yes, he was attractive, educated, and sounded good, but his break with the Liberal Party somehow struck her as selfish and ungrateful. That was more of a gut reaction, though, and Velásquez did not share it.

Velásquez recalled first meeting Uribe in person at a security summit held by the mayor of Medellín in the months after Escobar's escape from his prison-mansion of La Catedral. The war between Escobar's people and his enemies was in full swing, with bombs going off or killings happening every day. Uribe, then a senator, was seated next to Velásquez, who was inspector general of Medellín, and leaned over to ask whether there was any way to get Escobar to turn himself in. Velásquez pointed out that the difficulty was that the security forces were under orders to shoot Escobar; Uribe replied that he could bring together all the Antioquia members of congress to surround Escobar while he turned himself in, and in that way ensure his safety. Velásquez agreed that it was worth a try. He approached former Antioquia governor Álvaro Villegas, who lived in the same building as Escobar's mother-in-law and agreed to help. Through Escobar's wife, the three men sent the message to the drug lord. A few days later, on December 26, 1992, Escobar wrote a letter to the government offering to turn himself in, though insisting on extreme conditions—all the members of the Police Investigations Unit had to be fired—and making new threats of violence. The letter, which concluded with a note thanking Velásquez, Uribe, and Villegas for their "goodwill," was leaked to the press, and Los Pepes responded swiftly, setting off multiple bombs on or near properties belonging to Escobar's relatives. One of the bombs went off near Villegas's own house, and he was badly injured. The leak of the letter—which, in any case, President Gaviria rejected—and the bombings by Los Pepes derailed the three men's efforts. Escobar would be dead within the year.

Velásquez and Uribe did not stay in touch, but Velásquez continued to view Uribe as a serious, committed, and generally progressive man, even if they didn't agree on everything. Since becoming governor, however, Uribe seemed to have taken a turn toward the right, becoming much more militaristic and aggressive in his approach to security in the region, and particularly to fighting the FARC guerrillas. Velásquez was particularly concerned about a program the national government had authorized by decree a few years before, in 1994. The decree allowed groups of people in "high-risk" areas, where the military might have trouble providing support, to apply for licenses to provide private security services in those regions. The decree also authorized the groups, known as "Convivirs" (for Cooperativas de Vigilancia y Seguridad Privada, which means Private Cooperatives for Vigilance and Security), to use weapons that would normally be restricted to the military and law enforcement. In theory, the groups would not engage in combat, but rather would serve as a sort of "watch committee." They were to be in regular contact with the authorities, reporting suspicious activity.

The decree allowing the Convivir program had been controversial from the start. Some officials were afraid that it would simply create a new way for the military to legally establish paramilitary groups. In the 1960s and 1970s, the Colombian government had passed decrees and laws allowing the Colombian military to arm civilians to establish self-defense forces, supposedly to defend themselves from the guerrillas. But a number of those groups, in the 1970s and 1980s, had become powerful criminal enterprises, especially in the Middle Magdalena region along the Magdalena River and in the town of Puerto Boyacá, where they had begun committing heinous murders and massacres with military support. By the mid-1980s, the paramilitary group known as the Association of Middle Magdalena Ranchers and Farmers (Asociación Campesina de Ganaderos y Agricultores del Magdalena Medio, or ACDEGAM) was also working closely with drug traffickers —Gonzalo Rodríguez Gacha, aka "The Mexican," a powerful member of the Medellín cartel, underwrote them. In the midst of the bloodshed of the late 1980s, Colombia's government had passed new laws criminalizing the establishment of groups of assassins or death squads and suspended decree provisions that had allowed the military to arm civilians. But the 1994 decree, and regulations issued by President Ernesto Samper's administration allowing the establishment of the Convivirs, had created a new opening for government support of "self-defense" groups—and Governor Uribe enthusiastically embraced them.

In a later interview, former president Samper would say that he had viewed the Convivirs as "a space in which citizens could organize their own defense in a peaceful manner, but [Uribe] began to use them as an instrument of war, blindly defending them." Dozens of Convivirs sprouted up throughout Antioquia, with strong support from the governor, who portrayed the Convivir program as a harmless and legitimate way for civilians to cooperate with the military to further peace. Uribe's chief of staff, Pedro Juan Moreno, a businessman on the far right known for his quick temper and tendency to use harsh language and insult people, regularly held meetings with Convivir leaders and Fourth Brigade members to coordinate the provision of security and intelligence in the region. By 1997, according to one estimate, there were about 414 Convivir groups operating throughout the country with more than 120,000 members. Seventy-eight of those groups were in Antioquia.

The media, human rights organizations, and even the United Nations became increasingly critical of the Convivirs, especially in 1997. Samper's original decree had raised concerns about the risk the government was taking, if it was seen as supporting death squads, but

Uribe's aggressive implementation of the program was, in the eyes of many, confirmation of their worst fears, particularly as reports began to surface of Convivir members becoming involved in criminal activity. Uribe brushed off their concerns. "People imagine that the Convivirs are private, armed armies," he said to one news outlet in November 1997. "If only they knew how they operate in Antioquia. . . . [T]heir experience has shown the people of Antioquia that what's really needed is solidarity, in working jointly with public security forces and providing timely information." Convivir members who committed crimes should be brought to justice, he argued, but that didn't mean the whole program was flawed.

Uribe's backing for the Convivirs generated a great deal of criticism, but it also garnered him support in much of Antioquia—including from Velásquez's father. In arguments, Alberto Velásquez, who looked like an older, white-haired and blue-eyed version of Velásquez, kept going back to the same position, one that was reflected in some local papers and had become the talking points of some politicians: The country needed to find a way to strengthen security in the countryside. It was simply intolerable for farmers, landowners, and businesses to be constantly subject to the FARC's threats, extortion, and kidnapping. Lands were being lost, businesses shutting down. The highways were becoming so dangerous—because any minute you could be stopped by a FARC patrol and taken for ransom—that many people were choosing to give up travel entirely. For God's sake, the FARC were in Medellín itself, hiding out in plain sight, dressed as civilians. What was so wrong with the government supporting citizens who were simply trying to defend themselves? Something had to give!

Velásquez would sigh, getting increasingly irritated. He knew his father was exceedingly proud of him, and he had picked up a lot of his father's attitudes: the value of reading, hard work, and study; his disgust with officials who took bribes and broke the public's trust; his belief that, even when they were flawed, it was more important to try to make institutions of government work than to tear them down. But they parted ways on most policy matters. His father was so attached to protecting what he viewed as the country's established institutions (the Catholic Church, the military, business), and maintaining—or imposing—order, that he often ended up taking radical positions that Velásquez found appalling. For example, his father was still a great admirer of Laureano Gómez, a highly controversial figure who had led Colombia's Conservative Party from the 1930s to the 1960s, and who was known to sympathize with fascist governments, like Hitler's in Germany and Franco's in Spain.

In Velásquez's view, it was one thing to say the government had to protect its people and fight the guerrillas. It was something else entirely to let the military hand out military-grade weapons to civilians and get them directly involved in the conflict. And he agreed with many in the human rights community that the Convivirs could easily be used as cover for paramilitary groups.

Some, like Valle, even spoke interchangeably of the paramilitaries and the Convivirs, as though they were the same thing. In an August 25, 1997, speech commemorating the ten-year anniversary of the murder of Valle's predecessor, Héctor Abad, Valle described how he saw the situation in small towns across Antioquia:

> Dark forces appeared that replaced the mayor. . . . [T]hey were paramilitaries, Convivirs, self-defense forces. And the concept of public authority became ambiguous: people became friends or enemies of the Convivir, friends or enemies of the paramilitaries, friends or enemies of the guerrillas. . . . Today I can say that the meridian of violence courses through Antioquia. We are exporting, through a mistaken conception of public order, violence to other peaceful states . . . [and] to the whole country. And the paramilitaries and the Convivir[s] are confused in their uniforms, their headquarters, the vehicles they use. . . . I have seen it with my eyes, I have witnessed it with the people of my land, my towns. . . . Those people I saw born, those people with whom I heard the whistle of misery in the mountains, have been killed. And I have gone everywhere invoking the rights . . . of the peasants, and I haven't received a positive answer.

Velásquez took Valle's comments seriously. But he had yet to grasp their full implications.

As MARÍA VICTORIA drove the car up the Las Palmas highway, climbing the tall, densely forested mountains embracing Medellín, on that Saturday in late October 1997, the brakes gave out. "Stop," the normally serene Velásquez said, growing alarmed. But she couldn't stop, and the vehicle kept powering farther up the slope. If they continued, they'd soon be driving alongside a cliff.

But then Velásquez spotted a side street. María Victoria swerved onto it. "We're going to die," María Victoria thought, as she lost control of the car, hurtling down the steep incline. They turned upside-down as the car rolled, until finally it stopped, smashing against a wall.

"Is everyone okay?" Velásquez and María Victoria breathlessly asked, turning to each other and their children in the back. Catalina had a deep gash in her leg, and Laura was in pain: they'd later learn that one of her kidneys was bruised.

To this day, María Victoria grows enraged as she tells the story: "First they give him a car without brakes, then they tell him that he doesn't have a right to a driver [on Saturdays], and when we call the traffic police, people from the office beg us not to report that I was driving or that they had given us the car that way. Because there was, in fact, a driver for us to use."

It was evident to her that someone in Velásquez's office had sabotaged the car and deliberately arranged things so that Velásquez or his wife would be driving the car on Saturday. Someone wanted him dead.

Velásquez wasn't so sure about that. In any case, ever since his days as inspector general, his view had been that there was no point in worrying about security. In Colombia, if someone really wanted to kill you, they would.

CHAPTER 3

DEATHS FORETOLD

MILADIS TRIED NOT TO CRY. The paramilitaries had warned her that they would kill anyone who cried. But when she recognized Wilmar's limp body, tied to the mule the paramilitaries were leading to the church door, she couldn't stop herself. Disgusted, the armed men in camouflage pulled the boy off the mule and threw him to the ground. "Guerrilla! Your brother is a guerrilla," they cursed at Miladis, as they kicked the fourteen-year-old's corpse with their boots. When they finally let her get close to him, she saw machete grooves cutting into the center of her little brother's chest. One of his delicate hands looked broken. His teeth were clenched tightly on the Catholic scapular their mother had given to him, as though he'd prayed until the last instant to be saved. That was two decades ago, but Miladis and her sister, Maryori, remember it like it was yesterday.

"El Aro was a really good place, very calm. Everyone was very close," Miladis said of the three-hundred-person town in rural Antioquia, Colombia. She remembered the town square—the heart of the community—fondly; it looked like a painting, she said, with its coconut and lime trees, and the lush mango tree on the corner closest to her home. A statue of national hero Simón Bolívar, who liberated Colombia from Spain, stood in the middle, near another of the Virgin Mary. The large white church with its solid wooden doors sat at the top of the square, next to the priest's house and the police station. Also just past the square was the main town store, owned by Marco Aurelio Areiza, a friendly sixty-four-year-old man who seemed to have been

49

there forever, selling meats, beans, cleaning supplies, beer, coffee, and whatever else townspeople needed. Small mud homes squatted along narrow paths of overgrown grass radiating out from the town square, at the foot of which a single dirt road connected El Aro to the rest of the world.

October 25, 1997, had been shaping up to be a beautiful Saturday. The sun had finally burned off some of the clouds hugging the mountaintops, easing the morning's chill. But a somber mood had taken hold in the town. Other than the odd mule grazing or chicken pecking about the soil, little moved outside—everyone was staying indoors.

For days, Miladis had been hearing reports that paramilitaries were coming into the region. She didn't know much about them, except that they claimed to be fighting the left-wing guerrillas that roamed the countryside and occasionally came into town to buy food or supplies, or to press community members to pay the *vacuna*, or tax. The community members knew not to cross the guerrillas, or the army, which sometimes came through and stole a cow to eat. But the stories Miladis had heard about the paramilitaries were even more terrifying: it was said they carved people up with chainsaws, made their victims drink acid, and tied men, women, and children to the backs of cars, dragging them until they died.

Miladis, her mother, and younger siblings had discussed leaving, but now it was too late: early on Saturday, people from nearby farms called El Aro's telephone office to warn them that dozens of armed men were making their way up the road leading through the densely forested sierra to the town. If the family ran across them on their way out, the paramilitaries might get suspicious and accuse them of being affiliated with the guerrillas. And who knew what would happen then? At this point, there was little they could do but keep going about their business as usual. So Miladis helped her mother cook lunch for the town's schoolteachers in their wood stove—one of the many ways the family scratched out a living.

By noon, lunch was ready, but the teachers didn't arrive. Instead, "we started to hear shooting all over the place," Miladis recalled. They locked the door and huddled in the darkest corner of the back room, where the women normally slept. Distraught, they waited all day and night, listening to intermittent shooting outside, and sick with worry over Wilmar, the baby of the family, who had left that morning to work at a nearby farm.

He hadn't returned.

THE NEXT MORNING, while the rest of Colombia voted in local elections, Miladis jumped at the sound of men pounding on the front door. She had not slept all night, terrified and hoping that the paramilitaries would leave and not notice them. But the men hammering away at the door would not stop. Miladis opened it before they could break it.

Three paramilitaries stood in front of her, in full military attire and ski masks, and carrying huge weapons. Before Miladis knew it, they had shoved the family, still in their pajamas, out of the house and down the dirt path to the town square. "What a herd of guerrillas. How come we missed them yesterday?" Miladis recalled one of them hissing, mocking the family.

Soft-drink cans, rolls of surgical tape, beans, rice, toilet paper, medicine bottles, and more littered the streets. The paramilitaries had looted the town store and the pharmacy. As they walked by, the family saw three bodies on the square, shot to death under the mango tree. One was Luis Modesto, a municipal worker who had been drinking beer at the house next door to theirs just a few hours earlier.

When the men pushed the family into the church, Miladis was surprised to find it packed. It seemed like the whole town was there; people were crying, shaking, comforting each other, or simply silent. Miladis asked to go to the bathroom, and the paramilitaries directed her to the priest's home, next to the church.

As she walked from the church to the priest's home, Miladis had to step over a body, which she thought might belong to a paramilitary. From the church, she could also make out another corpse in camouflage on another corner of the square; it looked like it might belong to one of the guerrillas. "He was missing a piece of his head, and someone had cleaved a machete into him," she remembered.

As she moved through the crowd, Miladis kept asking about her brother, but nobody had heard from Wilmar. Finally, she found one of the teachers. "It's lucky you weren't here earlier," she remembers the teacher whispering. "They were raping the women." Another woman told Miladis that the paramilitaries had sent away some of the town's men to deliver soft drinks to their troops deeper in the woods, so the paramilitaries could do as they wished with their women. It sounded like they had raped some of the teachers, too, but in their very traditional community, it was too painful—not to mention frightening— for the victims to talk about it directly.

As the morning wore on, Miladis's mother asked a male cousin to approach the paramilitaries and ask for permission to go search for Wilmar. The cousin said they should wait, but Miladis couldn't wait any longer. She decided to go up to them herself.

One of the male teachers accompanied Miladis to the telephone office, where the troops gave her a hard look. "You can go look for your relative, as long as you don't cry," they said. "The first one who cries pays with their head."

They instructed her to talk to one of their bosses, a man called "Junior." Frightened but determined, Miladis walked across the square and found him. Except for his military fatigues, the twenty-five-year-old baby-faced man with thick brows and full lips looked like any other young man from the countryside, not a hardened killer.

"What does your brother look like?" asked Junior, businesslike, when she explained what she wanted to do. She described the skinny, fragile-looking Wilmar.

"Oh, son of a bitch," Junior said, looking at some of his men. "That's that kid who got killed."

"He was running away," said Junior, unapologetically, when he saw Miladis's reaction. "Yeah, you can go pick him up."

Junior ordered a couple of his men to collect the body. Miladis waited at the door to the church with her sisters while their mother prayed inside.

AFTER THE PARAMILITARIES brought Wilmar's body back, Miladis begged them to let the family leave town to bury his body. The paramilitaries said yes—a few could leave. Miladis walked out of El Aro with her mother, one of her sisters, her niece, and Miladis's small son that afternoon. The family mule carried Wilmar's ruined little body as they climbed down the steep mountainside, across a hanging bridge, and past empty farms where abandoned dogs barked at them. After several hours, they finally made it to the town of Puerto Valdivia, where they buried the boy.

The paramilitaries stayed in the town for five more days. Miladis later heard from other townspeople who fled to Puerto Valdivia that the day she left, they killed Marco Aurelio Areiza after accusing him of selling food to guerrillas. Ignoring the pleas of Areiza's domestic partner, who insisted that he had only sold the food under guerrilla threat, the paramilitaries had dragged him away. His body was later found tied to a tree near the town cemetery with his eyes gouged out, deep knife wounds in his ribs, and his testicles cut off and stuffed in his mouth.

She also heard that paramilitaries had forced a young woman to lead them to a guerrilla campsite nearby—Miladis heard that the young woman might have once belonged to the guerrillas but had deserted them. Later on, Miladis said, people found only the bottom half of her body. It was rumored that the paramilitaries had thrown explosives at her.

The paramilitaries raped more women after the family left, though the victims remained too afraid or ashamed to tell the authorities. Survivors did report that the paramilitaries had gang-raped Elvia Rosa Areiza, a woman who did domestic work in the priest's house. They had then dragged the young mother of five through the streets, transforming her face into a purple, bloody mess before tying her up in a pigsty, where they left her to die of thirst.

People said that the paramilitaries laughed as they talked about how they had killed Miladis's little brother. He kept crying, they said, calling for the Virgin Mary to protect him and for them to let him go back to his mother.

By the time they left, the paramilitaries had killed fifteen people. They finally ordered the remaining residents to leave as they burned down most of the town, leaving only eighteen houses and the church standing. In total, more than seven hundred people fled El Aro and the surrounding region as a result of the operation.

Over time, one of Miladis's aunts—an elderly woman whom the paramilitaries had forced to cook for them during their incursion—would tell her that she had seen a helicopter arrive nearby. Another young man talked about how the paramilitaries had forced him to tie the bodies of dead combatants to the legs of a helicopter.

During that entire hellish week, nobody—neither the military nor law enforcement—responded to pleas for help from the community. Nor did anyone stop the paramilitaries as they left, taking with them

El Aro, Antioquia, a few days after the massacre, October or November 1997. © Rainer Huhle.

as many as 1,200 head of cattle that they had forced townspeople to herd for them from neighboring farms.

Twenty years later, we know that senior military commanders—far from trying to stop the paramilitaries' expansion—assisted them and helped to plan the massacre. With the paramilitaries' enormous drug profits, it was easy for them to buy off public officials. But many members of the military were eager accomplices who equipped, funded, and jointly plotted operations with the paramilitaries, viewing them as essential partners in a dirty war against the guerrillas that they could not legally conduct.

Over the following years, El Aro became a typical example of the paramilitaries' operations during their massive expansion campaign in the late 1990s. The paramilitaries claimed to be going after the guerrillas, and in some cases, as in El Aro, there was evidence that they had engaged in combat with them. But in town after town, they committed gruesome massacres, apparently aimed at terrorizing the civilian populations near where the guerrillas were operating. Then top paramilitary chief, Carlos Castaño, later described the El Aro incursion as part of the paramilitaries' counterinsurgency strategy in the region, where many guerrillas were operating at the time: "Either the guerrillas come out of their sanctuaries or we will go in."

Years later, it became clear that there was another dynamic at play, too, though it was less obvious to Colombians at the time: as they wiped out entire communities, paramilitaries were seizing their land, keeping it for themselves or their cronies, or selling it—often to friendly landowners and businesses—at a profit. They placed friendly politicians in key local government positions, ensuring that nobody would interfere with their activities. And slowly, they asserted their control over key transit routes to seaside ports, which were essential for drug-trafficking operations and the movement of arms shipments. A decade later, another paramilitary commander who had been involved in the El Aro massacre, Salvatore Mancuso, would explain that one of their main reasons for wanting to seize control of the region was that it was in the middle of a key strategic corridor for transporting cocaine.

But none of this was evident yet in 1997, even to the people—including Velásquez—who were investigating the paramilitaries' crimes.

EL ARO SPAWNED an even greater rift between Jesús María Valle and the army's Fourth Brigade, joined by the office of Antioquia's governor, Álvaro Uribe. El Aro belonged to Valle's home region of Ituango—the very same region that he represented as a councilman, and which he had been pleading with the military and state government for over a year to protect.

Two days before the massacre happened, one of Valle's contacts from Ituango, Amparo Areiza, had called to tell him that she had heard that the paramilitaries were coming into town. Amparo was the daughter of the El Aro shopkeeper, Marco Aurelio Areiza, but she had moved to the town of Yarumal years before and married a lawyer who knew Valle professionally. She had been worried for months because of reports that paramilitaries had started to go through the region, sometimes with members of the army, and it was said they were planning to go into El Aro. She had begged her father to leave town, but he had refused, telling her not to worry: he was an honest man, and he didn't feel he should have to run away like a criminal. The guerrillas sometimes forced him to sell them groceries, but he had always done so under coercion. The Thursday before the massacre, Amparo learned that the paramilitaries had been seen traveling through Puerto Valdivia on their way to El Aro, and that they had killed her cousin, Omar Gutiérrez, when they had stopped at his farm at the edge of the river. Amparo had once again called her father and asked him to leave, but he still refused. She had then called Valle.

Valle and Amparo had immediately started calling all the authorities they could, trying to get someone to stop the paramilitaries on their way into town. They each called the Fourth Brigade, separately, but were told that because there were going to be elections on Sunday, all the troops were being confined to their barracks. They tried calling the police and the governor's office, but with the elections pending, they could get no answers.

Municipal officials from Ituango also later stated that they had been in touch with El Aro community members as the massacre was getting underway, and that as early as Sunday, October 26, while the massacre was in full swing, they had tried to get the attention of the governor's office, the army, and the police. But the governor's office only promised to hold a meeting about it three days later, the army said it had no troops available, and the police said they were under orders not to send any officers to rural areas because of security concerns. Meanwhile, the paramilitaries were free to continue their theft, murder, and destruction over several days.

As survivors of the massacre fled to Yarumal, Puerto Valdivia, and Medellín, Valle, along with Amparo and others, started collecting their stories, though Valle's trips to Ituango had to be very brief, as he himself was a target. Amparo had seen military helicopters land in Yarumal after the massacre, and she had been told the paramilitaries were on them.

Valle tried to convince survivors to tell their stories to prosecutors and other people who might do something about it. Many were terrified, but Valle kept saying that if only they told their stories, justice might be slow, but it would eventually come. At one meeting he organized in Medellín, with representatives of the Organization of American States, Amparo was surprised to see how, as survivors started to tell their stories, "pain turned into courage." The more they heard each other speak, the more emboldened they became.

Still, they were running enormous risks. Soon after she made her statement to the criminal investigators, Amparo heard that the report had somehow been shared with authorities in the town of Yarumal, where she lived, and that "Junior," the paramilitary from El Aro, had been seen in local government offices reviewing her statement. Around the same time, she noticed a skinny young man who seemed to be monitoring her, and she started getting threatening phone calls from a man claiming to be her father's killer, who said she should leave town "or we will chop you up just like we did with him." She fled to Medellín, where she kept meeting with Valle, but even there, as she waited for the bus one day, she once again saw the skinny man, who snatched her purse and told her he had been ordered to kill her, but he didn't want to do so.

Meanwhile, Valle had been doing his best to get the word out about what he was learning. He began saying publicly that witnesses had seen military helicopters flying over El Aro during the massacre. Once again, he accused the military of conspiring with the paramilitaries. A few days after the massacre, Governor Uribe called for a "security meeting" with representatives of the army and Valle. The Fourth Brigade's commander, Carlos Ospina, denied Valle's charges that the military was involved, saying the army had tried to help the community, but that its helicopters had been unable to arrive at the site in time to do so. But Valle didn't buy the story. In a sworn statement before a court in early 1998, he repeated his earlier accusations about the military's complicity: "The paramilitary groups could not commit so many abuses, kill so many persons, sow terror among my people if it weren't for the colluding behavior of the army."

MILADIS HAD NEVER met Valle, though she had heard a lot about him from others in the community, and viewed him as "the only one" who stood up for them in that whole time, by insisting on telling the truth. She and her family had lost nearly everything in the massacre: Wilmar, their home, their land, their animals, their entire way of life. Like millions of other Colombians who, fleeing the paramilitaries, flocked to the outskirts of Medellín, Bogotá, and other major cities, they did their best to build new lives for themselves. With help from Miladis's older brother, the family moved into a tiny house in Puerto Valdivia. They had trouble getting by—the government offered them no assistance—and after a year, they decided to move back to El Aro, which was essentially a ghost town. They tried to rebuild, but in 2004 and 2005, small groups of armed paramilitaries started going through the town again, stealing small things—good clothes, deodorants, hand lotion—as well as mules. After everything Miladis and her family had gone through, they could not stay and wait for another massacre. They fled again, never to return.

CHAPTER 4

FOR THOSE WHO SPEAK THE TRUTH

IVÁN VELÁSQUEZ PUSHED HIS WAY through the throng in front of the worn four-story building, the Colón, where Jesús María Valle kept his modest legal office. Ordinarily, he would not personally visit a murder scene—that's what criminal investigators did. As chief prosecutor, Velásquez reviewed the evidence they collected, directed their next steps, and crafted legal arguments from behind his desk.

But this was a special case.

"They didn't kill a man. They killed the dignity of Antioquia!" a man proclaimed outside the building. He was bony and pale, glasses perched atop a prominent nose and full mustache, and seemed to be holding back tears as he raised his arms. He was one of many mourners standing awkwardly among the downtown crowds, paying little heed to the afternoon sun pounding down on them, or to the street vendors hawking the usual dried packets of herbs, T-shirts, knock-offs of brand-name purses, and fresh fruit. TV crews and photographers were also on the scene, holding out microphones and cameras, eager to be the first to catch the latest tidbit of information about the attack.

At the entrance to the Colón, Velásquez drily greeted the police officers guarding the perimeter before stepping in. His eyes adjusted as he strode through the dim, narrow corridor past the front desk. Ignoring the creaky elevator, Velásquez climbed the three flights of stairs to the hallway leading to No. 405.

VALLE'S SPARROW-LIKE sister, Nelly, who had been his secretary for years, had first noticed her big brother was afraid in December 1997, two months after the El Aro massacre. At the end of the workday, Valle would look over his shoulder as they got into a taxi. He asked her to keep her son from watching TV in a room with a window overlooking the street, which he felt was too exposed. At one point, he urged her to find some other place to live. She had been hurt, thinking he was mad at her: she didn't realize it was because he didn't want her to be there when they killed him.

Velásquez and J. Guillermo Escobar had tried to convince Valle to seek protection: Valle was getting a lot of public exposure in the media, and his accusations against the military were the kind of statements, thought Velásquez, that got you killed. Valle's campaign was also making many people, not only members of the military, increasingly angry. As Velásquez waited to enter a meeting at the governor's office one day, he overheard Uribe's deputy, businessman Pedro Juan Moreno, speaking mockingly about Valle as "that nut-case with his accusations." Later on, Velásquez recalled that there had been "huge hostility by Pedro Juan and Uribe toward Valle. The minute Valle made an accusation, which he would make public through the newspaper *El Colombiano*, or radio stations, there would be a strong reaction from the military or the governorship."

International human rights organizations offered to buy Valle an airplane ticket out of the country. Even if it was just for six months, Velásquez and J. Guillermo argued, he should go—at least until things calmed down a bit. But Valle refused.

Why would Valle stay, knowing he might get killed? Years later, Velásquez agreed that it was hard to understand. But Valle was one of those people, he said, who "could die of sadness if he fled—no, more than sadness, shame." For someone as attached to his people as Valle was, leaving was not an option: "When he talked about 'my town,' 'my people,' he wasn't speaking rhetorically. He was talking about *his* people."

So Valle continued taking taxis to his office and walking from there to the courthouses and prosecutors' offices for hearings and meetings. At least, Velásquez and J. Guillermo agreed, they would try to get him some bodyguards.

With the exception of his closest friends, few people continued to associate with him; many of his acquaintances now kept their distance. Valle started getting phone calls from people who would then hang up—threats, or perhaps attempts by his enemies to keep tabs on him. But Valle was also filled with indignation: after his fight with Uribe and the Fourth Brigade over his claims about links between the military and the paramilitaries, "he had no more peace," recalled Gloria Manco, a former student of Valle's who was close to the activist. "He had his moments of reading—he was a man who loved books—but after that point he didn't have those pleasures. His last days were supremely difficult, because he could not derive joy even from the smallest things."

ON FEBRUARY 6, 1998, Valle had given a statement to prosecutors from Velásquez's office who were investigating the El Aro massacre. He had not minced words in his description of those he considered responsible for the massacre:

> I always saw, and understood, that there was something like a tacit agreement . . . cleverly arranged between the commander of the Fourth Brigade, the commander of the Antioquia Police, Dr. Álvaro Uribe Vélez, Dr. Pedro Juan Moreno, and Carlos Castaño [the chief of the ACCU]. All the power of the self-defense groups has become consolidated because of the support this group has received from people linked to the government, the military establishment, the police establishment, and to well-known ranchers and bankers from Antioquia and the country. . . . Because of the failure to act by Álvaro Uribe and Pedro Juan Moreno, I understood that in those three years there was an alliance in Antioquia that, with the pretext of acting against the guerrillas, had attacked the defenseless civilian population and had strengthened the drug trade.

Valle had also continued to fight the slander lawsuit that the Fourth Brigade member had started against him several months earlier: he wanted to use the lawsuit as a way to force the courts to investigate what was happening in Ituango. So on Thursday, February 26, 1998, at 2:30 p.m., he and Gloria Manco, who was representing him in the suit, went to the office of the local prosecutor (not under Velásquez's jurisdiction) handling the slander suit, and Valle repeated his earlier statements, only in greater detail: since September 1996, he said, there had been a paramilitary group operating right outside the town of Ituango, very close to where the army's Fourth Brigade and the police were based. Valle recalled that he had written to Governor Uribe, his chief of staff Pedro Juan Moreno, and former Fourth Brigade commander Alfonso Manosalva to request protection for the community, "but I found no answer," he said. Given how openly the paramilitary group operated—more than forty members, carrying rifles, had moved around the edge of the town—he believed they had to be enjoying the backing of the army and the police. He then recalled how, as councilman for Ituango, he had received information about how the paramilitaries worked jointly with the army: one would arrive, and the other would always be right behind. "That's why the La Granja massacre happened, as well as the deaths of what I estimate to be more than 150 people who were taken out of their homes, tortured, disappeared, and killed, and that's why the massacre in El Aro happened," Valle said. He added that he knew the chief prosecutor's office wanted to get in there to pick up the bodies, but that they couldn't because the military would not cooperate by providing helicopters. Not only that: "In El Aro, the peasants have said that army helicopters were present, which should be investigated. That's why I am saying that the army will not cooperate with prosecutors to even pick up the bodies."

As for the specific events that were the subject of the lawsuit—Valle's televised claim that the army had forced an Ituango driver to carry wounded paramilitaries with them in his car—he repeated his allegations and urged the prosecutor to try to determine who the paramilitaries and army members were in that case. Ultimately, Valle said, so long as prosecutors investigated "why my people are living in the shadow of terror, and how the peasants I knew as a child walking through the paths and small towns have died and their bodies have been dismembered," he would be at peace even if he was convicted.

After Valle made his statement, Gloria recalled, an official asked him why he hadn't just kept quiet. He blew up, furious: this, she recalled him saying, was why Colombia was the way it was—because the criminals had officials as their middlemen. How could someone ask him to keep quiet, when their rivers were bathed in blood? To Valle,

Gloria said, suggesting that he remain quiet "was the worst insult anyone could have given him."

THE MORNING OF Friday, February 27, 1998, Nelly and Valle went
into the office together. She took calls while he spoke to students and
clients. She stepped out for lunch alone—he had too much work.
While she was away, Valle took a call from Carlos Jaramillo, one of
his Ituango contacts, with whom he regularly met, along with
Amparo Areiza, to hear about what was going on in the region. They
had helped him piece together what had happened in El Aro and
identify links between paramilitaries and the military. According to
Jaramillo, the paramilitaries were also receiving support from two
brothers, the Angulos, who he said ran a cocaine-processing lab and
operated some of their drug-trafficking business in Ituango. In his
later statement to prosecutors, Jaramillo would say that when he
called, Valle immediately invited him to come by the office. After
greeting the doorman, Jaramillo took the elevator up, and Valle let
him into the office, where the two started drinking coffee and chatting as usual. Jaramillo remembered one statement that struck him
from their conversation: at some point, Valle said, "They haven't
killed me because they haven't wanted to. Whenever they want, they
can kill me, and nothing will happen."

WHEN SHE CAME back from lunch, Nelly saw two men at the door.
They were wearing suits and ties and carrying briefcases. Thinking
they were clients, she unlocked the door to the little reception area
that led into Valle's office. But as Nelly started to go into the office to
greet her brother, the men shoved past her, pushing her into a chair
across from Valle, who looked startled for a second. Then, realizing
what was about to happen, Valle turned to his sister and held her gaze
firmly: "Stay calm, Nelly, we're here now."

He let the men grab him. At some point, a woman slipped into the
office and helped them tie Nelly and Jaramillo up on the floor near the
door. Then one of the men pulled out a gun and put something on it:
a silencer. Be quiet, one of them hissed. They forced Valle to lie face-
down on the floor in a corner of his office, next to the window, and tied
him up there by his hands and feet.

Nelly couldn't tear her eyes away from Valle's face as one of the men put the gun to her brother's head. She screamed when they shot him.

VELÁSQUEZ KNEW WHAT to expect when he got to Valle's office later that afternoon, but the sight of his friend was still jarring. Valle's boulder-like figure remained unmistakable even as he lay face-down, crumpled on the floor by his desk. Dark blood confused itself with his thick hair and navy blue suit. His arms lay twisted into an arc behind him—later on, Velásquez would hear that the killers had used Valle's own shoelaces to tie his thumbs together before shooting him twice on the left side of his head.

That calm and strong voice that so many had relied upon to speak the truth, and which so many in power had dismissed, was now silenced for good.

PART II

THE HUNT

MEDELLÍN, COLOMBIA, 1998–1999

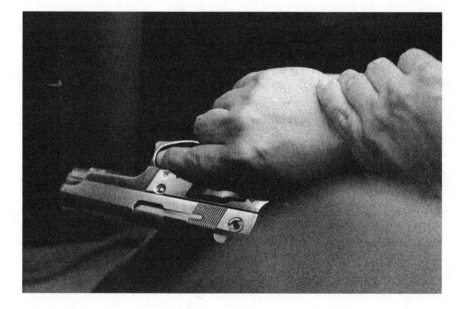

CHAPTER 5

THE INVESTIGATORS

"YOU WOULDN'T BELIEVE SOME OF the cases," J. Guillermo Escobar said to Iván Velásquez. The two men sat smoking in Velásquez's seventh-floor office in the concrete government complex known as "La Alpujarra" in downtown Medellín. La Alpujarra had little to recommend it—the clutch of gray, characterless buildings struck a somber note in the middle of a hectic city that, despite the daily string of murders, was still colorful and very much alive. But his surroundings were the last thing on Velásquez's mind.

His boss in Bogotá, Attorney General Alfonso Gómez Méndez, had instructed Velásquez that one of his top priorities as chief prosecutor was to investigate a large number of gruesome massacres and killings in Antioquia and Córdoba in which the paramilitaries were involved—previous prosecutors had made little headway in the cases. Because he needed someone he could trust to take the lead on these cases, Velásquez had asked J. Guillermo, his close friend and former thesis adviser, who was on the verge of retirement, to join him as a prosecutor, to coordinate the paramilitary cases.

They had started by taking an inventory of the case files involving paramilitaries that were littering the office, unsolved and, in many cases, untouched for months. In the case files involving the left-wing guerrillas, in contrast, there were signs that prosecutors had taken testimony, ordered searches and arrests, and even completed investigations. It wasn't clear yet whether the difference had to do with the relative difficulty of investigating the cases and the support they got from security forces and police, or lack of interest, fear, or corruption among prosecutors and investigators.

"I just found one file that's all about body parts: heads, arms, legs," continued J. Guillermo. The case records showed that the paramilitaries in the town of Puerto Berrío, on the banks of the Magdalena River, had collected all the bodies of people they killed, dismembered them, and then piled them up into a series of pyramids. He was particularly offended by how previous prosecutors had labeled the file: the case of the "big sausages." Other than that, they had apparently done virtually nothing to pursue the case.

JESÚS MARÍA VALLE'S murder, which came only a few days after the natural death of Velásquez's father, had also left Velásquez reeling with the anger and sorrow attendant to grief and flooded with an overwhelming sense of impotence. "It was about feeling very small in the face of it all, because you clearly knew who the enemies were," he would remember years later. To him, it was obvious that the paramilitaries had killed Valle, possibly with military backing. The meticulously planned, efficient operation also showed that the paramilitaries were no small-time groups roaming the countryside; this was a highly sophisticated criminal enterprise, and its reach extended deep into the city. By killing Valle, they were not just eliminating a problem; they were sending the message that anyone who got in their way—who exposed their atrocities or interfered with their expansion—would pay with their life. And, at that moment, Velásquez was facing the mammoth challenge of investigating their crimes.

But Velásquez's indignation at the injustice of Valle's murder won out over his fear. Valle, Velásquez was now convinced, had been right all along—the paramilitaries were an existential threat to the country's democracy and people. So instead of backing away, the prosecutor doubled down on his office's investigations of the paramilitaries. Besides, as he would write years later, he and his team in the prosecutor's office were "in the best moment of 'functional optimism,' that reaffirming feeling that makes us believe that it is possible to put an end to impunity, and not even the painful murder of . . . Valle . . . put the brakes on the almost frenetic momentum we had."

Velásquez had a way of putting the risks he might be running out of his mind, rationalizing that when his time came, that would be the end—there was not much he could do about it. Whenever he was asked whether he was afraid of getting killed, he would shrug, recalling what one of Pablo Escobar's men had said to him years before, when Velásquez was inspector general for Medellín: "If you're alive, it's not because we haven't been able to kill you, but because we haven't wanted to. If you have five guards, we'll send ten after you. If you have ten, we'll send twenty. If you have twenty—which is very unlikely— we'll send fifty, and you won't be able to resist." The bottom line was that if every public official who might come under threat resigned, then no change would ever be possible, and that, to Velásquez, would be intolerable.

COLOMBIA'S PARAMILITARY PROBLEM, Velásquez was also beginning to understand, extended well beyond Valle's beloved Ituango, and even beyond the borders of Antioquia. As Valle had said in a speech a few months before his murder, Antioquia was "exporting" paramilitarism to other Colombian states. And these paramilitaries seemed like different kinds of groups from those of the past.

There had been talk of "self-defense" groups backed by the military since the 1970s, and in the 1980s it was well known that at least some of them had forged strong ties with drug traffickers. One particularly infamous group was Death to Kidnappers (Muerte a Secuestradores, MAS), which members of the Medellín cartel established after members of the M-19 guerrillas kidnapped Martha Nieves Ochoa, sister of the cartel's Ochoa brothers. In the early 1980s, the MAS was believed to have killed more than two hundred people who in one way or another got in the way of their interests. But in those years, it had never been clear to Velásquez whether the groups involved in all these different activities were part of a single movement, or were operating independently of one another. It was also unclear what connection they had to the shadowy death squads that killed many activists—including Valle's predecessors at the Permanent Human Rights Committee—in the 1980s. The case files he was now reading pointed to a far larger and more organized force.

The group that was terrorizing its way across Antioquia and neighboring states, the Peasant Self-Defense Forces of Córdoba and Urabá, or ACCU, in the Spanish acronym, was named for the regions where it had started—Urabá is an area around the Gulf of Urabá that encompasses the northwest of Antioquia as well as parts of the states of Córdoba and Chocó. The ACCU's leader Carlos Castaño, was a short man, taut like a pitbull, with a crazed look in his eye. In a book he'd publish in 2001, *My Confession*, Castaño said that when he was a teenager, the FARC kidnapped and then killed his father, despite the family's payment of a substantial ransom. Castaño and his brothers Fidel and Vicente had then taken up the cause of arming ordinary Colombians so they could defend themselves against the guerrillas. While experts have later raised serious questions about Castaño's account of his father's death and the brothers' motivations, it's fairly clear that at some point in the 1980s they were working closely with the Medellín cartel, though eventually they turned on Pablo Escobar and joined Los Pepes, the death squad that targeted Escobar's people. By then, under Carlos's brother Fidel's leadership, the Castaños had also formed their own paramilitary group, named after their property, Las Tangas. "Los Tangueros," as they were known, committed a string of killings and massacres in the 1980s and 1990s in and around Córdoba. When Fidel was killed in 1994 under mysterious circumstances—Carlos blamed guerrillas—Carlos took over the group.

But they had now expanded much farther, across Antioquia and Córdoba and well into other regions. Sometimes known as the "head-splitters" (*mochacabezas*), the paramilitaries became famous for their gruesome and cruel tactics: tying someone up and dismembering them alive in front of their families; decapitating their victims and playing soccer with their heads; raping women with clubs while forcing their relatives to watch; scalping, burning, strangling, hanging— nothing seemed too vicious or too extreme for the ACCU.

Now in his mid-thirties, Castaño regularly exploded into lengthy tirades, barking orders and sermonizing about his war on the left. Yet the paramilitaries' motives were not purely political: it was widely rumored that the ACCU was involved in drug trafficking and organized crime. After Pablo Escobar's death, the former members of Los Pepes had been quick to pick up the reins of Escobar's drug-trafficking operations—as well as to continue applying his brutal tactics. By 1997, Castaño and his cronies might have been able to claim an even greater number of victims to their name than Escobar ever did. And based on what Velásquez was seeing in his office, law enforcement was doing little to stop them.

WHAT WORRIED VELÁSQUEZ the most was his own office: How could he ensure that his team of prosecutors, and the criminal investigators with whom they worked, was clean? Even before he started, people in the attorney general's office in Bogotá had warned Velásquez about possible corruption in the Medellín office. The lack of progress on the paramilitary cases raised real questions about whether some prosecutors and investigators might have ties to the very groups they were investigating.

So as a condition for taking the job, Velásquez had insisted that the attorney general allow him to name some of the senior prosecutors who would work directly with him. In addition to asking J. Guillermo Escobar to oversee the paramilitary cases, Velásquez asked Laureano Colmenares, a very respected senior judge who had already retired, to take over the equally sensitive drug-trafficking cases—despite Pablo Escobar's death, other traffickers had filled his shoes, and the number of murders in the city remained high.

Velásquez transferred more than a dozen other prosecutors he didn't trust or didn't know well out of the office. The transfers, he knew, had a cost: many of those prosecutors were well connected in Medellín, and he wasn't scoring any popularity points by getting rid of them. But he couldn't take any chances. So he hired a new batch of young lawyers recommended to him by friends and close colleagues. Among them was the cheerful and chatty Javier Tamayo, who was still in his late twenties and single, and who managed to thoroughly enjoy Medellín's nightlife even while pouring himself into his work. Another, Carlos Bonilla, was also young but already married and with small children. Bonilla had suffered polio as a child and walked with a limp as a result. Velásquez assigned him and J. Guillermo to the investigation of Valle's murder.

The situation with the criminal investigators was even trickier. Earlier that year, two investigators from the CTI—the special agency attached to the attorney general's office and charged with conducting criminal investigations alongside the prosecutors—had been killed. Another CTI agent, Diego Arcila, a sweet and shy young man who had been in a seminary, in training to be a priest, before becoming a wiretapping expert at the CTI, had given sworn statements to prosecutors in which he described evidence that paramilitaries had infiltrated the CTI: CTI agents may have given the assassins information about the dead agents' investigations and movements.

Velásquez had no authority over the CTI, which had its own regional director, who worked alongside Velásquez and answered to Bogotá. So he was relieved when, only a few weeks after he started, the CTI in Bogotá named a new regional director for Antioquia, Gregorio Oviedo. The forty-three-year-old Oviedo was a funny, outgoing guy, small, copper-skinned, and square-jawed, whose striking light blue eyes behind thick glasses suggested a quick intelligence. The two men hit it off right away—Oviedo could even get the usually impassive Velásquez to laugh at his jokes. Also, Velásquez knew Oviedo's wife, Amelia Pérez, who was doing good work as a prosecutor in the specialized Human Rights Unit in Bogotá that the attorney general's office set up in 1995 to handle major human rights cases.

A soft-spoken woman with brown eyes and hair and thick glasses, Pérez looked more like a librarian than a tough prosecutor who faced down organized crime, though there was a firmness about her chin and gaze that hinted at some hidden well of strength. Starting the previous year, Pérez had quietly been spearheading one of the Human Rights Unit's most difficult and dangerous investigations—the one that first brought the corruption within the Antioquia CTI office to the surface.

The case had started with the 1995 disappearances of three young men in different parts of Medellín, after men dressed in black and wearing ski masks had seized them from their homes. They also seized the wife and baby girl of one of the young men, but later released them. In interviews with the authorities, the young woman recounted being surprised at how one of the leaders of the kidnappers had treated her: he had given her money for her cab ride home, and clothes for herself and her little girl, and told her something like "Don't worry, he won't bother you anymore." The girl's husband had sometimes mistreated her, and she would often complain to her mother about it over the phone. Pérez took the exchange as an indication that whoever had carried out the operation had been tapping the family's lines. The father of two of the young men had also been killed after he gave a statement to prosecutors, in which he said he believed that members of the CTI and the UNASE, the elite kidnapping squad, were involved in the disappearance. Other evidence already collected by investigators, such as the descriptions of the cars of the kidnappers, also pointed to the involvement of government agents.

Another prosecutor had initially handled the matter, so when it got reassigned to Pérez, CTI agents in Medellín had already made some progress investigating the case. Their basic theory was that the disappearances were an act of retaliation: the young men who had disappeared were suspected of being involved in the kidnapping of another young man. The hostage's father, they said, had sought help from Gustavo Upegui, a wealthy soccer team owner from Envigado, a municipality on the outskirts of Medellín, who was said to have once handled Pablo Escobar's finances. People in Medellín whispered that Upegui was still involved in some of the assassinations that were happening all the time in Medellín, and that he was working with the fearsome criminal gang known as "La Terraza" and the infamous "Envigado Office," a drug-trafficking operation where, it was said, people in the underworld could hire the services of killers to settle scores and mediate disputes. But Upegui had never been convicted of a crime. The investigators believed that Upegui had arranged the disappearances with the help of members of public security forces—which would explain the hints of wiretapping in the case.

During an initial trip to Medellín, around April 1997, Pérez met the CTI team on the case: Jaime Piedrahita, Manuel López, Fernando González, and the former seminarian Diego Arcila, or "Dieguito," as she called him, whom J. Guillermo Escobar would later describe as "the smartest investigator" he had ever met. Pérez was taken aback when a more senior CTI official, after introducing Pérez to them, said that the CTI was transferring one of them—Jaime Piedrahita, a skinny young man with huge dark eyebrows and a slim moustache—out of town. He and the others, Pérez recalled the official saying, were "kind of crazy little guys," with strange ideas, off running investigations on their own. Pérez liked the investigators, and she found the comment troubling: Why was this official putting down good investigative work?

On July 4, 1997, a little after 5 p.m., as Piedrahita was leaving the office on his red Yamaha motorcycle, two men drove up to him on another motorcycle. Before he could react, in the middle of the busy street, they poured six bullets into his head and sped off. The night before, Piedrahita had called one of the other investigators, Fernando González, and told him that he had identified the armed gang through which Upegui was carrying out his criminal activities in the municipality of Itagüí, just outside Medellín.

Convinced that Piedrahita had been killed because of the Upegui investigation, Pérez went back to Medellín and met with the investigators. The problem, they told her, was that all of Medellín was under the thumb of the same criminals who had once belonged to Los Pepes, and who were close to the paramilitaries. One of them was Upegui. The investigators said they were especially concerned because they had evidence that some of their own CTI colleagues were on the payroll of organized crime.

Pérez agreed that they should look into it further, and in the next couple of months they sent her written reports. They described a store in a Medellín mall where current and former government officials who were on Upegui's payroll received bribes of as much as US$500 a month. They said a former CTI agent, Carlos Mario Aguilar, who was now working with the paramilitaries and Upegui, was in charge of recruiting CTI agents. Pérez also learned that the investigators suspected that Uber Duque, who had only just resigned as head of the investigations unit for the Medellín CTI in mid-1997, and was now setting up his own private practice as an attorney, was working with Upegui. Arcila noted that Duque had "expressed interest in the paramilitaries; he told me, literally, that in his view [and that of another official] . . . when it came to investigations, you had to play dumb, as that was a good way of collaborating with them." Duque was now in private practice as a lawyer in Medellín, but apparently he stayed in close contact with many of his former CTI colleagues.

In the first week of September, CTI agent Manuel López excitedly told Arcila that he had had another breakthrough: he had obtained incriminating recordings of Uber Duque, their former colleague, whom they now suspected of working closely with Upegui. He needed to meet with Pérez to share them with her. He never did: on September 5, López, like Piedrahita before him, was shot to death by unknown assassins; for López, it happened near a shopping mall as he was about to head to his office.

Shortly after López's death, the central CTI office in Bogotá changed the leadership in the Antioquia office—and that was how Gregorio Oviedo, Pérez's husband, ended up starting there as the regional CTI chief in late 1997, around the same time that Velásquez started as the regional chief prosecutor.

Aware of the infiltration of the CTI office, Oviedo and Velásquez selected Arcila and a few other CTI agents whom they believed to be trustworthy and started to channel all especially sensitive matters to them.

BY THE TIME Valle was killed, the team was already starting to make progress. It had all started a couple of months before, when Oviedo had given Velásquez some surprising news from the CTI office in Bello, right outside of Medellín. A young man had come into the Bello office saying he had recently joined the paramilitaries but was now terrified: he had overheard the paramilitaries talking about how they were planning to kill his grandfather, with whom he lived. So, he said, he had deserted the paramilitaries, and he was now seeking protection from the authorities. The head of the Bello office, Sergio Humberto Parra, interviewed the young man, who said he knew of a safe house where a lot of the paramilitaries stayed in Bello. Parra got the young man to give him the house's phone number.

Oviedo had jumped at the opportunity—now that they knew of at least one place where the paramilitaries were living, they could try to monitor their activities, and maybe start to build a solid case. Velásquez's prosecutors made sure they got the necessary warrants, and they entrusted Arcila with the sensitive task of wiretapping the paramilitary safe house. They asked a few others to help: one was Fernando González, who had worked closely with Pérez, Arcila, and the two murdered CTI agents, and whose specialty was investigating paramilitary crimes. His colleagues had jokingly nicknamed him "Paraco," a slang term for a paramilitary. González was also daring: working with Pérez on the Upegui investigation, he had taken a video recorder to the office of Upegui in Envigado wearing only sunglasses to make him harder to place, and had taken footage of the soccer magnate.

Oviedo also promoted Parra, appointing him to be his right-hand man as chief of the regional CTI's investigations unit. Despite his atrocious spelling—about which Oviedo teased him mercilessly—the chatty, slightly overweight, and perpetually disheveled forty-year-old Parra was the agent who had first obtained the phone number to the paramilitary safe house, and there seemed to be few doubts as to his honesty and commitment to the work.

The wiretaps started to produce results right away—the paramilitaries, it seemed, were so confident that nobody would pursue them that they talked endlessly on the phone about planned operations. They even mentioned individual members of the group (though always by their aliases), as well as the addresses they used. According to Arcila's reports, a bunch of the paramilitaries in the safe house were former army members—which was alarming but also made sense. The paramilitaries could afford to pay handsome salaries to people with military training, and many of the military men viewed the paramilitaries, in turn, as allies in their counterinsurgency campaign. Plus, Arcila found out through the wiretaps, the group in the safe house had contacts in multiple military units throughout Antioquia.

The team considered raiding the house, but decided against it. The wiretap was producing valuable information, and they could use it to learn more about the group's structure. They did, however, start to quietly arrest some of the group's members, including one active army soldier who was working with the group and was wanted for murder, though they were careful not to give away the existence of the wiretap.

They also tried to disrupt some of the paramilitaries' plots. One time, they figured out that the group was sending some of its members on a bus full of businesspeople traveling from Medellín to Ecuador, with the goal of holding up the bus and robbing its passengers on the road. So that the paramilitaries wouldn't realize that the CTI was on their heels, the team asked the police to take the lead: the police stopped the bus and confronted the paramilitaries on board, killing three and arresting several others who were following the bus in a car.

IT WAS LATE March 1998, and Oviedo was finishing lunch with a couple of colleagues at the apartment where he was rooming with the young prosecutor Javier Tamayo, when he received a call on his office cellphone: "Oviedo, I'm calling you from the ACCU," said the man on the other end of the line, referring to the paramilitaries by their formal acronym. "You are pursuing us too much and not the guerrillas. . . . If you continue, we will declare you, your family, and the CTI to be military targets."

As soon as they hung up, Oviedo put in a call to Amelia Pérez, his wife, saying only: "Keep your eyes open, because I just got a call." She understood immediately. She was having lunch out with two of her colleagues, who were watching her during the call. She told them nothing, but excused herself so she could contact the bodyguard who was assigned to protect her children as a result of the threats Oviedo had received in his previous job: please, she asked, be extra careful.

Oviedo put the phone down on his bed after calling her, walked out of the bedroom, and stared at his colleagues, waiting to see if they would notice anything in his face—they didn't. Excusing himself, Oviedo went straight back to the office to tell Velásquez about the call: "I came to tell you, because I interpret this call as being directed at you too," Oviedo told him. The seriousness of the threat sank in even more deeply a couple of weeks later, on April 13, when an assassin shot CTI agent Fernando González several times in the head one morning as he was leaving his house to go to work. Oviedo, Velásquez, and Pérez knew that the threat against Oviedo—and González's killing—were almost certainly connected to their investigations, though none of them could be entirely sure what had triggered them. None of them, however, viewed that as a reason to stop at that point: they had always known that their jobs were dangerous, and by now, they all felt they had a personal stake in seeing their investigations through.

And they were about to make their biggest discovery yet.

Chapter 6

In Plain Sight

Were it not for its history, the Padilla parking lot would be entirely unremarkable. A small neon sign on Tenerife Street in downtown Medellín announces "Parqueadero Padilla" in cursive script above the entrance to a paved lot with space for thirty or so cars, some of them partly covered, others in the sun. Much more memorable is the hectic commercial neighborhood—known as "El Hueco," or The Hole—surrounding the parking lot. Padilla is squeezed in among what feels like an endless stream of small businesses, selling anything you might need to build or furnish a house. Sinks, lengths of fabric, foam for mattresses, cement, ceramic tiles, doorknobs, hooks, tools, scraps of metal, are piled high, hanging from walls and doors and pouring out of the little warehouses that sold them. Every so often, the flow of stores is interrupted by an old barbershop, or a little restaurant serving coffee and a set and affordable "menu of the day" (usually your choice of meat or fish, juice, soup, and maybe some french fries or rice, plus a small dessert) for lunch.

Shoppers mill about, but there are also many men—ordinary men, in jeans and polo shirts—standing idly near stores, looking sharply at everything around them, staring at passersby. El Hueco is said to be one of the safest parts of the city, but according to some, that's because it is paramilitary territory. The men who stand around watching are lookouts, guarding the area and reporting back to their bosses if they notice anything unusual.

The Padilla parking lot, and its street, looked much the same when the CTI searched it on April 30, 1998.

Diego Arcila, the CTI agent who was a former seminarian, had picked up the address of the parking lot and one other location on the wiretap, but Oviedo had decided to hold off on searching it at first. He was still concerned that if they moved too quickly, the paramilitaries would realize that the CTI was listening to their calls.

Their plan that morning had simply been to stop and search a truck. Arcila had heard on the wiretap that the paramilitaries were planning to move some cargo that day on the road from Medellín to the Western Antioquia town of Sopetrán.

Sergio Parra and a few other CTI agents intercepted the truck on the road and pulled it over, pretending it was a routine search. And, sure enough, when they looked in the back, they found it was stuffed with what would turn out to be 150 military uniforms that, they surmised, were meant to supply the paramilitaries operating in Western Antioquia. They also found two beepers, ten .38-caliber weapons, and, under the driver's seat, US$20,000.

But the surprise came when they checked the names of the driver and two passengers. One of the men, a retired army officer, was, according to Arcila's analysis of the wiretap information, the paramilitaries' operational head for all of Antioquia.

It was a big blow—bigger than they had expected. And since the CTI, rather than the police, was conducting the arrests, Oviedo concluded, the paramilitaries would probably figure out quickly that the CTI was monitoring them. It was time to search the two Medellín addresses the paramilitaries had mentioned in their calls. To be safe, Oviedo instructed a massive number of agents to accompany them—as many as 120, as Oviedo later recalled it.

The first address they went to turned out to be a dead end: an ordinary diner. And when they first arrived at the second address, the Padilla parking lot, it looked like it, too, would prove to be nothing. It was just a small parking lot with cars in it.

But the investigators decided to walk around it anyway, and on the grounds they found a cheaply built two-story shack. They knocked on the door—nothing. They tried again, and still, nobody answered. Yet they could hear movement inside. Oviedo asked one of the CTI agents, a very large man, to kick in the door. And in they went.

Inside, they found two young women and a broad-faced man in his early thirties carrying a backpack. They all looked flustered, and Oviedo told them to wait while the investigators searched the space. He noticed a radio-telephone on a table in the main room and guessed that they used it to communicate with their commanders.

"Can I leave now?" asked the man with the backpack, getting impatient. "No," said Oviedo, "you wait here." In searching the space, the agents noticed that one piece of furniture, an armoire, looked like it had a fake backing. They pulled it off and found two detailed accounting books, carefully kept, detailing records from 1994 to 1998. In another piece of furniture they found a pile of propaganda material for the paramilitaries, a map of the organizational structure of the ACCU, and various other ACCU documents. They also found a laptop and a desktop computer, a couple of cellphones, and dozens of floppy disks sitting next to a shredder. Someone had managed to shred one of the disks, but clearly they hadn't had the time to finish.

When they finally searched the man's backpack, they found a Beretta pistol and two cartridges as well as a weapons license in the name of Jacinto Alberto Soto—the man's name—from the Fourth Brigade. They also found three checks in different names worth about 13 million pesos (around US$10,000 at the time).

The investigators put Soto and the two women under arrest and arranged to take all the materials to their offices.

AS THEY WRAPPED up the search, the normally affable Sergio Parra, who had joined the group during the search, looked worried. Oviedo would later recall that the two of them were standing alone in the parking lot when Parra gave him a fixed look: "You know what, boss? With this operation we just did, the two of us? We are *tuqui tuqui lulu*." Parra motioned with his hands in the shape of a pistol, pointing it first at Oviedo's head and then at his own to indicate that they were dead men.

But when he informed Iván Velásquez and other colleagues at La Alpujarra of his findings soon afterward, Oviedo found them in an exultant mood. J. Guillermo Escobar gave him a big hug: "Dr. Oviedo, with this operation you just justified your existence on earth. You have just saved not ten, not twenty, nor one hundred people. You have just saved thousands of people." Oviedo would cherish J. Guillermo's words, loaded with such emotion and coming from such an eminent figure, for years.

Over the next days, prosecutors and investigators pored over the documents they had found: it was hard to believe, but they appeared to be the entire accounting records for the ACCU for several years. "We had expected to find a place where they were making camouflaged uniforms, or to find weapons or money or drugs," recalled the prosecutor Javier Tamayo. This was the only time he could remember investigators finding such a significant cache of records for an armed group. The records included information about the ACCU's bank accounts, records of payments, and contributions of money and weapons made by various individuals, whose names were listed. There was a chart showing the ACCU's organizational structure, divided into dozens of blocks, or fronts, and lists of the expenses of each of these fronts (some of the documents sought to disguise the fronts by referring to them as various named "farms," but the investigators quickly figured that out). They also found records of extensive weapons purchases, labeled as receipts for purchases of ordinary items—nails rather than ammunition, clothes rather than military uniforms. The records showed that the ACCU was operating not only in their known haunts of Antioquia and Córdoba, but also on the eastern plains, the northern coast, Cali, and Bogotá.

Velásquez began to issue orders—around five hundred of them in just the first couple of days—to freeze the bank accounts of people and businesses that appeared on the paramilitaries' books. Oviedo dispatched investigators to personally carry the orders to banks in towns and cities across the country. If they could only spend enough time working with the records, Velásquez and Oviedo were convinced that they could identify and arrest not only the paramilitaries' members and leaders but also their financial backers. It could be a fatal blow to the ACCU.

In the following days, prosecutors also interviewed the three people they had arrested at the site, though the interviews were initially less than productive: the two women said they had only recently been hired to help Jacinto Alberto Soto; they were doing some accounting work related to what they had believed to be farms. Meanwhile, the heavy-set, green-eyed Soto acknowledged that he had been a member of the ACCU for a couple of years, and provided some more details about what the various documents meant. But for the most part, he

Iván Velásquez with bodyguards and investigators, 1998 or 1999,
Medellín. © Iván and María Victoria Velásquez.

denied knowledge of how the paramilitaries worked or who financed
them, pointing out that he simply did the accounting based on information provided by other contacts in the ACCU. Still, Oviedo kept
Soto in the CTI's jail and ordered that security around the jail be
strengthened—they didn't yet know how much information he had to
share, but the paramilitaries would have good reason to try to bust him
out or kill him.

IN BOGOTÁ, Amelia Pérez, the Human Rights Unit prosecutor in the
attorney general's office who was married to Oviedo, was juggling many
difficult cases. Not only was she still working on the Upegui investigation in Medellín, but she had also been assigned the El Aro massacre,
which senior officials had decided to move from Antioquia to the specialized Human Rights Unit. And she was making progress on an investigation into another paramilitary massacre from December 1996 in

the town of Pichilín, in the coastal state of Sucre (which borders Córdoba on the north). The story the survivors told was that around fifty
paramilitaries had come into town and sacked the homes of several of
its inhabitants, pulling more than a dozen of them from their houses
and killing them in public, then leaving their bodies strewn along a
main road.

In the El Aro investigation, Pérez found that she couldn't get to the
scene of the crime, which she wanted to inspect. She needed the governor's office and military to provide security and transportation support—
standard in other cases where crime scenes were hard to reach—but they
kept refusing, giving her different excuses. One day they would say that
there was combat going on in the area; another they would claim the
weather would not allow it. It was the same experience that previous
prosecutors in the case had had: Amparo Areiza, the daughter of the El
Aro shopkeeper and the woman who had tried to piece the story together with Jesús María Valle, had for months tried to get to El Aro to
pick up her father's body, but when she tried going on her own, the army
stopped her on the way, saying it was too dangerous. Prosecutors had
repeatedly told her they couldn't get cooperation from the military to
conduct exhumations. Finally, a prosecutor had called her in late March
1998 to tell her that they were taking advantage of the fact that the
Fourth Brigade commander, Carlos Ospina, was out of town to go into El
Aro. Areiza had gone on foot and met prosecutors there while they did
the exhumation. She then put her father's remains, now mostly bones,
into a suitcase, and left town carrying him on her back.

Months later, also facing what looked like obstruction from the
military and others, Pérez was doing her best to get information from
other sources. She started to compile information about the military
units that had been operating in the region at the time: given the military's failure to help the community during the massacre, and the fact
that the paramilitaries had been able to leave the region around El Aro
with around 1,200 head of cattle, without the military stopping them,
some level of collusion seemed likely.

She also interviewed survivors, who talked in detail not only about
the killings, but also about several rapes of women during the massacre. Many of them were afraid to come forward, out of shame or terror:
they had seen how the paramilitaries gang-raped, but also tortured and
killed their neighbor Elvia Rosa Areiza.

Around that time, Pérez also started interviewing a source who gave her leads about both the Pichilín and El Aro massacres: Francisco Villalba, a twenty-five-year-old former paramilitary member who on February 13 had turned himself in to the CTI office in Santa Rosa de Osos, Antioquia, saying he was tired of killing and was seeking protection. The head of that CTI office, Yirman Giraldo, had been the first to interview Villalba, and had then taken him in to Medellín, where Oviedo and a prosecutor from Velásquez's office also interviewed him. A skinny man from the town of Sincelejo, in the coastal region of Sucre, whose dark tan suggested he had spent a lot of time working or walking outdoors, Villalba said that he had been part of a paramilitary block run by Salvatore Mancuso that had carried out both the El Aro and Pichilín massacres. He provided extensive statements about both cases, recognizing his own participation in some of the killings—for example, he recalled beheading one young woman with a machete near El Aro.

Villalba said that he had joined the paramilitaries in 1994 because he was out of work, and Salomón Feris—who at one point headed a Convivir, but who Villalba said was the coordinator of the paramilitaries in Sincelejo—recruited him. Early on, Villalba recounted, he was sent to a ranch called "the 35" in Antioquia that belonged to the paramilitary leader Fidel Castaño, where the paramilitaries trained him. They taught him to use AK-47s, mortars, grenade launchers, and other equipment. The paramilitaries also required their trainees to prove their courage by dismembering people that the paramilitaries brought in from outside: "Every fifteen days they would take around . . . seven or eight people and throw them into the field to train. . . . They would tell one that you had to cut the person's arm off, or split them open alive."

Villalba identified some of the other paramilitaries who participated in El Aro, including the commanders known as "Cobra" and "Junior"—about whom the survivors had also spoken—as well as several of the men under him, including one known as "Pilatos." And he corroborated what Pérez and others had suspected about the military's involvement: he said that before entering El Aro, they had met with several members of the Girardot Battalion, along with paramilitary commander Mancuso. He also said that a military helicopter had stopped by during the massacre and dropped off more ammunition and medication. In fact, Villalba said, in response to one question, that he didn't even realize that his membership in the paramilitary group was a crime—"Since I always saw them working with the police and the army, I thought that it was legal, and to coordinate massacres and those things, you did it with the police and the army."

In El Aro, Villalba claimed, the town priest had also worked with the paramilitaries, talking with Mancuso in advance and giving Cobra a list of names of townspeople he thought were guerrilla collaborators (the priest denied this claim in his own testimony). He said that after the massacre, the paramilitaries left the cattle with Mancuso.

Pérez found Villalba to be a puzzling witness: she viewed him as a "cold being," and "very strange." Based on what she knew about the cases, she believed he often lied. But other statements he made did fit the evidence she was finding—including his statements about the involvement of the military, as well as his identification of other paramilitaries involved.

Much later, Amparo Areiza would learn that Villalba had admitted to being the man who had tortured and killed her father. When she saw his image, she immediately recognized him: this was the skinny man who had repeatedly threatened her, and finally told her that he didn't want to kill her.

ANOTHER WITNESS GAVE Pérez an important lead connected to the Padilla raid. The witness was a former member of one of the Convivirs who said he had realized that his Convivir, called Nuevo Horizonte (New Horizon), was in fact a front for the paramilitaries, and that its members were killing people. So he had gone to the CTI and begun helping Pérez on a number of cases, including that of Pichilín. As she started interviewing him one day, she recalled, he made a casual comment: "Ay doctor, what a blow they dealt to the paramilitaries in Medellín . . . " She paused. What did he mean? The witness explained: the man they had arrested in the Padilla parking-lot shack, Jacinto Alberto Soto, was no mere accountant. He was the man known by his alias as "Lucas," a heavyweight in the ACCU whose alias had come up repeatedly on the wiretapped calls from the safe house. Lucas was the group's chief for finances, and someone very close to Castaño himself. Pérez got a portrait sketched based on the witness's verbal description and sent it along to Velásquez.

CHAPTER 7

"THINGS THAT CAN'T BE INVESTIGATED"

TRAFFIC WAS HEAVY THAT FRIDAY, May 8, 1998, but twenty-nine-year-old investigator Augusto Botero was finally nearing the university on his Yamaha motorcycle. As usual, the streets were choked with smoke-spewing buses, decrepit taxis, the occasional expensive truck or SUV with tinted windows, and mobs of pedestrians who took their lives in their hands by throwing themselves across the street whenever they saw a small opening in the sea of vehicles.

Since the days of Pablo Escobar, motorcycles had had a sinister image in Medellín, since assassins so often used them. It was easy for a shooter to conceal a weapon under clothes while sitting in the back, holding onto the driver, and motorcycles made great getaway vehicles, as they could cut through the congested traffic easily. But they were also everywhere, as they were cheap and fast. So driving through town was a hair-raising experience, not only because of the risk of accidents, but also—especially if you might be a target for one of the city's armed groups—because you never could be sure whether a motorcycle coming up behind you carried a killer or just another person trying to get to work. Still, the motorcycle made sense for Botero, who needed to get around fast if he wanted to keep up with both his day job as a CTI agent and his accounting studies at the university.

As he got farther away from downtown, traffic eased up a bit, and the area got prettier, more residential, lined by palm trees and the other lush foliage reminding visitors that, yes, they were in the tropics.

Botero pulled up at a light at Forty-First Avenue and Fifty-Third Street—only a few more blocks to go before he got to school.

He had so much on his mind that he probably didn't even notice the killers pulling up beside him on the other motorcycle. Shots rang out and Botero's motorcycle swerved sharply, crashing into a tree. The assassins made sure to finish the job, following his bike and shooting him six more times by a tree. It was barely more than a week after the Padilla raid.

Botero had been one of two CTI investigators whom Gregorio Oviedo had assigned to Jesús María Valle's murder, because he had a reputation for being clean. He had also been working with Amelia Pérez on the investigation into the murder of CTI agent Jaime Piedrahita, in connection with Pérez's work on the Upegui case. So it seemed pretty obvious that the paramilitaries, or people linked to them, had ordered his killing, though it was hard to pinpoint exactly why. Another agent, Julio César González, who worked in the wiretapping room of the CTI, had died a few days earlier, in a supposed fight in Bello, and Oviedo was sure that he, too, had been assassinated.

Around that time, another CTI agent approached Oviedo: "Boss," Oviedo recalled him saying, "a source told me that the killings are based on a list of thirteen CTI members. Your name is at the top of the list." According to the source, the killings were being carried out by the La Terraza gang, which was working with the Envigado Office. Botero and González had both been on the list.

The threat to his life, Oviedo concluded, was now too serious. He asked for a transfer. Meanwhile, for security, he started to sleep in a different safe house every night. He barely went into the office, and was constantly on the move.

ON JUNE 10, 1998, a disheveled Sergio Humberto Parra walked into Oviedo's office, looking worried. Parra had been receiving death threats ever since he'd participated in that first operation, in which they'd stopped the paramilitaries' truck full of military uniforms. Earlier that day, he had also noticed a white Mazda following him. There was a little office party going on, so he and Oviedo chatted a bit while having a drink, and then Parra decided to go home. It was around 9:30 p.m.

A few minutes later, another agent ran into the party: Parra had been hit. He had been sitting in his gray Renault 12, stopped at a red light, when two men had gotten out of a parked green pickup truck and walked up to the front of his vehicle on either side. Before he could react, they had let fly a barrage of bullets into the windshield, hitting him sixteen times and eventually killing him.

Parra had been right, Oviedo concluded. They were both dead men.

ONE MONDAY NIGHT in June, Iván Velásquez hurried over to the house where Oviedo was staying with more bad news. A young woman he knew had come into his office that day to tell him about a conversation she had overheard while having lunch with her father on Sunday at one of the clubs that many of the city's prominent businessmen frequented. Velásquez explained: "A man, who she thinks was a rancher, was telling a group of people that you, Gregorio Oviedo, are 'screwing with them,' and that they 'have finally decided to take action.' She says that the man also said that they had 'already taken down one of them,' apparently referring to Sergio's [Parra's] death, and said that you only escaped his fate that weekend because you were traveling in Bogotá at the time." The two stayed up late into the night, discussing what to do. The answer was clear: Oviedo couldn't delay his departure any further. He had to leave town.

The very next day, Oviedo got a radio message from one of his agents: "Santacruz 901." It was code, meaning that an agent was down. Two assassins had killed yet another CTI investigator, Tomas Santacruz, as he was getting out of a taxi near downtown Medellín.

That week, Oviedo went back to Bogotá.

J. GUILLERMO ESCOBAR was walking into the court building in Medellín when a young man stopped him. His appearance—entirely bald, covered in freckles, with a wild look in his eyes—was striking, but J. Guillermo was even more surprised by what the young man said: "Master J. Guillermo, I accuse society and defend the mother." He was quoting a phrase J. Guillermo himself had written in a law journal article about one of his past cases.

"I see you're an intelligent man, because you remember this woman's case," said J. Guillermo, reaching out to shake his hand.

The young man introduced himself as "Edward," and J. Guillermo asked him where he worked.

"What if I told you that I'm not a lawyer but an assassin?" asked the young man.

"I wouldn't believe it," said J. Guillermo. "You look like a lawyer, and you have read legal articles. Where is your office?"

The young man paused, pointing to a nearby building.

J. Guillermo nodded: "Ah, you're not an assassin but a lawyer."

The young man hurried off. In discussing the incident later with Velásquez and Diego Arcila, both agreed with J. Guillermo that the young man was indeed an assassin, and that he had approached J. Guillermo to intimidate him, in an effort to derail his investigations.

J. Guillermo believed that his coordination with prosecutor Carlos Bonilla in the investigation of Valle's murder was probably the root of the threats against them. He and Bonilla had been making progress in the Valle case: they had discovered, for example, that the day before Valle's murder, the army's Fourth Brigade and the police had suddenly decided to "disarm" their forces and withdraw from important parts of the city the following afternoon—soon after Valle's murder. Had the killers counted on that to make their escape easier? They had also found witnesses who had identified the killers as members of the La Terraza gang, tied to the paramilitaries. Witnesses had spoken of the involvement of someone called the "Ñato," and had said that the Angulo brothers, powerful landowners from Ituango who were suspected of drug trafficking and of collaborating with Castaño, had been complicit in Valle's death.

J. Guillermo often got a ride in Bonilla's car, and he had noticed that they were routinely being followed: men were taking photographs and videotaping them as they drove. They would be walking down the street and notice that someone right ahead of them was waiting, and would start to walk in the same direction. At one point, J. Guillermo had picked up the phone to hear a cold voice telling him that he was conducting an investigation that he had to stop immediately. Otherwise, they wouldn't kill him, but they would kill "the daughter who lives on the third floor." The person calling him clearly knew that J. Guillermo's grown daughter lived with her husband and two children on the third floor of his building.

J. Guillermo warned his daughter that she was at risk, and soon afterward, she told him that someone had followed her when she was coming out of the University of Antioquia, where she was studying special education. Two days later, she and her husband stopped the car they were in so he could run into a store half a block from their house. Another car pulled up alongside theirs, and a bald, freckled man gave her a look. "That's not her," she overheard him saying, before he left.

The next day, J. Guillermo had her leave the university, and he made arrangements for her and her family to flee the country.

J. Guillermo, however, stayed on. He could not leave his work: it was "a mission for justice," he told his wife. And she agreed.

Carlos Bonilla, however, could not stay. Investigators listening to a wire had learned of a specific plan to have Bonilla assassinated. He left Colombia soon afterward.

MEANWHILE, JAVIER TAMAYO, the young prosecutor who had roomed with Oviedo, had been conducting investigations into the Envigado Office and La Terraza. At one point, a police officer who had gone to school with him warned him that he had obtained information about a prosecutor who was investigating the Envigado Office: members of the office were planning to seize the prosecutor, torture him, and kill him. Tamayo was sure the officer meant him.

One of the targets of Tamayo's investigations was a man named Alexander Londoño, who was better known as "El Zarco." El Zarco was both extremely good-looking and extremely vicious. He was said to have been an assassin for Pablo Escobar, and he had later become a senior member—and top assassin—for La Terraza, which at the time was working hand in hand with the Envigado Office and the paramilitaries. Working with CTI investigators, Tamayo had been wiretapping El Zarco's phone—it was a real coup. But then they realized that El Zarco had figured out who Tamayo was. In one of his calls, they overheard him ask about the prosecutor, how tough he was, and whether he followed a regular schedule.

Tamayo began to carry a loaded gun with him, just in case.

But the weapon was of no use when, one night, he walked into his apartment building late to learn that two assassins had just left, after murdering the building's security guard and dumping his body next to Tamayo's car. Tamayo read the incident not as a botched attempt on his life, but rather, as an effort to intimidate him.

MARÍA VICTORIA VELÁSQUEZ waited alone at the elevator bank on the first floor of her office building—strangely, hardly anyone was there that day. She had just finished lunch near the Medellín *personería*, a municipal office charged with looking out for city residents' rights, where she had been working for several years. She liked taking the elevators at the end of the bank, which were reserved for staff only, because, while less attractive, they were usually less crowded than the others, though at lunchtime there was normally some traffic on all of them.

Finally, one of the staff elevators opened and María Victoria got on, ready to head up to her office on the eleventh floor. One person joined her, a medium-sized man with wavy hair. She was surprised—she didn't recognize him, and he didn't look like most other people who worked in the building, though later she couldn't remember much about his face, as she deliberately tried to forget it. It was a small elevator that could not fit more than ten people, squeezed tightly. The doors closed and it was just them.

María Victoria waited to go up to her office, but the elevator didn't stop on her floor. Instead, it went all the way to the top floor, and then started to go down again. What was wrong with the elevator? Suddenly it dawned on her: he had locked it with a key.

And then the man started to talk to her. "You know there are things that can't be investigated. You're not deaf," he said. He told her that she could not keep pretending she didn't understand what was happening: "When we send a message, it's a message."

She stared at the man in silence, but she knew what he meant. For weeks, she had been keeping the threats to herself: The phone would ring, and she would hear a funeral dirge on the other end of the line. One time she received a funeral wreath with a card that she immediately tore up and threw into the garbage. "I didn't want to know what that was," she said years later. But she knew that they were threats against her husband: the killers had probably figured out that the best way to get to him was through his family.

María Victoria had also grown suspicious and tense around her colleagues. She recalled that one of them, who claimed to be friendly with Gustavo Upegui, the former Los Pepes member and businessman whom Pérez was investigating, kept telling her: "They're going to kill your husband, María Victoria."

"Why would you say that?" she'd ask.

"You have to be careful," the colleague would say. "Your husband needs to slow down. He has no idea about all those dark forces around here. Tell Iván not to get involved in all these things. I'm very afraid to be your colleague, you know more than anyone that they can set a bomb here and we're done."

Other times, her colleague would just say: "I don't know if your husband is brave or stupid. Maybe he doesn't value his family." María Victoria was left confused: Was he trying to help her as a friend and colleague, or was he delivering a threat?

María Victoria had kept all the calls, the flowers, and the comments from her colleague secret—she knew that if she shared the threats with Velásquez, he would feel he had to quit his job, to protect his family. She also knew that quitting would be devastating to him. So she said nothing.

But on the elevator, the horror of it all engulfed her, pounding on her like an inescapable, angry wave. Even though the man never touched her, to María Victoria, the experience felt like torture: going up and down the floors of the building, with no escape, while this man made what she clearly understood to be death threats against her husband.

He kept talking for what felt like an eternity: "We know what you don't know. We know what you do, what you eat, everything, we know everything. So tell him: that's enough."

She had no idea how long they had been in the locked elevator when the man suddenly pulled the keys out of the elevator controls and pressed a button. When they got to the ninth floor, he got off, and with the door open, said goodbye to her, affectionately adding, "but we'll see each other in English class." María Victoria stared, unable to move. She had just paid for a full course in English.

María Victoria never told Velásquez about any of it. Not the calls. Not her colleague's comments. Not even what the man on the elevator said. Velásquez would never quit out of fear for his own well-being, and she didn't want him to do so out of fear for her or the children.

María Victoria also avoided telling anyone in her own family about it at the time. She had grown so accustomed to keeping things to herself that it just seemed like the best thing. Why alarm anyone?

She couldn't always keep her emotions in check, though, and would sometimes break out crying at work. Concerned colleagues would ask:

Is Velásquez mistreating you? What's wrong? She couldn't even begin to explain.

From then on, she developed an intense phobia of elevators. To this day, she would much rather climb many flights of stairs than get on an elevator. Velásquez was unaware of the threats María Victoria had received, and he put all thoughts of danger to himself out of his mind. The way he later described his feelings about it, it sounded like he didn't just compartmentalize the fear: he deliberately banished it from his mind.

CHAPTER 8

THE ENEMY WITHIN

IVÁN VELÁSQUEZ WAS SMOKING ALL the time now, up to three packs a day sometimes. To others, he continued to appear calm. But the killings of the investigators, the loss of his father and Jesús María Valle, the difficulty of working in a place where he could never be entirely sure whom to trust, and now Gregorio Oviedo's departure, all within the space of just six months, had taken their toll.

At the same time, Velásquez knew that the threats and attacks on his team were happening because they were making progress against the paramilitaries. The arrest of Jacinto Alberto Soto, aka "Lucas," and the discovery of the records in the Padilla shack must have dealt them a serious financial blow, and Velásquez was convinced that, if they continued working at it, he and his team could crack open the ACCU's organizational structure, and eventually arrest its leadership and powerful backers. He had to continue.

To succeed, he would need a strong team; with Oviedo gone, he was again facing the problem of whom to trust in the CTI. Velásquez knew he could count on Jorge Fernández, Oviedo's deputy, and he had hoped Pablo Elías González, the national CTI director, would appoint Fernández to lead the regional office. Instead, González named a man named Fernando Márquez, who immediately struck Velásquez as a problem—in their early interactions, Velásquez thought Márquez seemed more concerned about keeping bureaucratic control of the investigations than in cooperating to make them succeed. The progress that Oviedo had been making seemed to stall. Worse yet, on July 31, 1998, Jorge

Fernández received notice that he was fired, though no explanation was provided (González later did not remember Fernández being fired, and instead said maybe the agent resigned). To Velásquez, it made no sense. Fernández had been a brave, reliable, and honest agent. There was no reason to let go of him.

So Velásquez put in a request to the main office in Bogotá for an entirely new arrangement: he wanted to have a small, specialized team of CTI investigators assigned to work directly within the prosecutors' office, under his supervision, on the cases involving paramilitaries. The arrangement would not only allow them to work more efficiently, but also provide greater security to the CTI investigators they trusted, as it would be harder for corrupt investigators in the CTI to know and report on their movements. The prosecutors' office also had access to more resources—more bulletproof cars, for example—to protect them.

It was a big ask, but he insisted, and finally Bogotá agreed. The new team, which included wiretapping expert and former seminarian Diego Arcila, started working with Velásquez shortly afterward.

A DOOR SWUNG open and a man in his early thirties emerged into the outdoors. The slightly pudgy, five-foot-nine man in blue jeans looked fairly harmless, unusual in Colombia only in that his eyes were green and he had a small scar, one and a half inches long, above his right eyebrow. It was September 29, 1998, and Jacinto Alberto Soto, aka Lucas, had spent over four months in the maximum-security unit of Bellavista prison in Medellín. During that time, Velásquez's prosecutors had repeatedly interviewed him, and Lucas had admitted to being a member of the paramilitaries for the past two years, and to managing some of the accounting for the paramilitaries from early on. He also claimed he had no alias. But the prosecutors knew, in part because of what Amelia Pérez's witness had said about Lucas being the paramilitaries' finance chief, that he was holding back. They would never learn what else he might have to say, though. Lucas left Bellavista through the front door and vanished.

Eleven days earlier, on September 18, Velásquez's office had received a telegram from the National Directorate of Prosecutors' Offices in Bogotá, which ordered the transfer of the Padilla case to a Bogotá prosecutor's office. "We were still in the process of going through the accounts, and doing other investigative activities, confirming facts," recalled

Velásquez. "But we were facing several logistical and personnel challenges, and that is what Bogotá took advantage of—instead of strengthening our investigation with additional resources and a support team, they decided to order the transfer."

The attorney general at the time, Alfonso Gómez Méndez, did not later recall the details of the transfer, but remembered that there had been a problem with paramilitary infiltration of the local CTI office. "When that sort of thing happened," he said, "the cases were sometimes brought to Bogotá," adding, "I had a national team that was and still is perfectly trustworthy." So Velásquez's team had to box up all the files, the checks, and the graphs that covered their office walls, tracking the route that the money followed and how the different accounts connected to each other, and send it to Bogotá. Someone else in Bogotá would now have to pick up all those threads.

Meanwhile, the transfer created an opportunity for Lucas. An unknown person replaced the transfer order from Velásquez's office with a different one, stating that Lucas was to be transferred not to Bogotá, but to the custody of a local prosecutor's office in Medellín. In turn, a prosecutor in that office issued an order to release Lucas, who then simply walked out, never to be seen again. The prosecutor was later convicted of helping Lucas to escape; he never explained why he did it, but the paramilitaries would later acknowledge having paid for Lucas's release. Nearly a decade afterward, a paramilitary leader known as "HH" would testify, without providing details, that Lucas's freedom had cost the paramilitaries millions of dollars—though he didn't specify whom they paid—and added that Carlos Castaño had insisted upon securing the release because Lucas had been his right-hand man. In the view of prosecutor Javier Tamayo, "Lucas was such a fundamental piece of the puzzle that if he had been neutralized at that time, I think much of what permeated Medellín, Antioquia, Córdoba," would have ended. Another former paramilitary leader and wealthy businessman from the Urabá region of Antioquia, Raúl Hasbún, also later confirmed that Lucas was very close to Castaño and his brother Vicente, and that the documents the investigators found at the Padilla parking-lot shack amounted to "all of the accounting records" of the Castaño brothers, including records of the paramilitaries' financial backers. So securing Lucas's release had been a top priority for them.

TO GET SO FAR in the Padilla investigation and to then have it snatched away, and have the key witness escape, was almost unbearable. But there was so much they could still do, and were doing. In the Valle investigation, prosecutors working under J. Guillermo Escobar concluded that they had enough evidence to order the arrest of the brothers Jaime Alberto and Francisco Antonio Angulo, as well as Carlos Castaño and two other individuals.

Toward the end of the year, Diego Arcila showed up in Velásquez's office, excited and somewhat nervous, to inform him of another breakthrough: he had identified one of the senior leaders of the Envigado Office—a sinister man known as "Ñato," and later on as "Don Berna," who was said to be behind much of the criminal activity in the city, including many of the killings of CTI agents. One of the witnesses in the Valle case had also said the Ñato was involved in the activist's murder. According to another prosecutor at the meeting, Arcila said that he had dressed up as a priest to sneak into the school where Don Berna's children went, and had been able to access the records listing the kids' parents' names and addresses. The man's true name, he said, was Diego Fernando Murillo Bejarano. Arcila had gone on to find official ID records for Murillo, and had even gone to the address he had obtained and knocked on the door. The discovery was a big deal: a former member of Los Pepes, Don Berna, as he would be most commonly known, was in fact the leader of the Envigado Office and the liaison between the paramilitaries and La Terraza.

Arcila was worried, however, because he had noticed a video camera by the entrance to Don Berna's house when he visited—what if Don Berna identified him? Arcila did not want to leave town, but at Velásquez's insistence, he went to Bogotá to hide out for a while.

YET FOR ALL their efforts, Velásquez and his team could not escape the fact that they still worked for a larger institution whose members did not necessarily understand or agree with their work. After the order from Bogotá transferring the Padilla case, the appointment of Márquez, and the firing of Fernández, Velásquez now viewed the main office, and particularly the national CTI director, González, with suspicion. The team's investigations—especially the Padilla parking-lot case—had threatened many powerful interests, not just the paramilitaries, and Velásquez could not help but wonder whether some of his colleagues were trying to put a stop to the investigations. Another senior official in the attorney general's office attributed the tension between Velásquez and González not to any effort to derail the investigations, but to a turf war between the two men, possibly because González, who was close to Attorney General Gómez Méndez, wanted more credit for the investigations underway. González, meanwhile, did not recall having had any issues with Velásquez.

In Bogotá, things were getting difficult for Amelia Pérez, too. She and her investigators had continued their research into Upegui and the disappearances of the three young men in 1995, and on November 3, 1998, she issued a warrant for the arrest of Colonel Luis Rodríguez Pérez, a police officer and former member of UNASE who had just been named police commander for Medellín and surrounding areas. Amelia Pérez believed strongly, based on the evidence the investigators had collected, that Rodríguez Pérez was involved in the disappearances. But that same day, a senior official in the attorney general's office ordered that the case be reassigned to another prosecutor. Soon after, the office also withdrew the arrest warrant. She never got a satisfactory explanation from her colleagues as to why they had made these decisions.

"DR. VELÁSQUEZ, sorry to interrupt you on your vacation, but something terrible has happened," Diego Arcila said at the outset of a phone call in early January 1999. Velásquez had finally taken a few days off after the holidays, and he and the family were trying to unwind on the beach in Coveñas, Sucre, a few hours from Medellín. "Jorge is dead."

Jobless and desperate after his firing, Jorge Fernández, Oviedo's former deputy, had decided to try to work as a taxi driver. He was shot and killed while doing his rounds. Velásquez was sure that it was another paramilitary hit.

Arcila knew that he was also in danger, even in Bogotá: he had noticed that several of the other CTI agents had been keeping their distance from him, looking at him suspiciously. A risk assessment conducted by the main CTI office in Bogotá had concluded that Arcila and Velásquez were the next likely targets for the paramilitaries. But, one of his colleagues recalled, Arcila didn't believe the witness protection system run out of the Attorney General's office worked. Pablo

Elías González, the national CTI director, later said that Arcila had been "desperate" to return to Medellín: he had insisted on leaving Bogotá despite González's objections.

But Arcila would not be able to work with Velásquez for long. In the weeks after Fernández's death, the small team of CTI agents working directly under Velásquez was finally disbanded, and all the specialized team's investigators were placed back under the leadership of the regional CTI office. Velásquez recalled that the orders came from González, and perhaps from the regional CTI director, Gilberto Rodríguez (who had replaced Fernando Márquez). González did not later recall the details of how it happened, but said that "normally, CTI people worked in the CTI. In Bogotá nobody worked in the offices of the prosecutors." To Velásquez, the loss of the special team meant not only that they would lose their focused, more confidential and productive way of working highly sensitive cases, but also that the investigators working on those cases would be at even greater risk as a result of the paramilitary infiltration elsewhere in the CTI office. "They're going to undo everything," he railed to J. Guillermo Escobar.

Arcila pleaded with the main office to let him keep working with Velásquez. He was convinced that he would only be safe if he could continue reporting directly to Velásquez, and working in his office, rather than back in the CTI's main office, where paramilitary informants would keep track of all his movements. Velásquez remembered sending messages to the attorney general himself, asking him to let Arcila stay on in his office. But he got nowhere.

As his transfer date approached, Arcila grew increasingly agitated. One day, he pulled J. Guillermo aside: "I think they're going to kill me very soon," he told the prosecutor. "And I have a favor to ask of you: When they kill me, please go to the funeral and find my father. . . . Tell him and my whole family that I love them very much, I respect them, and I'm grateful for their offer to help me leave my job to save my life." J. Guillermo tried to interrupt, but Arcila would not let him. "Tell them I could not accept it," he said. "I've been working on some very important investigations that are on the verge of producing results, and it's my duty to see them through. So I couldn't agree to their offer to help me set up a business. I've been putting my life on the line, but it is out of love for justice."

Iván Velásquez and J. Guillermo Escobar continued trying to find ways to keep Arcila safe. They sent him to the countryside to take a break. But they could not stop the transfer.

On Monday, February 15, 1999, Arcila's first day back at the CTI's regional offices in Medellín, he got into a cab and headed to work. For several weeks, he had been carrying a loaded handgun wherever he went, and it was in his lap, covered with a manila envelope, then. The taxi stopped at a light, and out of nowhere, two men on a motorcycle pulled up next to the cab and shot him. Arcila died there, his hand on a gun that he had not even had the chance to draw.

Velásquez was in his office, a few blocks away, when he got the call about Arcila's death. Later on he would watch the killing, which had been caught on tape by one of the video cameras set up on the street, and he would see the motorcycle with the anonymous killers, their faces indistinguishable in the distance, turn the corner and get lost in the chaos of the city.

VELÁSQUEZ'S RUN AS chief prosecutor for Antioquia finally came to an end in April 1999. As he and one of his colleagues later remembered it, Pablo Elías González—who at that point was the acting national director of all the prosecutors' offices—called and told him that the office was asking all regional directors to tender their resignations, as the attorney general was considering a nationwide restructuring of the agency (González did not recall this happening, and Gómez Méndez said he never gave instructions along those lines, but neither offered an alternative explanation for Velásquez's departure). Velásquez thought it was strange, but he complied, and Gómez Méndez accepted his resignation. Only later did Velásquez call two other regional directors and find out that they had not been asked to resign.

Afterward, María Victoria was terrified to learn that the attorney general's office was apparently planning to withdraw Velásquez's security detail, since he would no longer be working for the agency. Shortly before Diego Arcila's murder, the CTI agent had told María Victoria that he was concerned not only about his own life, but also about Velásquez's, and even her own security. One of his colleagues at the CTI, he had said, had been asking Arcila and other CTI agents about María Victoria: where she lived, what her car was like, what her schedule was. She had not paid too much attention to what Arcila was telling her at the time, but after his death, she had grown alarmed about her family's security, and had contacted the attorney general's office in Bogotá to express her fears. At the time, they had strengthened Velásquez's security detail. But two months later, it seemed, Velásquez was going to be stripped of all protection.

In desperation, she drafted an urgent petition to Attorney General Gómez Méndez on April 20, describing the many killings and threats that people around Velásquez had received, and noting that Jorge Fernández had been killed even after he was no longer working for the office. She asked that Gómez Méndez inform her about how he was going to keep her husband safe. Soon afterward, she followed up, reporting that a low-level official had denied her first request, and that she assumed the attorney general was not aware of the denial. "I apologize in advance for the way in which I am going to express myself," she wrote, copying Amnesty International, the United Nations office in Colombia, and the newspaper El Colombiano, "but I find no other way to say it, which is that I hold you responsible in the future if anything happens to my husband or to me."

María Victoria and Iván Velásquez recalled that soon afterward, Velásquez got his security detail reinstated.

IN THE FOLLOWING years, things would only get more difficult for those investigating paramilitary crimes. On August 1, 2001, a new attorney general, Luis Camilo Osorio, took over, and almost immediately he began criticizing the investigations, saying there was a "distortion" in the way that prosecutors were handling the cases. He argued—despite extensive evidence to the contrary—that they were neglecting cases against the guerrillas and instead were overly focused on the paramilitaries. Almost immediately, he began purging the office of prosecutors who had been involved in major cases against paramilitaries. One of them was Gregorio Oviedo, who had been working at the office in Bogotá: on August 8, just one week after Osorio took over, Oviedo received a letter notifying him that he was being fired.

Others, such as Amelia Pérez, found it increasingly challenging to do their jobs. After Velásquez's departure from Medellín, Pérez had continued investigating the El Aro massacre, and had charged both Salvatore Mancuso and Carlos Castaño. Her work had clearly angered the paramilitaries, and in April 2002 a CTI investigator informed her that a letter was circulating in which the paramilitaries were announcing their plans to kill several prosecutors, including her. Pérez asked the office to provide her with some form of protection—the bulletproof vehicle that had been assigned to her and her family for years for their security had been suddenly reassigned to someone else after Osorio took over—but she never received a straight answer. Instead, she was transferred in May to the Counterterrorism Unit of the office, where she would have to work with members of the very same security forces she had previously been investigating. Several months later, a bombing took place in El Nogal, an exclusive club in Bogotá. Pérez, assigned to the investigation, began working on several hypotheses, but later said she began to feel pressure immediately from her supervisors to focus only on members of the FARC as possible perpetrators. Eventually, she was removed from the case, with no explanation, and reassigned to the Anti-Drug Trafficking Unit.

Meanwhile, Oviedo had also received new reports that Carlos Castaño had ordered his assassination. With Oviedo out of the attorney general's office, and Pérez sidelined, it was clear to both of them that they would receive no protection. Neither would their two small sons. Finally, they decided, it was time to go. They requested asylum in Canada, and fled with their children to Quebec in April 2003. Like many other prosecutors who had been forced to move there, Oviedo and Pérez had a difficult time: they had never experienced such cold in their lives, they had to learn a new language, and they could not practice law, so they struggled to get by financially, doing odd jobs to support their kids while studying French. They missed their country. But they had no choice: exile was better than death.

THE PADILLA parking-lot investigation never produced the results it could have. In Bogotá, prosecutors divided it into a number of smaller cases. One of the Medellín investigators who had worked on the case with Velásquez said that, in his view, they "distorted" the direction of the investigation and the case essentially got lost in the office. Nobody else was arrested for years. In 2001, one of the cases did lead prosecutors to conduct a search of the "Foundation for the Peace of Córdoba," an entity that had been mentioned in the Padilla records, and that turned out to be a cover for the Castaño family, so that it could move its money. But hundreds of other leads in the Padilla records seemed to have been abandoned.

To those who had worked on the case, the outcome was appalling: "With that small group we had, if we had continued, we would have done the twenty searches in Córdoba, the ones in Antioquia, and we would have found just how rotten the country was," said Javier Tamayo. With all those hours they put in, all the sacrifices they made, they should have achieved something. But instead, he and others felt, "after weighing everything that we had done, we reached the conclusion that all we did was to put at risk men who were assassinated."

Oviedo felt similarly: when he had started the work, he had been idealistic about what they could achieve, but his ideals had collided with a very different reality. In the end, he thought, he and Velásquez had been "Don Quixote and Sancho Panza tilting against windmills. That is how we ended up, I think. At least we weren't dead."

The investigation they had started into Valle's murder also seemed to go nowhere. In March 2001, a Medellín court convicted Carlos Castaño in absentia in connection with Valle's murder, but the conviction was one of several against the paramilitary leader that had no practical consequences: there seemed to be no real effort underway to arrest him. To the disappointment of the prosecutors who had worked on the Valle case under Velásquez, the court acquitted the Angulo brothers. There seemed to be no ongoing effort to identify others who might have been involved, or to dig into whether the military—which Valle had criticized so sharply—had any role in his assassination.

After his dismissal in 1999, Velásquez continued living in Medellín, but he was constantly looking over his shoulder. He worked as an administrative law judge until May 2000, when he got a job as an assistant justice on the Colombian Supreme Court, in Bogotá. It was only when he walked off the airplane in Bogotá, with no security detail, that he realized the burden he had been carrying. "It was like recovering my freedom," he recalled. Medellín would always be home in a way, but it would also forever be tied to the losses he suffered there. In Bogotá, finally, he could walk the streets calmly, without guards, without worrying.

PART III

HOPE

BOGOTÁ, COLOMBIA, 2000–2008

CHAPTER 9

HEROES

"HAVE YOU EVER SEEN SOMEONE be eaten alive by ants?" The question took investigative journalist Ricardo Calderón aback, but the man beside him kept talking, matter-of-factly pointing at an anthill surrounded by four stakes with chains attached to them. "They tie up informants and guerrillas there and coat them with *panela* [a form of cane sugar]. They last about three days while the ants eat them." The lawyer was giving Calderón a tour in early 2006 of a vast ranch on a mountaintop near the Magdalena River owned by his client, a paramilitary leader known as "The Eagle." The Eagle's lawyer had invited Calderón several times to visit the ranch and talk to his boss. In addition to the anthill, Calderón noticed a large board to which the paramilitaries tied their victims before doing target practice on them, a swimming pool shaped like a guitar, with a bar and jukebox next to it, and a massive house. Farther out, the lawyer had told Calderón, The Eagle had several cocaine-processing labs. On his fairly short drive from Bogotá to the ranch, Calderón had also noticed several large plaster statues of eagles perched along the road, as well as a couple of wrecked Toyota and Ford pickup trucks—The Eagle's son, the lawyer said, enjoyed drinking and crashing vehicles, then leaving them by the side of the road. His father always replaced them.

THE SON OF A POLICEMAN, the scrawny, prematurely balding, chain-smoking Calderón had grown up during the heyday of the Medellín cartel. He had attended a school in Bogotá for the children of police officers, so, ever since he was a small child, he had heard macabre stories about drug lords and police raids. He had attended many funerals for fathers of his classmates, including the one for Colonel Jaime Ramírez, who in 1984 had discovered Pablo Escobar's cocaine-processing lab, Tranquilandia, and was then gunned down by assassins. Calderón also developed a sense of which kids' fathers might be on the take, based on how much money the children could spend on going out for ice cream or to play pinball.

He had always been intrigued by that world. He had even thought of becoming a policeman himself, but his father warned him away from it: "You're very lazy, you don't like getting up early, and you don't like cold water." Lazy may not have been the best description for Calderón, who had worked every summer since he was fourteen, packing glass and crystal cups for a local company, or stretching lengths of chain out on the city's streets, to take measurements for the official transit agency. But it was true that he hated waking up early, and couldn't stand cold water, and, sure enough, Calderón found out that if he joined the police, he would have to get up at 4 a.m. and take very short, cold showers. So he decided to go to college instead. He started out studying biology, but did very poorly. When a family friend offered to find him a spot at a new college that was opening on a beautiful campus in Bogotá, he jumped at the chance to transfer. The only catch was that the new school only offered two majors: engineering and journalism. Calderón was bad at numbers, so, to his father's dismay—at the time, journalism was known as the career of choice of Colombian beauty queens, and his father viewed it as a frivolous profession—Calderón picked journalism. He was, he claimed later, a terrible student, though one of his classmates, Mónica, who would one day become his wife, disagreed, remembering that even in college the shy, quiet Calderón would throw himself into his journalism projects, usually working alone, with passion.

In 1994, during one of his final years in college, a classmate told him about an opening at the newsweekly *Semana*, covering sports. Unlike many Colombians, Calderón had little interest in sports—soccer, to him, was just a group of men running around with a ball—but he jumped at the job and got by, at first by writing about the only sport he knew a bit about: Formula One car racing. It was a great opportunity. The magazine had a very small writing staff, so Calderón got to see how it put together an entire issue, and to see how politics, crime, and public order issues, which he found fascinating, got covered.

The following year, a massive political scandal began to unfold over what became known as "Proceso 8,000," a wide-ranging criminal investigation started by the attorney general's office into alleged ties between the Cali cartel and various prominent public figures, including several members of Congress, as well as Santiago Medina, the treasurer for President Ernesto Samper's 1994 presidential campaign. (The unofficial name, which meant "Process 8,000," referred to the case number.) After his arrest, Medina began testifying against other former campaign officials who were now in the Samper administration. The president himself soon came under investigation in Congress. Meanwhile, the accountant for the Cali cartel, Guillermo Pallomari, turned himself in to the US Drug Enforcement Administration and started to hand over evidence against Colombian politicians. Although Samper was eventually acquitted, the case would continue to present new twists. It dominated the news for years.

Semana's political journalists poured themselves into coverage of the rapidly changing scandal over the Proceso 8,000, but that meant nobody was available to cover the ongoing war. So Calderón volunteered to start going to the country's "red zones," where the conflict was hot, even while he continued to cover sports. Soon, he was traveling to far-flung parts of the country and filing reports about FARC killings and—increasingly—paramilitary massacres, alongside his still-required stories about the local soccer team.

Throughout the decade, the paramilitary groups had slowly been gaining in strength, but now they were engaged in a coordinated and terrifying campaign to seize control of key regions of the country. Moving beyond Antioquia and Córdoba, where Carlos Castaño's ACCU had first started its expansion in the 1990s, they were now spreading out over most of the country's northern states, and even venturing into the center and south of the country. The ACCU had also joined forces with other paramilitary groups, organized under a single umbrella as the AUC (Autodefensas Unidas de Colombia, or United Self-Defense Forces of Colombia), which had multiple "blocks," each under separate leadership.

The areas that were hit the worst included the Middle Magdalena Valley and the oil port city of Barrancabermeja, a traditional ELN stronghold that Calderón visited repeatedly, and from which he wrote numerous articles about increasing paramilitary killings. In one, he described how, on May 16, 1998, around fifty paramilitaries had entered the northeastern section of the city, murdered eleven people, and kidnapped another twenty-five, labeling them "guerrilla sympathizers." In a statement delivered to the government, ACCU leader Carlos Castaño later announced that the paramilitaries had summarily "tried" and executed the twenty-five before burning their bodies. The massacre was so brazen that it got national public attention, but it was far from unique. Across the region and much of the country, paramilitaries were growing fast. With the promise of high wages, which were easy to pay with their profits from cocaine, the AUC had enticed thousands of underemployed young men to join their ranks, and they were killing tens of thousands of people in grisly ways, including beheading, clubbing, or dismembering their victims, often in front of their families and neighbors. Calderón lost track of how many mass paramilitary killings he wrote about at the time. In the aftermath of massacres, remaining community members fled in terror, leaving behind ghost towns throughout much of the Middle Magdalena region, Antioquia, and the northern coast.

Meanwhile, the FARC and the ELN, too, were engaging in ever more ruthless tactics. They had taken people hostage for ransom or political gain for years, but now kidnappings were a daily occurrence. Travel by road throughout Colombia had become so hazardous that many people gave it up entirely. The guerrillas took advantage of the absence of law enforcement on many lonely roads to conduct *pescas milagrosas* (miraculous fishing), where they stopped drivers and kidnapped those they thought might be worth something. The kidnappings affected Colombians of all stripes and backgrounds, wealthy and poor alike, and by paralyzing travel, damaged the economy and frustrated city residents, for whom going to the countryside was a common pastime. To secure their territory, the guerrillas had also deployed antipersonnel landmines, which maimed not only soldiers, but also peasants, children, and animals that walked in the wrong place.

Calderón's own family had been the target of the FARC's cruelty: his mother had come from a comfortable family from Yarumal, Antioquia. They had owned a very good piece of land on which they had processed panela, which was a traditional Colombian sugarcane product. There was also an asbestos mine on the property. As a small child, Calderón had spent his school breaks on that farm, playing with his cousins and surrounded by vegetation and farm animals. But in the early 1980s, the 13th Front of the FARC came into the region, forcing Calderón's uncles to flee and seizing the farm, depriving the family of what his grandfather had built up over an entire lifetime. A few years later, one of his cousins visited a nearby community and started talking about the land with a store owner; another man in the store, who turned out to be a FARC member, overheard him and shot Calderón's cousin on the spot.

By the 1998 presidential elections, many Colombians were eager to find a way to end the war. Andrés Pastrana, a former TV news anchor, and a Conservative, was elected president on a platform promising to seek peace with the FARC. Immediately after the elections, Pastrana launched negotiations, and by 1999 the government had ceded a de-militarized jungle area the size of Switzerland, in the region known as El Caguán, in the southern state of Caquetá, to the FARC. However, the talks got off to an inauspicious start when Manuel Marulanda, the FARC's top commander, stood Pastrana up on the opening day of ne-gotiations, claiming there was a plot underway to kill him. Things got even worse when, in March 1999, two months after the start of the process, the FARC murdered three US indigenous rights workers.

Calderón began traveling regularly to the town of San Vicente, in El Caguán, to cover the talks, joining an assortment of foreign digni-taries, international media, and movie stars who were traipsing through the demilitarized zone. But, while many seemed to get a kick out of hanging out with the guerrillas, Calderón was more interested in what was happening with the people from the region, who had not had any say in the establishment of the zone. He met one man, for example, who said the FARC had blown up his house. In another case, the FARC had kidnapped and killed an affluent rancher, Arnulfo Amaya; they later also kidnapped his wife, but released her after she paid them half of the ransom they required. When the peace negotiations started, the FARC used the remaining "debt" she owed them as a justification for seizing the family's house, which was spacious, attractive, and con-veniently perched on the top of a hill overlooking San Vicente. They used it as a meeting space, forcing Amaya's wife and daughter, who were still living in the house, to host the FARC leadership, which meant, essentially, becoming servants for the guerrilla leaders. Calderón also saw family members of hostages showing up to pay ransoms, or to ask about their relatives: in one case, a rice farmer from the neighboring state of Huila, who clearly had limited resources, drove to San Vicente in his truck—he had already paid a ransom, but the FARC was still holding his father, and he wanted to convince them to take the truck as further payment.

In the last few pieces he wrote from El Caguán, Calderón reported about a curious infrastructure project underway: a group of wealthy Iranians was getting ready to build a multimillion-dollar slaughterhouse and refrigeration plant in San Vicente, from which meat could be shipped directly to Iran. It seemed like a bizarre idea, but the Iranian embassy told Calderón that they were making the investment to help Colombia's development. When Calderón interviewed Colombian ranchers, they argued that the plant made no sense; it would harm other plants that were already in operation. Building on Calderón's reporting, *Newsweek* went further, reporting that the project was a cover for Iranian weapons sales to the FARC. Within a few weeks, the Iranian embassy announced that it had canceled the project.

Calderón was then living at his parents' home in Bogotá, and one day, as he took his car out of the underground garage, a funeral wreath dropped from the top of the garage door onto his car. It was his first death threat. He was sure it was connected to his reporting on the Iranian meat plant. Mónica, who was then his girlfriend, recalled that Calderón didn't say much about the threat, but he did leave town for a period of time: he had a great fear of flying, so he drove to Medellín. To her, that seemed like going into the lion's den, given all the violence wracking the city, but it was a way of letting the immediate threat from the FARC subside.

Unable to return to El Caguán, Calderón once again began writing about paramilitary crimes. In November 2000, it was a massacre in the picturesque town of Nueva Venecia, one of a handful of Colombian villages made up entirely of buildings on stilts. It was in the swampland near Santa Marta on the northern coast. When he heard about the killings, Calderón started making phone calls, and he was struck by one woman's description of what had happened: "As soon as the *paracos* [slang for paramilitaries] arrived, they started shooting us like ducks. It was a duck hunt."

Three days after the massacre, Calderón took a boat into town from Barranquilla. Nueva Venecia smelled like death. There was still blood on the soccer and basketball field the community had built among the houses, though the victims' bodies were gone. The people he interviewed didn't understand what had happened: Nueva Venecia had always been a peaceful town. It only had around 450 houses, and most of its 4,000 inhabitants lived off fishing. "Here we lived as if every day were a holiday," the man who sold ice in the town told Calderón. "In this town we never had thieves, and we never needed the police." But late at night on November 21, a group of sixty paramilitaries on five motorboats had made their way toward the town with a list of six names of people they claimed worked with the ELN. On their way in, they stopped a group of sixteen fishermen and asked them what they knew about the people on their list. When the fishermen couldn't answer, the paramilitaries knifed eleven of them to death; they took the other five with them into town. They later ran into another boat with twelve fishermen on board. After making the men throw all their catch back into the water, the paramilitaries forced all twelve to go back into the town with them. Then, in front of the church, a group of the paramilitaries interrogated the men about the six names on the list. After, again, not getting any answers, the paramilitaries killed them all. Another group of paramilitaries shot indiscriminately at the houses in town. Yet another group looted the shops, homes, and fishermen's boats, taking home electronics, food, and boat motors. They then kept going, and, according to the remaining residents, slaughtered several more people on the water. Not all the bodies had been recovered, but the official death toll stood at thirty-eight. Calderón estimated that the paramilitaries had killed more than fifty people during the incursion. More than five hundred others fled the town in the following days.

Paramilitary massacres had become so commonplace that the media never even covered many of them. *Semana* itself often just mentioned them in the "In Brief" column. Despite the groups' savagery, to Calderón it seemed as though many Colombians had concluded that the paramilitaries were the solution to the guerrillas' violence. With FARC kidnappings and attacks at their peak, and with important parts of the military and various business sectors quietly backing the paramilitaries, it was easy to look away from the massacres and killings, or to accept the paramilitaries' lines about the victims simply being members of the guerrilla groups.

But Calderón felt strongly that the public needed to grapple with what was really happening. He wrote a piece, entitled simply "Barbarism," describing the Nueva Venecia massacre in detail.

A few days later, he got his first phone call from the paramilitary commander Salvatore Mancuso: the fishermen, Mancuso said, were exaggerating. Not that many people had been killed. Mancuso wanted a correction. Calderón argued back and held his line. But from then on, he and Mancuso began to speak regularly—in the past, only Castaño had spoken publicly for the paramilitaries; now, several commanders were starting to engage more with the media, always presenting themselves as saviors and accusing their victims of being guerrilla collaborators.

Later, Calderón met Mancuso in person at his posh, three-story house in Montería, the capital of the state of Córdoba. Mancuso was strongly built, with a large, bulbous head squarely set into a thick neck and a face that could easily become intimidating. But he dressed suavely, his thinning hair was neatly trimmed and slicked back, and he had good manners. Calderón thought Mancuso looked more like his idea of a drug lord than a paramilitary leader. Mancuso came from a well-off, half-Italian family from the ranching region of Córdoba, and he had studied engineering at a Bogotá university for a few years before joining the paramilitaries in the early 1990s. His home housed a jumble of Louis XV furniture and rococo-style ornaments, Chinese vases, Japanese sabers, and a collection of fine Italian wines. On one floor, there was a gym and an office from which to conduct AUC business. As Calderón approached Mancuso's house, he noted police standing guard around it—not to arrest Mancuso, but to protect him.

Calderón got the impression that in their interview Mancuso was making a special effort to come across as a decent person who had had no choice but to go to war in response to the pressure from the guerrillas. Years later, his authorized biography would explain that guerrilla threats against his family had led him to work with a member of the military, Walter Fratini, to establish the paramilitaries in Córdoba in the early 1990s. But he glossed over the bloodshed—including the El Aro massacre—in which he had been implicated.

Mancuso confirmed the paramilitaries' ties to the public security forces during their conversation, explaining how they "had" people in the police and army, and that one of their more prominent commanders, known as "Double Zero," was a retired army officer. Through Mancuso, Calderón met Double Zero and other commanders, who began inviting him to meet with them at their campsites or homes. During those visits, Calderón regularly saw members of the military, the intelligence service, or the police with the paramilitaries—the close ties between the paramilitaries and sectors of the public security forces were evident.

Calderón also noticed another trend: a growing fissure within the paramilitary groups over their involvement in the drug trade. Even though the AUC had from its inception been involved in drug trafficking, and the Castaños had been members of Los Pepes, Carlos Castaño had recently been urging his fellow commanders to give it up. Castaño expressed concern that drug trafficking was somehow tainting their "political" objectives of defeating the guerrillas, and that some sectors of the paramilitaries were more interested in seizing territory for cocaine trafficking than in confronting the FARC. Double Zero, who considered himself a "pure" paramilitary, took Castaño's side. But they were the minority, and Double Zero's "Metro Block" of the paramilitaries soon found itself at war with another sector of the paramilitaries headed by Diego Murillo Bejarano, or "Don Berna," who until recently had headed the Envigado Office that had been involved in the CTI killings in Medellín a few years earlier.

Calderón began publishing stories about what he was seeing at his meetings. The paramilitaries didn't like it, but he had always been clear with them that just because they were meeting and chatting didn't mean he would refrain from publishing. And from their perspective, it was still worthwhile to try to get their views across to a journalist from a prominent publication like *Semana*; the massacres were hard to cover up entirely, but at least they could try to divert attention from their savagery and confuse the public. Some of them, like Mancuso and Castaño, also seemed—like Escobar had many years before—to aspire to some form of public approval or even admiration. In their polarized society, in many cases, they got what they were seeking.

MEANWHILE, the FARC peace talks went from bad to worse, finally collapsing in February 2002, when a FARC unit hijacked a commercial airplane and kidnapped Senator Jorge Gechem Turbay, who was on board. A few days later, they kidnapped the French-Colombian presidential candidate Íngrid Betancourt and her campaign manager, Clara Rojas, as they traveled by road to the demilitarized zone. To the vast majority of Colombians, the FARC's continued kidnappings and cease-fire violations were the final nail in the coffin for the guerrillas' image: these were not romantic revolutionaries, but a bunch of thugs who cynically took advantage of the talks and demilitarized zone to add thousands of new fighters to their ranks, carry out more kidnappings and killings, and enrich themselves at the expense of ordinary people.

With the end of the peace talks, Colombia's conflict only intensified. In late April, Colombia's "public advocate" issued a written report to the heads of the armed forces and other government officials, warning that three hundred paramilitaries were traveling along the Atrato River near the municipality of Bojayá, in the deeply impoverished Afro-Colombian region of Chocó, with the apparent objective of seizing the region from the FARC's control. The public advocate urged immediate action to protect the people of Bojayá from the imminent violence, but no action was taken. On May 2, FARC guerrillas, in the midst of fighting with paramilitaries in Bojayá, lobbed a gas cylinder bomb into the town of Bellavista, hitting the town church, where hundreds of townspeople had taken refuge from the fighting. The bomb exploded, killing seventy-nine people, including forty-eight children, and injuring another one hundred. Terrified of further bombs, thousands of people fled, many never to return.

IN THE MIDST of the bloodshed, Colombians lost any shred of the hope that had fueled President Pastrana's efforts to seek peace. Instead, they grew increasingly desperate for someone to bring order to the country. Former Antioquia governor Álvaro Uribe, who was now running for office, seemed to fit the bill: though he rarely smiled, he had a sincere, honest air—fine features and pin-straight posture, neatly parted and combed hair, and upturned brows—that inspired confidence. The way he spoke conveyed strength and commitment. In the autobiography he published after leaving office, Uribe recounted an

episode that occurred when he was performing a particularly dangerous move in bullfighting: he was on his knees, but when the bull came
out of the pen, the creature charged in another direction. Uribe's father called out to him: "Álvaro, stay on your knees, stay there." Uribe
did, and eventually the bull came around and charged, and Uribe completed the move. Upon reflection, he later said, he thought that his
father was teaching him how to stand up to a threat: to "look it straight
in the eye and wink." Ultimately, he said, "there are only two dignified
ways of leaving the bullfighting ring: in a casket on the way to the
cemetery, or on the shoulders of the crowd. In this type of life, there is
no middle road." Uribe, it seemed, viewed the entire country as his
own enormous bullfighting ring, and he had no intention of leaving it
until he succeeded. Over the years, Uribe's sense of purpose—to lead
and save Colombia—seemed to have eclipsed nearly all of his other
interests. He later said that the last film he saw was *The Lone Ranger*,
and he gave up drinking and smoking in his twenties. Although he had
been a superb horseback rider in his youth, later in his political career
he rarely took the time to engage even in this pastime. His long hours
and willingness to travel across the country became legendary, as did
his willingness to hold conversations with any and all Colombians: he
traveled to countless small towns on the campaign trail, and seemed to
connect with people in a way that many politicians from Colombia's
traditional elite were incapable of doing.

His message, too, resonated: the former Liberal was running for
president as an independent that year, promising a "firm hand, and a
big heart" when it came to the guerrillas, including through commitments to dramatically bolster the size of the military and police forces,
to recruit thousands of citizens as informants for the government, and
to engage in peace talks with the FARC only if they implemented a
full cease-fire, including an end to all kidnappings. According to Uribe
adviser José Obdulio Gaviria, Uribe's position on the FARC ever since
he had become a governor was clear: there was no point in negotiating
with the FARC, because it was a "terrorist organization that has no
interest in changing the political system through negotiations." During
the Pastrana years, Gaviria said, nobody had wanted to listen to Uribe,
because politicians and the public were enamored of the idea of negotiating for peace. But in the aftermath of the failed Caguán negotiations, Uribe's message was perfect: the public was now thoroughly

disgusted with the FARC and saw no way out of the war except by escalating it.

Not that Uribe escaped all criticism—some journalists dug up old allegations that Uribe's father had been a friend of the Ochoa family, some of whose members, the infamous brothers Jorge Luis, Fabio, and Juan David, had become major figures in the Medellín cartel, along with Pablo Escobar. Uribe acknowledged that his father and Fabio Ochoa had known each other many years earlier, in the world of horse fairs, but he firmly denied any connection to the Ochoa clan's drug trafficking. Others charged that when Uribe had run the Civil Aviation Agency, he had granted licenses to pilots working with Escobar. Uribe denied the claims, stating that the record was clear—he could only grant licenses to people who had relevant certifications from the Ministry of Justice and the military.

Critics also accused Uribe of being, at a minimum, tolerant of the paramilitaries, based in part on his support of the Convivir program when he was governor of Antioquia. In 1999, Uribe had also publicly spoken at an event to honor General Rito Alejo del Río. Then president Pastrana had recently dismissed Del Río over serious allegations that he had colluded with paramilitaries, and had been involved in atrocities in the Urabá region when he had commanded the Army's 17th Brigade. The United States had also reportedly canceled Del Río's visa on similar grounds. Yet, at the event, Uribe strongly defended Del Río, whom he had met when he was governor.

But much of the public paid little attention to these concerns. In May 2002, Uribe was declared the winner of the elections in the first round after getting just over 50 percent of the vote.

BY THE TIME Uribe was elected, the paramilitaries were at the peak of their power. Official estimates by the Ministry of Defense put their membership at 12,000 troops—almost as many as the FARC—though it was hard to tell how reliable the numbers were. After their offensives in the late 1990s, the paramilitaries had effectively seized control over much of northern Colombia, establishing a significant presence in large chunks of the coastal areas and Antioquia. In recent years they had even been expanding into the eastern plains of Meta and Casanare, and into territory in the southern states of Nariño, Cauca, and Putumayo. And while on the surface things might have looked normal in many of these regions—local government and businesses were still active, and people seemed to go about their daily activities as usual— residents knew not to cross the paramilitaries or the landowners, businesspeople, and officials who were close to them.

The paramilitaries had thrived in part because they had never had much to fear from Colombian authorities—Carlos Castaño, for example, had at least one conviction for murder hanging over his head, and had admitted his involvement in numerous other crimes, yet he had never been arrested. That began to change on August 5, 2002, two days before Uribe took office, when Colombia ratified the Rome Statute of the International Criminal Court. The court would not have jurisdiction over past crimes, but, in theory, paramilitary atrocities committed after ratification could one day come under the court's purview.

What may have been even more significant was an announcement, just a few weeks later, by the US attorney general in the George W. Bush administration, John Ashcroft. At a press conference, Ashcroft announced the unsealing of a US Department of Justice indictment against AUC leaders Carlos Castaño and Salvatore Mancuso, as well as against a man described as an "AUC member," though in Colombia he was mainly known as a drug trafficker, Juan Carlos "El Tuso" Sierra, on five counts of drug trafficking. Ashcroft made a point of noting that the AUC was on the State Department's list of Foreign Terrorist Organizations, stressing that the indictments underscored "the convergence of two of the top priorities of the Department of Justice: the prevention of terrorism, and the reduction of illegal drug use." "As today's indictment reminds us," said Ashcroft, "the lawlessness that breeds terrorism is also a fertile ground for the drug trafficking that supports terrorism. To surrender to either of these threats is to surrender to both."

As Calderón had noticed in his meetings, the paramilitaries were increasingly divided over the issue of drug trafficking, and some had recognized the danger of getting involved in the trade. In a July 2002 letter to his fellow commanders, Castaño noted that "the money from drug trafficking is employed primarily for personal enrichment, and not to fund the organization. Those I'm referring to know it and their wealth is impossible to hide; the only way to legalize it would be through a serious negotiation with the government." But Castaño didn't think the paramilitaries were going to succeed against the

FARC: despite the AUC's expansion, the FARC, which had an esti-mated 13,500 troops, remained strong in many of its traditional strongholds. "We have occupied territory where there were no guer-rillas and won others where there were some . . . but we haven't eradicated them completely from any state in the center and north of Colombia, which we claim publicly to be under our control, and we prefer to go start groups in other areas in the south of the country, not exactly in search of the enemy but of coca, and we falsely pretend like we're growing . . . ; these are lies, what is growing is drug traffick-ing dressed up as self-defense forces." And, perhaps above all, Castaño was concerned that, if the paramilitaries didn't seek a negotiation now, they risked extradition and imprisonment in the United States: "The drug traffickers, whether guerrilla or self-defense forces, are be-ing sought for extradition," he said. "I think that if we can demon-strate that in the self-defense forces there are no drug traffickers, but rather there was a need to resort to that money to finance the strug-gle . . . we could find a solution for everyone."

Ashcroft's announcement of the indictments and extradition re-quests made the threat real. Unless they wanted to risk spending de-cades in a US prison, the paramilitaries needed to find a way to evade the US charges. Castaño's preferred solution—to embark on "peace" negotiations with the government—seemed like one promising way out, and the Uribe administration quickly engaged. By November 2002, the AUC had declared a cease-fire, and by July 2003, the AUC leadership and the Colombian government, represented by Peace Commissioner Luis Carlos Restrepo, had entered an agreement. In this pact, known as the Agreement of Santa Fe de Ralito (named for the province in Córdoba where the negotiations happened), the paramili-taries promised to demobilize all their troops by the end of 2005.

But the very next month, in August 2003, Uribe introduced a bill in the Colombian Congress that was so lax on the paramilitaries that it made some people question the government's motives. The bill would protect the paramilitaries from prosecution for all their crimes—including the worst massacres and atrocities, as well as drug traffick-ing—if they agreed to put down their weapons. The paramilitaries would not have to serve any time in prison or even confess their crimes. Nor would they have to give up their illegally acquired wealth, or dis-close any details about their accomplices and drug-trafficking networks. All they were asked to do was to provide some form of reparation to the victims, but what that meant was unclear. Victims' and human rights organizations both within and outside Colombia were horrified at the proposal, which they viewed as a complete pass for some of the worst killers in the country's history, and began immediately organizing to fight it.

That would not be easy. The president's popularity had only increased since the elections, as he had quickly moved to strengthen security in Colombia, particularly in areas where the FARC posed a threat. Early on in his term, Uribe decreed a one-time "security tax" on wealth, which helped him to increase defense expenditures substantially. He bolstered the police and military presence along major roads, and during holidays he implemented a new initiative, called "Live Colombia, Travel Through It" (Vive Colombia, Viaja Por Ella), designed to promote internal tourism: the government would organize large caravans of vehicles to drive together, escorted by security forces, to get to their destinations. At the same time, Uribe was building a strong relationship with the United States. By the end of the 1990s, Colombia had already been the third-largest recipient of US security assistance, after Israel and Egypt. Toward the end of the Pastrana administration, the United States had pledged to substantially increase that aid through a package known as Plan Colombia. President Bill Clinton promised a $1.3 billion influx of aid, overwhelmingly focused on counternarcotics assistance and military aid, over three years starting in 1999. By 2003, the US embassy in Colombia was the largest US embassy in the world, with thousands of embassy staff and US military advisers, as well as civilian contractors who were there to train and support their counterparts in Colombia (it would be surpassed in size by the US embassy in Afghanistan in 2004). Within his first few weeks in office, Uribe visited Washington to meet with President Bush; the meeting was the beginning of a friendship between the two ranch-loving presidents, and solidified the assistance package.

Questioning Uribe would only get more difficult over time, as official statistics pointed to substantial drops in violence. In a 2004 op-ed in the *Boston Globe*, the Colombian ambassador to the United States, Luis Alberto Moreno, reported that "since 2002, homicides have declined by 25 percent; kidnappings have declined by 45 percent; and incidents of terrorism have declined by 37 percent." Uribe's popularity

rating was hitting 78 percent. Colombia, it seemed, was turning a corner. And after all those decades of tragedy and despair, who was to
question the man who had made that possible?

IN THE AFTERMATH of the US indictments of Castaño and Mancuso, Calderón began receiving numerous invitations to meet with
the paramilitaries, who were obviously on a charm offensive, trying
to convince the public that they were heroes. One of the leaders he
got to know was Rodrigo Tovar Pupo, also known as "Jorge 40," who
was said to head the "Northern Block" of the paramilitaries, which
operated primarily in the coastal states of Atlántico and Magdalena,
as well as the state of Cesar, on the border with Venezuela. The
bearded, strident, compact Jorge 40 was a member of the elite in
Valledupar, the capital of Cesar, and had even worked for the city
government before joining the paramilitaries in the early 1990s—
like Mancuso, he told Calderón that he had joined in response to the
guerrillas' increased presence in the region, which included threats,
kidnappings, and extortion against members of his landowning family. He gave Calderón a long and whitewashed story about himself,
telling him that both he and Ricardo Palmera (aka "Simón Trini-
dad," a FARC commander) had been members of the Valledupar
Club, where they had known each other. Although they had taken
different paths, they had both, he said, been forced by war to abandon their families. Unlike Mancuso, though, Jorge 40 made no effort
to come across as a gentleman; instead, he had a harsh, almost militaristic manner of speaking. Calderón first met him at a small farm,
and they spoke for about five hours. Calderón asked Jorge 40 about
some of his block's massacres, which by then numbered in the dozens, and included the particularly gruesome February 2000 massacre
at El Salado, in which 450 paramilitaries had killed 60 townspeople,
scalping, raping, dismembering, torturing, and beheading them on
and around the soccer court. But Jorge 40 pushed back hard, blaming
the guerrillas for his actions. Like other paramilitary leaders whom
Calderón met in those days, Jorge 40 tried to convince him that the
paramilitaries were a force for good. They would trot out community
members to tell Calderón that, thanks to the AUC, they now had
water, or other benefits. It was time-consuming to sit for the inevita-
ble dog-and-pony show. But it was worth it for Calderón: he knew

that if he stuck around long enough, he would pick up bits of information that were useful.

That included information about the rising tensions among the paramilitary leaders negotiating with the government. In the eyes of Castaño, and of some officials, a number of the leaders at the negotiating table in Santa Fe de Ralito, including El Tuso Sierra and Francisco Javier Zuluaga (aka "Gordolindo"), were not paramilitary leaders at all, but rather drug traffickers who had bought franchises within the AUC, and who should be excluded from the process. Castaño was anxious for some kind of deal to work out soon, as he had recently had a baby daughter who suffered from a serious genetic disease known as the *cri du chat*—ideally, it was rumored, Castaño wanted to get her care in the United States. He feared that the inclusion of drug traffickers would doom the peace negotiations. But he and Double Zero were increasingly alone in their purist position, and many of the other commanders had started to view them with hostility.

Calderón also continued to see more evidence of the tight relationship between the paramilitaries and public officials, including during what became fairly regular visits to The Eagle, which Calderón set up through the commander's lawyer. A big fan of deceased Medellín cartel member Gonzalo Rodríguez Gacha, aka "The Mexican," The Eagle sported a thick mustache and a heavy gold chain with an Eagle on it. The Eagle's group was not yet within the AUC, but he had joined the negotiations at Santa Fe de Ralito.

The day that Calderón was getting a tour of the anthill by The Eagle's ranch, Calderón saw a helicopter touch down filled with about thirty paramilitary troops. The Eagle later explained that his men had been in a battle with the guerrillas, and had been having trouble, so Castaño had sent him reinforcements. The strange thing, Calderón realized later, was that to get to that location, the helicopter would have had to refuel at the air force base of La Dorada. Another source close to The Eagle told him that the paramilitaries eventually defeated the guerrillas with support from a sector of the army.

During another visit to The Eagle, Calderón was surprised to see some people he knew—members of Colombia's intelligence service, the DAS (for Departamento Administrativo de Seguridad, or Administrative Department of Security)—arrive at The Eagle's campsite. "They almost had a heart attack when they saw me," recalled Calderón.

The DAS members had come to sell stolen weapons and vehicles to the paramilitary commander, whose son, they said, wanted a new Ford Explorer. They didn't speak to Calderón at the time, but a couple of days later, he walked to his office in the afternoon and found them in the lobby, where they had been waiting for him for almost six hours. "Look, you know, intelligence people need to get together with the bad guys," Calderón recalled them saying. He knew that they were lying to him, but decided not to publish anything at the time. These people could be good sources, and, he suspected, there was a lot more to the story.

CHAPTER 10

THE COMMANDERS' "FRIENDS"

IVÁN VELÁSQUEZ READ THE FEW words on the piece of paper and considered his next move. Outside his window on the fourth floor of the dilapidated Palace of Justice, where the Supreme Court sat, he could just make out through the gray haze the bulky silhouette of the yellowing congressional buildings, and then the expansive grounds of the Presidential Palace in the heart of downtown Bogotá. In the narrow streets below, cars were snarled in the never-ending traffic. Government and service industry workers, professionals, and students made their way around in a glut of ramshackle buses, taxis, and the occasional gleaming SUV with tinted windows shielding the passengers from potential attackers.

If he could have seen farther, into the southern margins of the landlocked city, he would have glimpsed the bleak and crowded slums stretching endlessly into the distance. Many of their residents were peasants who, having lost everything to the country's war, had sought refuge in the large city's anonymity and relative safety. To the north, there were wealthier residential districts, with block after block of modern red-brick buildings and comfortable, stately houses where the affluent lived. Restaurants and cafés, ever more luxurious malls (with the greater security, they were increasingly opening boutiques for Louis Vuitton purses, Hermès scarves, and Dior jewelry), beauty salons, and bookstores lined the streets, which were shaded by tall ash, oak, and walnut trees. Dark green mountains towered all around the city, a lush yet forbidding landscape spreading out for miles along the Andes

Mountains that cut across the whole of South America's western flank, until they descended to the Caribbean or Pacific coasts to the north and west on one side, or the plains and then the Amazon rainforest on the east.

Velásquez had been in Bogotá for five years, leading a quiet life and working as one of three assistant justices supporting Justice Álvaro Pérez in the criminal chamber of Colombia's Supreme Court. Mainly, his job consisted of supporting Pérez in reviewing appeals from lower courts, but on rare occasions, he worked on criminal investigations against members of Colombia's Congress, over whom the court had jurisdiction. The position had a lower profile than his job as chief prosecutor in Medellín, but Velásquez enjoyed working with the sharp and straightforward Pérez. It was also a much less dangerous job, at least so far.

The complaint Velásquez had received that morning in June 2005 was not much to go on, really—"insignificant," Velásquez told himself, and "impossible to prove." The content was so simple it was almost laughable: Clara López—a lawyer, academic, and left-leaning politician who had dated President Uribe in her youth—was asking the Supreme Court to investigate the truth of recent statements by paramilitary leaders Salvatore Mancuso and Vicente Castaño, in which they claimed that they controlled a substantial portion of Congress. That was it. The complaint referred to a lengthy interview that *Semana* magazine had just published with fearsome paramilitary chief Vicente Castaño, Carlos's brother, in which, in response to a question by the interviewer about the paramilitaries' connections to politicians, Vicente had stated that the paramilitaries had "as friends" more than 35 percent of Congress, "and in the next elections, we will increase that percentage." Mancuso had made similar statements around the time of the 2002 elections, claiming that the paramilitaries had exceeded their goal of winning 35 percent of the seats in Congress.

Velásquez knew better than most that the paramilitaries had friends in powerful places. The hundreds of names in the Padilla files were proof enough, even though that case had fallen apart. But it also stood to reason: for all the thousands who had died at their hands, there must be many others who had gained a great deal from their control, from their theft of land, and their killings of union and community leaders. That had to include politicians, at least at a local level. A member of Congress from the opposition party Polo

Democrático Alternativo (Alternative Democratic Pole), Gustavo Petro, had given an impassioned speech on the floor of Congress just a few weeks earlier in which he accused a number of prominent politicians from the region of Sucre of having conspired to create paramilitary groups, and even to carry out massacres. Citing evidence buried in old case files and media reports, he painted a picture of an entire region under the thumb of what he called "local mafias," which combined "economic elites, political leaders, and criminals who had been turned into commanders of private armies" with "one goal: to control through terror . . . the society in which it is based," and ultimately, to secure "their illegal enrichment . . . the capture of public resources, natural resources, land, and cocaine."

Vicente Castaño's statement, while far from clear, could be read to suggest that the dynamic Petro had described was in place not only in Sucre, but in more than a third of the country. If the paramilitaries in effect controlled that many congressmen, it meant they had a big say in the passage of legislation: it might help to explain why Congress seemed poised to pass the so-called "Justice and Peace Law" that President Uribe was backing.

Under international pressure, Uribe had backed off his original proposal to give the paramilitary leaders a complete pass on their crimes, but, in Velásquez's mind, the newly revised bill he had now put on the table was still deeply flawed: it would allow paramilitary commanders who entered a "demobilization" process to serve as little as three to five years for all their crimes, apparently on farms rather than in prisons. It would be one thing if, to get these benefits, the paramilitaries had to take apart their powerful criminal networks, give up their illegally acquired wealth, and tell the full truth about their crimes and accomplices. But as written, the bill required none of those things—and given Uribe's history of minimizing military-paramilitary links and endorsing the Convivirs, many viewed the bill as a gift to the paramilitaries rather than a serious effort to demobilize them. Victims' groups and critics of the government, including Senators Rafael Pardo and Gina Parody, who had once been Uribe supporters, had repeatedly pointed out the bill's flaws. Even in the United States, senators from both sides of the aisle—Republican Richard Lugar and Democrats Patrick Leahy, Edward Kennedy, Christopher Dodd, Russell Feingold, and Joe Biden—were calling on Uribe to reform the bill. In a letter to

Uribe, Lugar insisted: "We want to see the armed groups demobilize, but this law rewards some of Colombia's worst terrorists and drug traffickers without any assurance that their criminal organizations will be dismantled." But the US ambassador to Colombia, Bill Wood, seemed to support the bill, and it was now sailing through congressional review. The thought that the paramilitaries might have corrupted Colombia's democracy to such a degree that they could even get the government to wipe their records clean was alarming, but not, to Velásquez at least, surprising.

Still, the comments by Mancuso and Castaño did not directly accuse anyone of illegal acts. So even if Velásquez wanted to investigate, where would he begin? The Supreme Court also had limited resources—unlike the prosecutors in the attorney general's office, Velásquez had no support from professional investigators to track down leads and interview witnesses. Virtually all the work would have to fall on his shoulders. And what was the point? After Velásquez's attempt to go after the paramilitaries in Medellín, he had ended up feeling like Don Quixote, a sculpture of whom stood next to the crucifix in his home office—not that he had been tilting at windmills, but perhaps he had been naive to believe that the justice system could really rein in the paramilitaries. And the price had been so high.

It would be easy enough to just set the complaint aside, concluding there wasn't enough to go on. In any case, with the majority of Congress belonging to the president's party, it would be next to impossible to get any real movement on an investigation like this. Many others would have done exactly that. Not Velásquez.

SINCE HIS DAYS as inspector general of Medellín, in the early 1990s, Velásquez had carried in his memory the image of a young man he met one day at his offices. He first caught sight of the youth sitting alone on a battered metal chair in the worn, bare office of the Human Rights Unit, his blackened cheekbone swollen so badly that it looked as though he had two cheekbones on one side of his face, his wrists a mess of deep, raw gashes, still wet with blood. He could not have been older than twenty-five, a skinny kid in tattered jeans, staring at his sneakers as he waited. He looked up when Velásquez walked in and eagerly started telling him the story: "I just got away from the UNASE," Velásquez recalled the young man saying, as he lifted his T-shirt. "Look at what they did to me." Long welts like red ribbons, some bright and fresh, others older and darker, ran up and down his back, from where he had been whipped with the side of a machete. He had caused the wrist injuries himself when he had slipped out of the knots tying him to the floor.

In a short time, the UNASE, the elite anti-kidnapping unit, had developed a stellar reputation for quickly finding and rescuing hostages, and the Colombian government liked to tout UNASE's successes as proof of the effectiveness of its security policies. The UNASE's headquarters were three blocks from Velásquez's office in downtown Medellín.

"I want to file a complaint against those *hijueputas*," swore the victim, his voice thick and raspy. Velásquez said he would take it down and investigate, but warned the young man that it was risky. The victim's response stuck in his mind: "Yes, I know. They'll kill me," he said, matter-of-factly. "But they're going to kill me anyway, and if I report this I can keep them from doing to others what they did to me." It was true: chances were that whoever had been torturing this boy would eventually track him down and kill him. Realistically, Velásquez knew he could do little to protect him, especially if the UNASE really was behind this. All he could do was put all his energy into finding the torturers and trying to keep them from doing it again. And that was a very long shot. But this sort of case really got under Velásquez's skin: when officials who were supposed to be protecting people instead became yet another threat. So he promised to investigate.

To Velásquez's surprise, he and one of his colleagues, Guillermo Villa, had very quickly made progress—they located a space that the UNASE was using as a torture chamber, and then collected enough evidence to file disciplinary charges against several UNASE members. The case seemed to be going extremely well, until one day Velásquez read a shocking story in the paper: Villa, whom he had known since law school, was under investigation for secretly leaking information to the Cali cartel. Immediately, the national inspector general's office announced that all the cases Villa had worked on would be put on hold. Eventually, the office decided, against Velásquez's wishes, to shutter the investigation into the UNASE's practices, despite the strong evidence they had collected.

Velásquez later looked up the tortured young man who had sought his assistance in the case. When he introduced himself to the woman who opened the door to the youth's house, she grew enraged: "You! It's your fault!" he recalled her saying. "My son is dead. They killed him, and it's all because of you!"

Throughout his life, Velásquez had repeatedly heard people in Colombia say: "La justicia, pa' que?" (Justice, what's the point?). He had always pushed back, saying it was important to have hope and try. What happened with the UNASE investigation, like what happened later with his investigators in Medellín and the Padilla parking-lot case, had sometimes made him despair and wonder whether others were right to be cynical. But ultimately, Velásquez was an idealist. He did not believe things would always turn out well, but he believed that justice was at least possible, and that it was still worth fighting for. He wanted to give others—like the mother of that young man—a reason to believe. To give up was, in his mind, a betrayal. "I act out of conviction, and having to act against those convictions would be a denial of myself that would be very complicated," he later tried to explain. "If I got to that point, I might as well just sit around and read all day. I would lose all authority before myself. Fortunately, I don't think too much about that. It's something you just live."

So when Velásquez had to decide what to do with the complaint about the paramilitaries' influence in Congress, he didn't really have to think about it much. He started to investigate.

SITTING BEFORE Supreme Court Justice Álvaro Pérez, Vicente Castaño did not look like a sinister figure. Unlike his younger brother, Carlos, he had avoided the spotlight, and before the interview with Calderón that was published in *Semana*, only one photo of him was publicly known. But he was said to be one of the more ruthless and powerful of the paramilitary commanders—and deeply involved in the drug trade. He was also said to be behind the mysterious disappearance of Carlos, who had gone missing in April 2004, in the midst of the paramilitaries' negotiations with the Colombian government. A month later, Double Zero, the only other paramilitary commander who had taken Carlos's side on the issue of whether the paramilitaries should break with drug trafficking, had been killed.

But that day, there was nothing about Vicente Castaño's appearance or manner that hinted at the terror that he and his fellow commanders had inflicted on much of Colombia. He was mild mannered and looked like an ordinary man, of medium build, tan, with a balding head and stern gaze that made him look older than his forty-eight years. Salvatore Mancuso, who, along with Castaño, had flown in a private jet to Bogotá for the interview with the Supreme Court justice, appeared even more smooth than Vicente. He had dressed for the occasion in an expensive suit and tie—Pérez recalled that the court's secretaries seemed to swoon when he arrived.

Once Velásquez had secured Pérez's approval to start investigating the complaint, one of their first steps had been to call Castaño and Mancuso to explain their statements. But, not surprisingly, they extracted little in the way of new information from the commanders, who spoke in generalities and cast themselves as heroes. While Vicente Castaño repeated what he said to *Semana* about the 35 percent of members of Congress who were the paramilitaries' "friends," he refused to name any specific individuals who were collaborating with the paramilitaries, or to explain what he meant by calling them friends. The two men seemed unconcerned by the investigation: if the Justice and Peace Law was passed, they would soon get to wipe their records clean, with little more than a slap on the wrist, and without having to tell the truth about their crimes. The Uribe administration seemed to be in no rush to rein them in: labeling Mancuso and Castaño as "peace negotiators," it was still allowing them to move around the country freely.

If the court was going to make progress in these investigations, Velásquez would have to find other leads. With Pérez's backing, Velásquez began to go back over old case files in the court—complaints that were unresolved, cases that were stalled, unfinished investigations. All he needed was one loose thread, one concrete allegation that he could follow up, or one witness from inside who would talk.

IT WAS MERCIFULLY warm when Velásquez arrived in Canada that summer—he had never been in Canada before, but he knew of many people who lived there. The country to the north had for years been a top destination for Colombian refugees, including, in recent years, several former prosecutors who had attempted to investigate the paramilitaries. These included Velásquez's old friends from Medellín days, the investigations chief Gregorio Oviedo and his wife, the human rights prosecutor Amelia Pérez, who were struggling to get by, and whom he managed to see for lunch in Quebec at the end of his visit. But Velásquez was not in Canada to see his old friends; instead, he was there to interview a former paramilitary member, Jairo Castillo Peralta. Also known by his alias as "Pitirri," Castillo had been living there since 2002, when he fled Colombia after offering extensive testimony to a local prosecutor about paramilitary activities in his home region of Sucre, Colombia. When Velásquez dug up Castillo's testimony, he had also found statements about several politicians' links to paramilitaries in the area.

The sweltering, cattle-ranching, coastal region of Sucre and the neighboring state of Bolívar had been the scenes of a savage paramilitary onslaught throughout the 1990s and early 2000s, including multiple large-scale massacres in the lush stretch of small mountains known as the Montes de María, which straddles the two states, and which guerrillas and paramilitaries had long used as a strategic corridor to the Caribbean coast. Some of the cases were so grotesque that they were infamous throughout the country, such as the 2001 massacre in Chengue, Sucre, in which paramilitaries systematically killed twenty-four men on the town plaza, bashing their heads in with a sledgehammer, and then bringing their families out to witness the carnage.

Nor did the paramilitaries just swoop in, commit massacres, and leave. The local paramilitary commander in Sucre, Rodrigo Mercado Peluffo, also known as "Cadena" (or "Chain" in English), disappeared mysteriously in July 2005 as he was leaving the paramilitary leadership's negotiation site in Santa Fe de Ralito. His car was later found burned by the side of the road. In subsequent months, some of his victims started to come forward to speak out about the horrors he had inflicted on them—particularly in the municipality of San Onofre, where he had a vast farm called "El Palmar." Tips led criminal investigators from the attorney general's office to go to the farm, where they found more than seventy bodies in mass graves. Community members, however, claimed that the investigators had done an incomplete job, and that hundreds of their "disappeared" family members were also buried there. Victims described Cadena or his men regularly showing up in small towns, pulling young men from their homes, and shooting them on the spot or taking them away. The killers were said to have chopped up their victims' bodies and thrown them into rivers, left them on the sides of roads, or buried them in El Palmar. Cadena was also rumored to have abused large numbers of young women, whom his men would rape or hold as sex slaves.

In his culling of old case files, Velásquez had found an anonymous complaint stating that in Plan Parejo, a small town in San Onofre, Cadena's men had forced the inhabitants to attend a rally in support of a couple of congressional candidates, Jairo Merlano and Muriel Benito. One of Cadena's lieutenants had also participated in the rally. The same complaint claimed that the paramilitaries had later driven the inhabitants to their voting locations, instructing them on how to vote; Merlano and Benito were both now in Congress. Here was a concrete allegation of paramilitary manipulation of elections to favor politicians—exactly the sort of thread Velásquez had been looking for—so he decided to dig into the region further.

First, though, Velásquez had to talk to Justice Álvaro Pérez: Velásquez and the two other assistant justices working for Pérez could not conduct a massive investigation into Sucre on their own. Remembering how in Medellín he had created a separate team of trusted investigators to focus on the paramilitary cases, Velásquez suggested contacting the attorney general's office to see if the court could borrow a couple of investigators; he insisted that the court should be able to pick the investigators and should have full authority over their investigations. Pérez reached out to Attorney General Mario Iguarán, who agreed, and now Velásquez had two criminal investigators working with him who could travel to Sucre, conduct interviews, and start building a case.

Velásquez had also found another investigation pending in the court into Sucre senator Álvaro García's alleged involvement in the 2000 massacre of Macayepo, in which paramilitaries clubbed and stoned fifteen peasants to death. In 2002, in *Semana*, Ricardo Calderón had reported on a recording he had obtained of a phone call that had taken place a few days before the massacre between the senator and a prominent Sucre landowner, Joaquín García, in which they appeared to be discussing plans to move paramilitary troops into the area of

Macayepo. The court's investigation had failed to focus on the recording and was on the verge of being closed—but Velásquez reactivated it.

Eventually, Velásquez and his team also found a couple of other investigations, long ago forgotten, in which a witness had talked to prosecutors about politicians organizing a paramilitary group in Sucre in the late 1990s, and even ordering the murder of a young elections monitor, Georgina Narváez, to keep her from reporting voting irregularities in local elections in 1997. That witness was Castillo.

A skinny, small man with a scraggly mustache and elfin features, Castillo was still in his thirties, but he had a serious, tired cast to his face, as though he had seen too much in his life already. Castillo spoke extremely quickly, jumping from one issue to another and going down multiple tangents in an overwhelming flood of information. He was illiterate, but Velásquez was impressed by his memory for details like names, dates, and places, and by his consistency. What Castillo told Velásquez in Quebec—and expanded upon in later statements—was almost exactly what he had told investigators and prosecutors in Colombia six years earlier.

Castillo had grown up poor in Majagual, Sucre, but had had to flee his hometown because of extortion by the guerrillas. Later, in the regional capital of Sincelejo, he met some military officers who convinced him to become an informant for them, since he came from an area with a strong guerrilla presence and knew what they looked like and how they operated. They also recommended him as a guard to a powerful local landowner, Joaquín García, who had repeatedly been the target of guerrilla attacks and kidnapping attempts, and who also happened to be one of the primary backers of paramilitary groups in the region. García was also close to many prominent politicians in the region, funding their campaigns. Through García, Castillo became privy to meetings between paramilitaries such as Salvatore Mancuso; local politicians, including Salvador Arana and Álvaro García; and members of the military and other officials. Eventually, he also began to run errands for Joaquín García, Arana, and the paramilitaries, taking messages back and forth and collecting financial contributions for the paramilitary group.

According to Castillo, in the 1997 elections Joaquín García had backed Eric Morris, now a member of Congress, as a candidate for governor of Sucre. When initial results indicated that Morris was losing,

Joaquín García and Senator Álvaro García made arrangements to fix the results. But Georgina Narváez, an elections monitor for the opposing candidate, reported irregularities in the voting in her region, which could have thrown the results and gotten them into trouble. To keep her from testifying about them, Castillo said, Álvaro García and Joaquín García had ordered her murder. An assassin killed her outside her home shortly afterward. Morris went on to become governor.

Castillo also said that in 1998 he had been present for a meeting at a popular steak restaurant called Carbón de Palo in Sincelejo, the capital of Sucre, at which Joaquín García met with several senior paramilitary leaders and well-known political figures, such as Salvador Arana—who would later replace Morris as governor of Sucre, and whom President Uribe would eventually name as ambassador to Chile. At the meeting, the men agreed to create a new paramilitary unit to operate in specific areas, including Majagual; Castillo said they agreed that Álvaro García would get financing for the group with the help of the governor, Eric Morris. Castillo later provided a copy of a check for thousands of dollars related to a municipal contract that he said he was asked to cash, to help finance the group.

Around the same time, Castillo said in other statements, he was asked if he would lead a local paramilitary group. He refused, but Mancuso grew angry and—according to Castillo—ordered his murder. Fearing for his life, Castillo approached the CTI in Sincelejo and began to give them information about the paramilitaries in exchange for protection. Soon thereafter, he began to speak with prosecutor Yolanda Paternina, sharing detailed information, including names and phone numbers of paramilitary commanders and politicians involved in massacres and other crimes, the names of ranchers who contributed money to them, and evidence about police officers, prosecutors, and members of the military who were cooperating with the paramilitaries. With his testimony, the investigators began to carry out a number of successful operations against the paramilitaries in Sucre.

But the paramilitaries caught on to what was happening and killed three CTI investigators who had been working with Castillo. In October 2000, assassins shot Castillo himself in front of his house, puncturing a lung—but he survived. After the attack, Paternina got him into a witness protection program and moved him to Medellín. She also began to receive threats herself, and repeatedly wrote to her supervisors in 2001, pleading with them to protect her or transfer her to another office. In one letter she said that the local paramilitary commander, Cadena, had given orders that she be kidnapped and brought before him. Her supervisors ignored her repeated requests or turned them down until August, when she was finally assigned a bodyguard. On August 29, however, she called her children from the office, saying that she couldn't find her bodyguard and would have to take a taxi home. As she arrived, two men approached on a motorcycle, and one shot her to death at her front door. Castillo left Colombia a few months later.

After Paternina's murder and Castillo's departure, the cases in which he had testified stalled under Luis Camilo Osorio's leadership of the attorney general's office, and the part about the politicians' involvement—which was pending in the Supreme Court—gathered dust.

To Velásquez, it was clear that the statements Castillo had made were so serious, and so detailed, that they could only have been ignored for so long through gross negligence or outright corruption. In one case, the investigators working with him looked up a case file in Sincelejo that involved the congressmen and found that the entire file had disappeared. It seemed as though the paramilitaries and their "friends" in Sucre controlled everything that happened in the state.

THE INVESTIGATION of Sucre was the Supreme Court's first major step toward scrutinizing paramilitary influence in the political system. But if what Castaño and Mancuso had said about 35 percent of Congress was true, then Sucre was just the tip of the iceberg. And now there was an analysis of how that might have happened: a few months after Velásquez received the complaint about Castaño's and Mancuso's statements, a tiny, determined thirty-five-year-old political analyst named Claudia López (no relation to Clara, the author of the complaint) published an article in Semana pointing to highly unusual voting patterns in the regions where paramilitary violence had been most acute. With a detailed slideshow of maps showing voting patterns in regions with high rates of paramilitary massacres, López explained how her analysis suggested that paramilitaries had backed specific pairs of candidates—one for the Senate, and one for the Chamber of Representatives—in each electoral district where they exercised control. In those districts, she found, the pair of candidates backed by paramilitaries won by highly atypical majorities of as much as 98 percent. She went on to provide a list of names of members of Congress who had obtained their seats in the irregular elections. López pointed out that "the [paramilitaries'] political consolidation was not achieved by giving out kind pieces of advice so that people could 'freely' decide, as Mancuso has cynically stated before the Court and the media. . . . The pattern that appears to repeat itself is that of entering with massacres, carrying out selective homicides, securing military control, going into the political system and local economies and consolidating their political hegemony in elections, and economic hegemony in multiple businesses spanning the use of public resources, the state lottery, palm [oil], contraband in gasoline and drug trafficking."

López's analysis was not hard evidence of corruption, but the patterns she identified were extremely suspicious, and they offered a useful lens through which to look at the problem. So, early on, the court called on López to testify, and Velásquez began to take a closer look at some of the regions she had highlighted.

As the 2006 elections approached, López's article in *Semana* was causing enough of a stir that members of the opposition to Uribe began accusing some of the political parties affiliated with him of including politicians who were closely tied to the paramilitaries. In particular, they named congresswomen Rocío Arias and Eleonora Pineda, who openly and proudly spoke about their friendship with Mancuso and other paramilitary leaders, and had been among the strongest proponents of the demobilization process. Public pressure led Juan Manuel Santos and Germán Vargas Lleras, then the leaders of two pro-Uribe parties, the Social Party of National Unity (Partido Social de Unidad Nacional, known as "la U," for Partido de "la U," or Party of the U), and Cambio Radical (Radical Change), respectively, to announce in early 2006 that they were purging the parties of a handful of candidates who were suspected of having paramilitary ties. But the changes were small, and they were far from accounting for the percentages that Mancuso and Castaño had mentioned.

BY EARLY NOVEMBER 2006, Velásquez and his team had compiled enough evidence to issue arrest warrants against three members of Congress from Sucre, Senators Álvaro García and Jairo Merlano and Representative Eric Morris, on charges of conspiring with paramilitaries. García was also charged with aggravated homicide in connection with the Macayepo massacre and the murder of Georgina Narváez.

Soon afterward, the attorney general's office also issued an arrest warrant for Salvador Arana—over whom the court had no jurisdiction—in connection with the 2003 murder of Eudaldo Díaz, a former mayor in Sucre. Díaz had opposed the paramilitaries in his state and had publicly said that Arana and others in the state government wanted to kill him. A few weeks before his murder, Díaz had even told President Uribe, at a televised community meeting at which Uribe was seated next to then governor Arana, that he was going to be killed for reporting on corruption within the state government. Uribe had then asked him to be quiet, saying that the attorney general's office and inspector general's office would take his complaint. But Díaz never received an answer to his complaint, and on April 10, his tortured body was found with several bullet wounds in it. His body was arranged in the shape of a crucified man, with the identification documents for his mayorship thrown on his face.

The arrest warrants were an unheard-of step and a blow to Uribe's coalition in Congress, of which Álvaro García, Merlano, and Morris were a part. But Uribe's initial reaction to them was positive: a US embassy cable from the time reported that at a November 17, 2006, event commemorating the Supreme Court's anniversary, Uribe said that Colombia "had to proceed with 'more severity' when public officials were accused of violating the law." Uribe had "stressed [that] 'where there are congressmen, political leaders or Executive officials involved in crime, they must go to jail,'" and that "the GOC [Government of Colombia] supported the Justice system's ongoing investigations 'without hesitation.'"

Still, Velásquez knew that the "parapolitics" investigations had the potential to be much bigger, and that he needed more help. Velásquez and Justice Pérez had made progress on Sucre by trying to concentrate all of the court's investigations involving that state in Pérez's office, but going forward, they would face difficulties: it would be hard to be efficient and make consistent progress if different justices kept handling different cases. So they proposed an ambitious and novel approach: creating an investigative commission within the court made up of one assistant justice from each justice's chambers. The commission would be dedicated exclusively to investigating paramilitary infiltration of the political system, with support from CTI investigators borrowed from the attorney general's office. The criminal chamber agreed, and they designated Velásquez as the coordinator. The court also asked the government for more resources to fund the team of investigators for these new cases. Uribe, expressing support for the investigations, approved the increased funding. It was an encouraging start.

CHAPTER 11

CLOSE TO THE BONE

JOURNALISTS STOOD EXPECTANTLY AT THE February 19, 2007, press conference at the Casa de Nariño, the presidential palace, wondering what was about to happen. The attractive, elegantly dressed young foreign minister at the podium, María Consuelo Araújo, had been under pressure to resign for months, ever since the Supreme Court announced in late 2006 that it was investigating her brother, Álvaro Araújo, a former soap-opera star and now a senator representing the state of Cesar, for colluding with paramilitaries. The foreign minister had a good reputation and was rumored to be very close to President Álvaro Uribe, who spent weeks defending her even as he attempted to distance himself from her brother, who had been part of Uribe's coalition in Congress. The investigations against Senator Araújo and other members of that coalition were starting to raise questions about Uribe's choice in political allies. Meanwhile, the scandal involving the Araújos had snowballed, with news stories and investigations implicating other members of the Araújo family, including the siblings' father.

Four days earlier, the court, building on Iván Velásquez's investigations, had ordered the senator's arrest, along with that of four other members of Congress from the states of Cesar and Magdalena. The "parapolitics" investigations, as they were now known, had begun to make waves not only within the country, but also outside—Defense Minister Juan Manuel Santos pointed out to the media that he was trying to raise international funding for Colombia, but that at "every meeting [with foreign dignitaries], we had to explain the foreign minister's situation." Ultimately, the political pressure for her resignation overwhelmed even Uribe's objections, with not only opposition parties, but also leaders of "la U," one of the main political parties supporting Uribe in Congress, calling for her to leave.

At the press conference, the foreign minister briefly announced her departure: "My certainty of the innocence of my father and brother forces me to leave so I can be free to be by their side and support them." She took no questions.

BECAUSE OF HER closeness to the president, María Consuelo Araújo's resignation was by far the worst blow yet to the Uribe administration stemming from the parapolitics scandal. It had all started, in a way, with a series of articles by Ricardo Calderón.

In late 2005, Calderón had published a front-page story in *Semana* titled "The DAS and the Paras," based in part on the information he had been slowly drawing from the intelligence agency sources he had met at The Eagle's home. The article started by reporting on the recent exit from the DAS of the agency's head, Jorge Noguera; his deputy, José Miguel Narváez; and the intelligence director, Enrique Ariza, after Noguera and Narváez had a falling out over allegations of corruption and ties to the paramilitaries within the agency. Calderón cited claims that Ariza had been trying to set up a DAS office that would work for drug-trafficker-turned-paramilitary-leader Carlos Mario Jiménez, aka "Macaco." But, Calderón reported, far from being the exception, corruption like what was being described in the Ariza case was "the norm" at the DAS. Calderón described how the DAS was providing armed guards to protect a paramilitary known as "El Pájaro" (The Bird) as he went about his business in Bogotá; how DAS officials had established "satellite offices," where they would meet regularly with paramilitaries or drug traffickers to share information, and even to conduct wiretapping on their behalf; how senior DAS officials had warned The Eagle of imminent raids on his house on two occasions, allowing the paramilitary leader to escape; and how the DAS had shared intelligence information with one of the notorious heads of the Norte del Valle cocaine cartel, Diego Montoya.

A few months later, in April 2006, Calderón published even more details about paramilitary infiltration of the intelligence service, based on interviews with Rafael García, a former IT director for the DAS. A tubby, round-faced, brown-skinned man with a very open, frank manner of speaking and a strong *costeño* accent (the accent of people from the Caribbean coast), García came across as a cheerful and sharp man, despite his sordid history: he had been arrested for allegedly tampering with DAS databases and erasing the records of arrest warrants for various criminals. García felt that former DAS director Jorge Noguera, who had been his friend, had made him a scapegoat, so García turned on him.

According to García, the paramilitaries' influence in the DAS had extended to the very top of the agency. Under Noguera, he said, the DAS, since 2002, had collaborated extensively with paramilitaries under the command of Rodrigo Tovar Pupo, or "Jorge 40." This collaboration had included sharing lists of names of labor union leaders and academics with the paramilitaries, so that they could be threatened or killed. Among the names García mentioned was that of Alfredo Correa de Andreis, a prominent sociologist who had been researching the plight of displaced people in the states of Bolívar and Atlántico. Assassins had killed Correa de Andreis as he was walking down the street in Barranquilla in 2004.

García also described an elaborate process by which, he said, the paramilitaries from the Northern Block of the AUC had carried out massive electoral fraud in the 2002 congressional elections. García confirmed Claudia López's analysis about the paramilitaries dividing up the municipalities and backing specific pairs of candidates in each one. He said that politicians allied with the paramilitaries had illegally purchased a copy of the registrar's office's records of all the voters for each voting site in the states of Cesar, La Guajira, Magdalena, and Bolívar. The paramilitaries had threatened local populations, ordering them to vote for the specific pairs of candidates they had selected for that municipality. They had also forced the local registrars' offices to appoint certain individuals as voting officials in each voting site. Many voters, terrified of the paramilitaries, either followed their orders or stayed home. So at the end of election day, the paramilitaries had their handpicked voting officials use the registrars' records of voters for each site to fill out ballots in the name of all the voters who never showed up. In Magdalena, the fraud had been so blatant that in some cases more than 90 percent of the votes in a given municipality went to a particular pair of candidates. If what he said was true, it could mean that the congressional representatives of four states had been installed there by the AUC.

Not only that, but before joining the DAS, Noguera had been Uribe's presidential campaign manager for the state of Magdalena, and García said that he had worked for Noguera on the campaign. Because the paramilitaries supported Uribe, he said, they decided to use the same techniques that they had used in congressional elections to conduct fraud in favor of Uribe during the presidential elections in Magdalena. Calderón and his colleagues followed up with other sources and found witnesses who confirmed García's claims with respect to several municipalities. Calderón wrote about the example of the impoverished and tiny municipality of El Difícil, Magdalena, where Uribe supposedly got 9,858 votes, and his main opponent, Horacio Serpa, got 1,102. A voting official told one of Calderón's colleagues that at the table he was manning only forty people cast ballots. However, at the end of the day, the local paramilitary boss ordered him to fill out another four hundred ballots for the other people who were registered to vote at that table. Another official said they were also made to damage the ballots cast for Serpa, so they would be voided. In yet another municipality, El Pozo, *Semana* reported, out of seven hundred people who were eligible to vote, all seven hundred were recorded as having voted—a highly unusual outcome in a municipality where there had always been people who abstained.

Calderón's articles, including an extensive interview with García in *Semana*, as well as coverage by other media, sparked a major scandal: How did Noguera get to that position? The head of the DAS worked directly for the president—how much did Uribe know about what was happening within the agency? And how much did he know about the electoral fraud?

Noguera, whom Uribe had recently named Colombia's consul in Milan, denied all the charges, though he admitted to having met with paramilitary commander Jorge 40 "for institutional reasons." Uribe also denied all the allegations. He stood by his former intelligence chief and lashed out against the media with fury, calling it "dishonest and malicious" and saying that *Semana* had published a "frivolous and silly" story.

García provided extensive testimony before the Supreme Court, which, combined with Claudia López's analysis, and an anonymous 2002 complaint about fraud in the congressional elections in Magdalena, allowed Velásquez to move forward with investigations into the members of Congress from some of the northern states. In the state of Cesar, the court zeroed in on the two senators who won during those elections: Mauricio Pimiento, a former governor of Cesar, and Álvaro Araújo, the brother of the foreign minister.

Investigating Araújo meant taking on one of the state's most powerful political families: Álvaro's father, also named Álvaro, was a former congressman; the senator's uncle, Jaime, had served on the Constitutional Court; and his sister, María Consuelo, of course, was foreign minister. His aunt, Consuelo (better known by her nickname, "La Cacica"), had been a journalist and then minister of culture under President Andrés Pastrana. She was also famous for having founded—alongside former President Alfonso López Michelsen and the Vallenato music composer Rafael Escalona—the "Festival of the Vallenato Legend," a beloved celebration of the region's trademark Vallenato music that every year drew thousands visitors from around the country to Cesar's capital, Valledupar. Many members of Bogotá's political and economic elite had enjoyed attending the festival's four days of music, contests, and parties. Still, Cesar had not escaped Colombia's war, which had ravaged the Arhuaco, Wayuu, Kogui, Wiwa, and Kankuamo indigenous peoples who made their homes in the nearby Sierra Nevada Mountains, as well as many other communities in the region. La Cacica herself had been kidnapped by the FARC in 2001, and was killed during a rescue attempt. Her surviving husband, Edgardo Maya, was now inspector general of Colombia.

But when Velásquez and the other investigators looked into the voting patterns in Cesar, they found serious irregularities, including two unusual concentrations of votes, with the bulk of municipalities in the south of the state voting for Araújo, and those in the state's mining region voting for Pimiento. Together the two candidates received more than 38 percent of the votes in the state—no other candidate got more than 3 percent. Velásquez and his team started to look for witnesses, and soon they began turning up local politicians and others who testified about the pressure that members of the Northern Block of the paramilitaries had put on them during the elections. For example, Cristian Moreno, a candidate for governor, told them he had been forced to withdraw on account of the threats by Jorge 40's men against him—the paramilitaries, he said, were backing candidate Hernando Molina (another member of the Araújo family) for the office.

Another politician, Alfonso Palacio, from the municipality of La Jagua de Ibirico, said that it was widely known that the paramilitaries or local leaders close to them were giving instructions to communities about which candidate to vote for, based on a predetermined division of municipalities. As a result, even though most of the inhabitants of La Jagua de Ibirico would have naturally voted for Álvaro Araújo, they were instead forced to vote for Pimiento, because that municipality was supposed to go for Pimiento, based on the paramilitaries' map. Voters who did not follow instructions would suffer the consequences.

Velásquez was particularly moved during Palacio's testimony before the court, when he reminded everyone in the courtroom of the very real human costs of parapolitics by speaking of the paramilitaries' murder of community leader Jorge Arias shortly after the elections. Turning to Mauricio Pimiento, he said: "Jorge Arias was killed for not voting for your candidacy, Dr. Pimiento. As a liberal, he voted for Álvaro Araújo. . . . That cost him his life."

EVEN AS THE parapolitics investigations gathered steam, Calderón was looking at the paramilitary demobilization process with concern. Multiple drug traffickers who had had little connection to the paramilitaries had managed to sneak into the negotiations, hoping to get off the hook for their crimes. As early as 2004, Calderón had reported on major drug traffickers, including Francisco Javier Zuluaga ("Gordolindo") and the "Mejía Múnera" twins, who had managed to purchase paramilitary blocks so they could have a seat at the negotiating table. He was also tracking the behavior of the leaders still in the "negotiating zone" of Santa Fe de Ralito, who seemed to be free to move around the country and go shopping and partying.

Part of the problem was the lax terms of the demobilization process, which had been proceeding at a brisk clip on two tracks: On one hand, there were the demobilizations of low-ranking paramilitary members, which had started in 2003 with a ceremony at which more than eight hundred members of the "Cacique Nutibara Block" of the paramilitaries, under the command of Don Berna (Diego Murillo Bejarano), supposedly demobilized. On the other, paramilitary commanders or members who were already facing charges for serious crimes were applying for reduced sentences under the country's Justice and Peace Law, which had sailed through Congress in July 2005.

The demobilizations of troops were questionable, because all the authorities did was take down the young men's identifying information, without conducting any meaningful investigation to determine if they had been involved in crimes other than membership in the group. They were pardoned for their membership in the group, however, and by mid-2006, the Uribe government claimed that more than 30,000 paramilitary members had demobilized in 37 different ceremonies, turning over 17,000 weapons.

The number of individuals demobilizing was surprising, given that just a couple of years earlier the Ministry of Defense had believed there were only 12,000 paramilitaries in the country. One possible explanation for the discrepancy was that the paramilitaries were inflating their numbers by recruiting nonmembers to demobilize—and possibly disguising the fact that some of the real members were staying active. One blatant example was the Northern Block of the paramilitaries, under the command of Jorge 40. Shortly after nearly 5,000 members of the block supposedly demobilized, in March 2006, CTI investigators arrested a man known as "Don Antonio," one of Jorge 40's henchmen, who had participated in the demobilization ceremony but was apparently still running his group's operations on the Atlantic Coast. The investigators seized multiple digital files, including numerous emails and instant messenger discussions saved on CDs or USB drives. Some of the discussions apparently involved Jorge 40: he was ordering his men to recruit as many poor peasants as possible to pose as paramilitaries for purposes of their block's demobilization ceremony in exchange for money, and to train them in how to answer questions from prosecutors. For example, they should make clear, if asked, that there were no "urban" members of the Northern Block, even though that was obviously not true. Don Antonio's files made clear that Jorge 40 and his men were exerting tight control of towns on the Atlantic, including Barranquilla; they also included records of more than five hundred murders by the group just in the state of Atlántico, several of them committed after the Justice and Peace Law's approval. But the Uribe administration rarely said anything in response to concerns about fraud in the demobilizations: when asked about the evidence of fraud in Jorge 40's computer at a congressional hearing in October 2006, the minister of the interior, Carlos Holguín, insisted that the official number of demobilized individuals was correct, and that the high numbers were due to the fact that many of those demobilizing were not paramilitary troops, but rather collaborators of the paramilitaries. He also denied reports of killings, insisting that the homicide rate was substantially down according to official figures.

Meanwhile, though, the terms of the Justice and Peace process that applied to paramilitary leaders and those charged with serious crimes had changed dramatically. When the law was first approved, it seemed certain that commanders would be able to get away with making some vague, general statements about their activities, and serving a few years under lax detention conditions before being set free. Once they completed their light sentences, they would be allowed to enjoy their wealth, with their records clean—and the core of their illegal operations intact. But victims' and human rights groups in Colombia filed multiple legal challenges to the law, and these challenges made their way all the way up to Colombia's Constitutional Court. (Colombia has four high courts; the Constitutional Court reviews only select constitutional challenges to laws and rulings, whereas the Supreme Court reviews other types of appeals from lower courts.) In a May 2006 ruling hundreds of pages long, the Constitutional Court upheld the Justice and Peace Law, but on the condition that it be implemented with substantial amendments that gave the legislation more teeth: to be valid, the court held, the law had to require that the paramilitaries give full confessions about all their crimes and turn over all of their illegally acquired assets. If the paramilitaries failed to comply or committed new crimes, they risked losing the sentence reductions and having to serve the entirety of their original sentences.

The ruling fixed many of the key problems that activists and victims had been pointing out in the law. Of course, whether the law was implemented in the way the court envisioned—whether paramilitaries fully confessed, turned over their assets, or lost their benefits when they committed crimes—depended heavily on prosecutors' ability or willingness to enforce the law. But still, for the first time, the ruling had created an incentive for the paramilitaries to talk to prosecutors about their crimes. And starting in December 2006, Salvatore Mancuso began to do so.

IN HIS EARLY STATEMENTS, Mancuso spoke broadly about his decision to join the paramilitaries and his collaboration with sectors of the army in setting up his groups, but he gave few details. Little by little, he started giving more information, as though he were testing the waters of how much he could say.

In a statement in January 2007, Mancuso admitted to planning the El Aro massacre—the same crime in which Valle had, so many years ago, accused the army of complicity. Validating Valle's accusations, Mancuso said the paramilitaries had indeed planned the massacre with members of the army, and he specifically mentioned Alfonso Manosalva, the former Fourth Brigade army commander who had been based out of Medellín, as a coconspirator. Manosalva had died a few months before the massacre.

Later in 2007, Mancuso said that he had met with Senator Mario Uribe, the president's second cousin and longtime political ally, a couple of times to discuss a plan for the paramilitaries to support him in the 2002 elections. He also claimed that Vice President Francisco Santos had met with Carlos Castaño and encouraged him to create a paramilitary group in Bogotá. And Mancuso said that Minister of Defense Juan Manuel Santos—the vice president's cousin—had met with Castaño in 1997 and asked for the paramilitary leader's support for a "sort of coup" in which the paramilitaries would reach a cease-fire agreement with the FARC. The agreement would allow them to set up a constituent assembly, with Santos at the helm, and remove then president Ernesto Samper from office.

But there were reasons to doubt what Mancuso was saying. The vice president acknowledged meeting with Castaño as a journalist, but purely for journalistic purposes, and he vigorously denied the claim that he had encouraged Castaño to create a paramilitary group. As for the allegations against Juan Manuel Santos, the media would later report that the defense minister, along with several witnesses who had been present at the meetings with the paramilitaries, had stated that although Santos had met with the paramilitaries and other armed groups, he had only done so as part of an effort to get them to agree to a cease-fire, not to remove Samper. The attorney general's office looked into the allegations and eventually decided not to pursue an investigation into the defense minister.

During those early statements, Mancuso turned over a copy of what came to be known as the "Ralito Pact," a written agreement from 2001 that had been signed by several AUC leaders, including Mancuso, Jorge 40, and Don Berna, as well as thirty-two politicians. The pact loftily announced the signatories' goal of "re-founding" the nation, and signing a "new social contract" to build "a new Colombia, in a space where every person has the right to property, and has duties with respect to the community." The signatories agreed to divide up into "working groups" that would present their results at their next meeting, in October. The politicians who signed included the governors of Córdoba and Sucre at the time (the governor of Sucre, Salvador Arana, was already under investigation by the time the pact was revealed), several senators and members of Congress, and various mayors and councilmen. Senator Miguel de la Espriella had already mentioned the pact in an interview with the newspaper El Tiempo in November, and Eleonora Pineda, a former congresswoman, and one of Mancuso's most vocal and open supporters, corroborated De la Espriella's statement, saying she had been proud to sign the agreement in the name of Colombia's "peace." The pact allowed the Supreme Court and the attorney general's office to move forward in their investigations against some of the politicians mentioned in it. In May 2007, the court ordered the arrest of five senators, and the attorney general's office ordered the arrest of Pineda (who was no longer in office, so not under the court's jurisdiction at the time).

Velásquez's team would later find more agreements between politicians and paramilitaries. During a visit to the coastal town of Santa Marta, Velásquez recalled, some of his colleagues heard about material sitting in a prosecutor's office that the army had found during an operation several months earlier in Magdalena, in territory under Jorge 40's control. When they opened the sealed boxes, the investigators found a large number of documents about the paramilitaries' links to politicians—so many, in fact, that they sealed the boxes up again and brought them to Bogotá, where they spent a couple of days reviewing the contents. Among the documents they found was one that came to be known as the "Pivijay Pact," which listed various plans about the candidates for various elected positions in the 2002 elections, who would support them, and how they would use their resources. In addition to being signed by multiple politicians, every page of the agreement bore Jorge 40's signature—it was the same signature that appeared on the Ralito Pact. Jorge 40 refused to speak to the court, but the details of the pact seemed to corroborate some of Rafael García's testimony about how the paramilitaries' electoral fraud in Magdalena had worked, so Velásquez's team opened investigations into the politicians under the court's jurisdiction. Another agreement, known as the "Chivolo Pact," provided further details about Jorge 40's ties to politicians in Magdalena. Also around that time, Velásquez was approached by a Liberal politician, Dagoberto Tordecillas, who talked about how the "Élmer Cárdenas Block" of the paramilitaries had also struck deals with powerful politicians in Urabá—leading the court to open additional investigations in that region.

By mid-2007, it was clear that the court's investigations extended well beyond the original Sucre indictments, and there was no telling how much further they would go. Up to that point, nearly all of the politicians under investigation were part of Uribe's coalition in Congress.

IN RETROSPECT, Velásquez later thought, the Araújo arrest marked a turning point in the Uribe government's view of the parapolitics investigations. The indictments of the Sucre politicians, Eric Morris, Álvaro García, and Jairo Merlano were significant because of the power these men had at a local level, but nationally they were barely known. By contrast, the Araújo family was extremely well-established and close to the president. To many, the Araújos seemed untouchable. Even if the investigation was uncomfortable for the government, however, Velásquez felt it would have been inconceivable to ignore the evidence against Araújo: "It would upset me my whole life if someone could say to me: 'Why didn't you investigate so-and-so when you knew there was evidence against him? That would forever put me to shame." Plus, by showing that the court was willing to investigate even the most powerful people in the country, Velásquez thought, it could start to inspire trust among members of the public who had never believed that institutions of justice could work.

Velásquez was paying less attention to the effect that his investigations were having on Colombia's international standing, and, in

particular, on a free trade deal that the Uribe administration had negotiated with the administration of George W. Bush in the United States.
Colombia and the United States had negotiated the United States–
Colombia Trade Promotion Agreement—which Uribe described as a
"national priority"—in 2006, and the Uribe administration had campaigned hard for its approval, with senior officials repeatedly traveling
to Washington and meeting with US lawmakers. But early on, Democratic members of the US Congress had been expressing concern over
the large numbers of labor union members who had been killed in
Colombia—more than 2,000 since the mid-1980s, many at the hands
of paramilitaries. Hardly any of the cases had ever been solved or even
meaningfully investigated. The AFL-CIO, the large US trade union,
was calling Colombia the world's most dangerous country for trade
unionists. The parapolitics scandals only deepened opposition to the
deal among many Democrats, who had taken control of the US Congress in January 2007. In subsequent trips to Washington, Uribe and
his advisers were on the defensive, constantly trying to focus attention
on the thousands of paramilitaries they had demobilized, the overall
reduction in official rates of violence, and a decline in the rate of union
member killings to argue that the free trade agreement should be approved. But on June 29, 2007, House leaders issued a stern statement
expressing "widespread concern in Congress about the level of violence in Colombia, the impunity, the lack of investigations and prose-
cutions, and the role of the paramilitary," and noting that they could
not support the trade deal until there was "concrete evidence of sustained results on the ground." A few weeks later, the House and Senate
leadership together repeated the same points.

WHILE VELÁSQUEZ continued to plug away at his investigations of
members of the Colombian Congress, another Colombian would soon
try to train the spotlight on the president himself.

On April 17, 2007, the Colombian opposition congressman Gustavo Petro stood up in front of Congress, looking cool as he started his
widely anticipated hearing on paramilitarism in Antioquia. Twenty
years earlier, Petro had been a member of one of Colombia's guerrilla
groups, the M-19, which was known for being more urban and appealing to young people. Petro had joined the group as a teenager and had
spent several years as a member before demobilizing as part of a peace

process with the government in 1990. He had gone to college after that, and then quickly entered politics. In recent years, he had become known for his public criticism of the Uribe government's policies on paramilitaries and his accusations concerning the influence of paramilitaries in the political system. It was Petro who in 2005 had held a hearing on the links between paramilitaries and public officials in Sucre, a few weeks before Velásquez started his investigations.

Some of the buzz around that day's hearing stemmed from reports that Petro was going to talk about President Uribe's family. A couple of years before, Petro had publicly stated that Uribe's brother, Santiago, had once been the subject of a criminal investigation for paramilitarism in connection with a paramilitary group called the "Twelve Apostles" in the Antioquia region of Yarumal. In December 2006, Uribe acknowledged that his brother had indeed been the subject of an investigation, but said he had been cleared of all charges. Now, it was said, Petro was going to go into a lot more detail.

A lean man in his early forties, wearing thick glasses over his heavy-lidded eyes, Petro started the April hearing by arguing that the paramilitaries were not merely self-defense groups, who emerged in the state's absence, as the Uribe government often liked to say. Instead, they were a military, social, and economic project that rested on three pillars: "the alliance between anticommunist members of the military and landowners; private vigilante groups carrying out 'social cleansing'; and . . . drug trafficking." He cited letters and statements by AUC members, military officers, prominent politicians, drug kingpins, and powerful landowners going back to the 1980s to support his view that members of all these groups had formed alliances, initially at a local level, but eventually at regional and then national ones, to further their interests. He spoke about the Convivirs that Uribe had backed as governor of Antioquia, reading off multiple names of members and leaders of the Convivirs in the mid-1990s who later turned out to be paramilitary commanders—these included Salvatore Mancuso and Rodrigo Mercado Peluffo (aka "Cadena," the head of the paramilitaries in Sucre).

Petro also talked extensively about the evidence that Velásquez's team had collected during the raid at the Padilla parking-lot shack in 1998. According to Petro, it contained all the evidence that was needed to take down paramilitarism at the time—until the investigation was closed by Attorney General Luis Camilo Osorio. That evidence, Petro said, included "beeper" messages between Jacinto Alberto Soto, aka "Lucas" (the financial chief of the paramilitaries, whom Velásquez's team had arrested, and who later escaped), and thousands of people, including many messages with a man who headed a Convivir called "The Condor." He then cited a witness's testimony from the criminal case files about a meeting between this man and local paramilitary groups at the ranch called Guacharacas—which belonged to then governor Álvaro Uribe. The same witness said that groups of paramilitaries used Guacharacas as an operating base, from which they went out to kill people.

Petro also cited various witness statements about paramilitaries operating out of a ranch called "La Carolina," in Yarumal, which was run by the president's brother, Santiago Uribe. According to some of the testimony that Petro cited, Santiago was the boss of the Twelve Apostles group, which Petro claimed may have been behind as many as sixty-four killings in Yarumal, a massacre in a neighboring municipality, and at least two disappearances between 1990 and 1997. Digging further into the past, Petro also showed a photo of Santiago Uribe smiling with a group of men, including famed Medellín cartel member Fabio Ochoa Vásquez. According to Petro, the photo was taken in 1985, when it was widely known that Ochoa was a member of the cartel, and after the cartel's murder of the justice minister, Rodrigo Lara, had prompted the government of Belisario Betancur to declare an all-out war against the cartel.

Uribe initially allowed others to respond to Petro's statements. Presidential adviser José Obdulio Gaviria reportedly said that the hearing was truly vulgar; he had "never before seen such a disorganized, libelous debate, in which there was such an abusive lack of respect for justice, for people, for Colombians, and even for President Uribe." Santiago Uribe also quickly issued a statement in which he challenged Petro to provide evidence to back up what he was saying. Santiago did not deny he was in the photo with Ochoa, but he said that it was a photo he had taken in the open—he had nothing to hide; in an interview with El Tiempo, he said that it was "no secret" that his father had grown up close to the Ochoa family and that they had traded in horses together.

But Petro's hearing, coming on the heels of the parapolitics investigations, had an almost immediate effect: former US vice president Al Gore, who was supposed to participate alongside Uribe at an event in Miami, canceled his appearance, expressing deep concern about the allegations against Uribe, and noting that he had not been told that Uribe would be participating in the event when he received the invitation.

Two days after the hearing, Uribe convened a press conference that ended up lasting nearly two hours. To the assembled reporters he denied Petro's allegations about his links to paramilitaries, saying his family had repeatedly been investigated by the authorities and that nothing had ever been found. On TV, Uribe referenced Gore's cancelation as evidence that Petro was undermining Colombia's international standing, and argued that this was all part of a systematic effort to discredit his government and prevent approval of the free trade deal.

THE PETRO HEARING marked the first time Uribe had been personally accused of being involved in the parapolitics scandal, but in his response, he avoided talking about the Supreme Court's investigations. In fact, Uribe had mostly appeared respectful of the court in his public statements, with the exception of a falling-out he had had with a former president of the court, Yesid Ramírez, in mid-2006. When the parapolitics investigations first started, Uribe had expressed support for them and, according to Velásquez, as well as two justices at the time, Álvaro Pérez and Mauro Solarte, went so far as to provide resources to the team conducting them. Attorney General Mario Iguarán, however, said the government kept referring his requests for more funding to Congress, where "we were left with absolutely no voice."

It was only in January 2007, once the Araújo investigation was underway, that Velásquez started to notice that the government and the court might be working at cross-purposes. Rumors were going around that the administration was exploring the possibility of legislation that would free the politicians under investigation for working with the paramilitaries if they admitted their offenses. After initially denying that there was any such plan in the works, in April Uribe started speaking publicly about the idea, though he met with a lot of resistance from critics who said this was simply a way for Uribe to help his allies.

Things changed in July 2007, after the court ruled that, unlike the offense of "rebellion" with which guerrillas were usually charged, the conspiracy offenses with which paramilitaries were charged could not be considered "political" crimes, because they were not committed against the state—instead, they were committed alongside state actors. As a result, they could not be the subject of an amnesty, as the government was arguing. Uribe lambasted the court, saying the ruling reflected an "ideological bias" that would undermine his government's peace process with the paramilitaries. Already, he said, thousands of paramilitaries had demobilized on the assumption that they would not have to serve any prison time simply for their membership in the group (the reduced prison terms in the Justice and Peace Law only applied to those charged with additional offenses, such as homicide, forced displacement, or drug trafficking—everyone else was getting a pass).

The new president of the Supreme Court, César Julio Valencia, a bookish man who spoke little and chose his words with care, later recalled attending an event at around that time: Uribe was also there, and he was enraged. Uribe called the court an obstacle to peace, and asked what he was supposed to do with the 19,000 young men who had demobilized, placing their trust in him: now he would have to stand by while they were sent to prison. The government eventually found a legal fix by passing another bill that suspended the demobilized individuals' sentences or arrest warrants so long as they met certain conditions, such as completing a reintegration program and not committing new crimes.

Velásquez also started noticing strange events: people were following him, his phones made unusual noises—were they being tapped? One day, when he was conducting various meetings for his investigations in the city of Manizales, in the coffee-growing region of Caldas, he met with a friend who worked in the inspector general's office there. His friend asked about his bodyguards: Where were they? Velásquez explained that he didn't have any bodyguards. His friend looked surprised: Hadn't Velásquez come with the DAS? No, said Velásquez. Why? The local prosecutor had just called Velásquez's friend to let him know that two DAS agents had just stopped by after Velásquez's visit, had asked about him, and had followed him. The prosecutor thought they were Velásquez's bodyguards, and he had called to let the friend know they had gotten lost and were trying to reach Velásquez.

The incident troubled Velásquez—why would the DAS be following him? Was this a one-time occurrence, or something more systematic? He became more guarded, but he didn't have much time to focus on it. His investigations were only getting more sensitive.

CHAPTER 12

"I'm Calling You from Prison"

WHEN RICARDO CALDERÓN WALKED INTO the decrepit little Bogotá bar at 10 p.m. on a Sunday in October 2006, he had no idea what he was getting into. All he knew was that a person had written to the general email account for *Semana* claiming to have information the magazine might find interesting. Calderón wrote back, and the person asked him to meet at this bar.

Calderón was easy for his contact to pick out: "I'm skinny, bald, and have a big head," he had said. Once the man found him, they chatted a bit—the man said he had information about the paramilitaries, and might even have audio recordings, which he would like to sell. Calderón explained that he did not pay for information, but he figured out pretty quickly where the man had come from: "You're from police intelligence, right?" Yes, the man confirmed, and then launched into a long explanation about how unfairly the institution was treating him, and the difficulties he was having getting medical care for his sick child. Calderón sympathized, and they kept talking. Little by little, the man started disclosing more information, and they agreed to meet again. Soon, they were meeting regularly on Sunday nights, at the same place and same time. Eventually, Calderón gave him a series of flash drives, and at each meeting, the source gave one back to him, loaded with recordings of phone calls and copies of email exchanges involving the paramilitary leaders.

BY THE TIME the source contacted Calderón, several of the paramilitary leaders had relocated to a low-security "detention center" in a building that had previously served as housing for Jesuit seminarians, and then as lodging for tourists, in the municipality of La Ceja, Antioquia. President Álvaro Uribe had announced the move on August 14, 2006, in a four-point statement alluding to the need for the peace process to progress in order to maintain its "national and international credibility." He called on the paramilitaries to "immediately go to the detention centers, which are dignified, sober, and austere, even if they are temporary, while a decision is made about the permanent ones."

The media portrayed the move in part as the government's tough response to a "crisis" in the negotiations. The Constitutional Court ruling on the Justice and Peace Law had led several of the paramilitary commanders to worry about whether the new version of the law left them too exposed to prosecution and extradition to the United States, and some of them threatened to leave the negotiating table. Uribe's statement called on the paramilitary leaders to put themselves at the disposal of special courts set up to review the charges against them, warning that "those who have benefited from suspension of their extradition orders must follow this decision, or they will lose that benefit." But Uribe also paired that warning with a promise: "The government will issue a decree providing regulations for the implementation of the Justice and Peace Law. If necessary, it will once again go to Congress. The official will is to save the process . . . with the cooperation of those who are participating in it." The minister of interior and justice, Sabas Pretelt, went further in separate statements, indicating that he believed—as the paramilitaries were arguing—that the court ruling was not retroactive, so the paramilitaries could benefit from the law as it was drafted, and not as amended by the court.

But another factor likely contributed to the decision to relocate the paramilitary leaders: an article in El Tiempo, published on July 22, had triggered a public outcry by describing in detail the "jet-setting" lifestyle of some of the paramilitary commanders in the negotiations. Mancuso was regularly spotted in high-end shopping malls in Medellín, buying expensive clothes and—it was said—his favorite Salvatore Ferragamo shoes. He had recently left his wife of more than twenty years to marry a much younger woman, and the article described his wedding as a massive party, with five orchestras and specially built cabins to house the guests. The former commander claimed to have lost all his assets to the war, but it was said that he was still traveling across the country in privately chartered flights and helicopters. In his hometown of Montería, the news report said, his convoy of pickup trucks (which included multiple armed guards provided by the DAS and police, as well as several paid for by Mancuso himself) regularly paralyzed traffic—only top members of the cabinet could usually tie up traffic that badly. Also disturbing, the article reported, without providing much detail, was that Rodrigo Tovar Pupo (aka "Jorge 40") and Carlos Mario Jiménez (aka "Macaco," known as one of the commanders most deeply involved in drug trafficking) were continuing to run their criminal operations even in the midst of the negotiations with the government.

Whatever the reason, the paramilitaries who moved to La Ceja were apparently not forced to go there: Mancuso reportedly turned himself into police in a gleaming new Toyota pickup truck, accompanied by his pregnant young wife and escorted by men in two other trucks. And both he and Iván Roberto Duque, known as "Ernesto Báez"—a senior commander of the AUC—made statements indicating that they had "voluntarily" chosen to go to La Ceja, based on an agreement with the government. Not all the paramilitary leaders agreed with the decision: Vicente Castaño, who had long been a critic of the process and did not trust the government, disappeared. A few months later, *Semana* published a letter from him in which he complained to Peace Commissioner Luis Carlos Restrepo about the government's failure to follow through on promises to pass stronger laws or decrees to protect them from extradition. Meanwhile, in August, prosecutors announced that six paramilitaries had confessed to having murdered Vicente's brother Carlos, along with five of his bodyguards, in April 2004, on Vicente's orders. Salvatore Mancuso and Jorge 40 had also allegedly been involved in the decision. The killers later chopped up the bodies, covered them in gasoline, and set them on fire in common graves. Investigators would eventually exhume the bodies and confirm the younger Castaño's death. The grisly news seemed to confirm that the more overtly pro–drug-trafficking wing of the paramilitaries, which included Vicente, had prevailed in their internal battles over who should be allowed to demobilize. But it also made it even less likely that Vicente would reappear.

Jorge 40 also failed to turn himself in with Mancuso and the others in August, but he did so in September, after *Semana* published an article about the computer and files that prosecutors had seized from his lieutenant, "Don Antonio," which included evidence of ongoing crimes and apparent fraud in the demobilizations. Oddly, the evidence did not prompt the government to lift the suspension of the extradition order against him, or even to withdraw him from the list of people who could benefit from the Justice and Peace Law. Instead, he was simply taken to La Ceja along with the other leaders.

In December, the government suddenly announced that it was moving all the paramilitary leaders from La Ceja to the Itagüí maximum-security prison. Carlos Holguín, now minister of the interior, claimed that they had received information about a plan to escape from La Ceja. The paramilitary leaders expressed surprise, pointing out that they had gone to La Ceja voluntarily. Earlier that week, Uribe had also made a comment about a couple of murders of lieutenants of the paramilitary leaders, indicating that the murders might have been ordered from La Ceja. He warned that those involved might lose the benefits offered under the Justice and Peace Law. Still, the government took no action to take away those benefits, and it was reportedly allowing the paramilitary leaders unrestricted use of cellphones from Itagüí.

"EVERY DAY THIS is getting worse. Here, orders change every day. I say no, and immediately they call the director general, the commissioner, the minister, or, if not, the president," Calderón wrote, quoting the recorded statements of a former director of Itagüí prison, Yolanda Rodríguez, in a front-page article in *Semana* in May 2007. Armed with around 8,000 hours of recorded phone conversations that he had obtained during his Sunday-night meetings with his source, Calderón had put together a short but explosive story: the supposedly demobilized paramilitaries, including some who were now serving reduced prison terms, were running entire criminal operations from behind bars—even in Itagüí.

Calderón quoted recordings from the previous four months in which the right-hand men of the top paramilitary commanders, who were sharing the same *patio* (prison yard) as their bosses in Itagüí, ordered the purchase and sale of large cocaine shipments, instructed troops to dig up the weapons they had hidden at the time of their "demobilizations," so that they could reassert their control over key neighborhoods, and told their associates to continue their extortion of small businesses in order to help fund their operations. "And what's most terrifying," Calderón wrote, "is that, calmly, on cellphones, they talk about the murders and acts of torture that they keep committing; for example, in [one conversation involving a paramilitary known as 'El Mosco'], men report the murder of a man, saying, 'Believe it or not, nobody cried or anything for that son of a bitch. You know, sir, that as long as that's done with your approval and on your say-so, then that's how it is.'"

Calderón noted that the evidence flatly contradicted a statement that President Uribe had made a few months before, in which he had said that the paramilitaries' detention in Itagüí stood in stark contrast to what had happened with Pablo Escobar's lavish prison in La Catedral. Regarding the latter, Uribe said—perhaps in a reference to former Colombian president César Gaviria—that "many of our critics have yet to explain [it] to the country." Calderón wrote, "Now the country needs another explanation. For Itagüí."

The morning *Semana* ran his story, Calderón heard from General Óscar Naranjo, who headed the Criminal Investigations Directorate of the police. Naranjo was said to have been involved in some of the police force's most successful operations against the Medellín and Cali cartels. Now, he told Calderón that there were rumors going around that he was Calderón's source—which, as Calderón knew, was false. If he was asked, could Calderón please set the record straight? Calderón, who knew and thought highly of Naranjo, agreed.

Soon afterward, Calderón got a call from Minister of Defense Juan Manuel Santos, who asked point-blank whether Naranjo had something to do with the story. Calderón said no. But Santos then asked him to come to his house. Calderón tried to reach his editor, Alfonso Cuéllar, to ask him to join him, but there wasn't enough time, so Calderón went alone. As Calderón recalled it, Santos said the situation was very serious—he claimed he had had no idea that the paramilitaries were doing these things. He tried to probe for more details as to Calderón's source, but Calderón refused to give him any more information. At one point, Santos asked Calderón how much material he had—was it 8 or 10 transcripts? It was more than 8,000, Calderón replied. And what if the government came out and said it wasn't true?

Calderón made clear that he had enough material to keep publishing for months on end. At that point, Santos went back to stating that this was very serious, and he would need to shake up the police. He began asking Calderón who would make for a good chief of the national police, but Calderón said that was his decision. Calderón left feeling worried: Was the government going to do anything about the paramilitaries' crimes?

The following Monday, Santos issued a statement saying that the government had not known about the crimes reported in the *Semana* article beforehand, and that once it verified the authenticity of the recordings, it would withdraw Justice and Peace benefits from those who had continued committing crimes. But instead of addressing what had happened in Itagüí, the rest of the statement focused on the source of the recordings: "Unfortunately, it has been confirmed that the recordings and leaks were conducted by personnel from the Directorate of Intelligence of the National Police [DIPOL, for Dirección de Inteligencia Policial]." And then it changed the subject of public debate entirely by announcing that the government had discovered that "personnel from the DIPOL had, for over two years, been recording people who were not the subjects of any investigation, including members of the government, opposition, and journalists. This manner of proceeding is entirely unacceptable, illegal, and contrary to the policy of the government. . . . An internal investigation has been ordered to identify those responsible for such deplorable facts and punish them accordingly." In the meantime, given the "gravity" of the situation, Santos announced, he had asked for the resignation of the chief of police, Jorge Daniel Castro, and named General Óscar Naranjo to replace him. In the process, he was also removing eleven generals who were senior to Naranjo to clear the way for Naranjo's promotion.

ONE EVENING A few days later, at 8 or 9 p.m., Calderón got into his car to drive the few blocks to his apartment from *Semana*'s offices in a small red-brick building in the north of Bogotá. As he rolled up to a corner, a man in a black leather jacket walked into the street directly in front of his car, forcing Calderón to stop. Calderón stared, and then heard a tapping sound. Another man, also in leather, was by his window, showing him a gun. They looked at him for a few seconds, then the two men turned and walked away. Neither one had bothered to cover his face.

It was a warning—Calderón was convinced these were plainclothes police. But the incident, while unsettling, just added to his anger. Ever since he had published his article on the paramilitaries' phone calls, Calderón had been hearing members of the Uribe administration on the radio denying that anything was happening. At one point, Calderón recalled later, Uribe himself even accused *Semana* of paying money for material, though he later retracted that claim. Now that he was being threatened, too, Calderón knew how he wanted to reply.

The following week, *Semana* published more details about the recordings, running an article by Calderón stating that the police had been illegally recording many people who were not under investigation, including the former foreign minister, María Consuelo Araújo, the opposition leader Carlos Gaviria, and multiple journalists. The article even included excerpts from a phone call Araújo had had with one of her brothers, in which she joked that if the neighboring country of Ecuador didn't allow Colombia to fumigate coca crops along their border, Colombia would cut off its energy supply.

Publishing the second article was, to Calderón, the only way to defend himself from the government—if the police were going to go after him for the first article, then he was going to open five more holes that they would have to deal with. And, as the government knew, Calderón had thousands of additional recordings that he could make public if necessary.

His tactic worked: the attacks on *Semana* for the first article stopped. But Calderón later felt conflicted about the story: certainly, reporting on the police's illegal surveillance was important, and the scandal did apparently lead to reforms within the police. But the focus on the police actions distracted the public from the scandal Calderón had reported on in the first place, over the paramilitaries ordering crimes from prison. And despite Santos's promise to remove the paramilitaries from the Justice and Peace process if the government "verified" the crimes reported by *Semana*, as far as Calderón could tell, nothing was happening.

CALDERÓN'S STORIES MAY not have led to the results he thought they should, but they did get the attention of someone he didn't expect. Antonio López, also known as "Job," was a supposedly demobilized paramilitary member who, because he had never been charged with any crimes, remained free. But the heavy-set man, his bushy eyebrows hovering like rainclouds over a penetrating glare, was known to be close to Don Berna (Diego Murillo Bejarano), the head of the Envigado Office, who had demobilized in 2004, claiming to be a paramilitary. Job was also one of the leaders of the "Corporación Democracia" (Democracy Corporation), an organization in Medellín supposedly set up to assist demobilized paramilitaries, though many Medellín residents said it was in fact a tool through which Don Berna continued exerting control over the city.

A fellow journalist at Semana had asked Calderón to meet with Job in her place one day when Job was at a nearby restaurant, as she was away and could not make it. Job already knew who Calderón was, and soon after meeting him, asked Calderón how much it would cost to buy the recordings about his "papa"—referring to Don Berna—and his friends. Calderón told him they weren't for sale.

But Job had other fish to fry. His main goal, it seemed, was to offer Calderón what he said was very important information about the parapolitics investigations and the Supreme Court—something to do with corruption on the court. Was Calderón interested? asked Job. Calderón said it depended on whether there was evidence.

And so began a series of meetings between Calderón and Job at restaurants near Semana's offices. The meetings quickly became tiresome to Calderón: Job provided no concrete information, instead making only vague statements about judges who he claimed were asking for money from politicians. Meanwhile, the long-winded Job was endlessly boring Calderón with his speeches about the wonderful projects he claimed the Democracy Corporation was implementing in Medellín.

At one of their meetings, Job launched into his usual spiel about how Uribe was such a great person, who was trying to follow through on his promises on the demobilization, but the Supreme Court was so corrupt. But then Job added a detail that intrigued Calderón—he started talking about one assistant justice in particular: Iván Velásquez, whom "they" knew from Medellín. Job went on for a long time, repeating that Velásquez was making stuff up, that he was persecuting the government and the business community, and that he was using false witnesses. He also kept adding that Velásquez was terribly corrupt, though he provided no solid details to back up his claims.

The intensity of Job's attacks on Velásquez struck Calderón as strange. The journalist had never met Velásquez before, though he had been meaning to contact him to see if the assistant justice had any information he could share about some of the politicians in the recordings that Calderón was still analyzing. Through another journalist, he reached out to Velásquez, who agreed to see him.

The first meeting between Velásquez and Calderón, sometime in mid-2007, was very short—no longer than thirty minutes. Calderón shared some information with him from his own investigations about members of Congress whom Velásquez was also investigating, and told him about some of the things Job had said. Velásquez thanked him, but he was his usual formal, dry self, and hardly said anything.

CHAPTER 13

FRAME JOB

BOGOTÁ, COLOMBIA, OCTOBER 9, 2007.

Colombian president Álvaro Uribe sounded aggrieved. He spoke slowly, choosing his words with care, but he couldn't quite mask the rage brewing underneath. "We're dealing with one of three possibilities here," he said on La FM radio station's popular early-morning news show. "Either the president of the republic is a murderer; or the prisoner . . . is lying; or there is some machination, a machination by an assistant justice . . . against the president."

The story had already been all over news shows the previous night, after Uribe first issued a press release about it and then proceeded to make multiple media appearances on the topic. But that morning, he explained yet again why he was so concerned: some time earlier, Uribe had received a letter from a man named José Orlando Moncada, who went by the alias "Tasmania." A low-level member of the paramilitaries' "Southwestern Antioquia Block," Tasmania was serving time in the Itagüí maximum-security prison on the outskirts of Medellín on charges of extortion and kidnapping. In the letter, which was publicly released and dated September 11, 2007, Tasmania reported to Uribe that Assistant Supreme Court Justice Iván Velásquez had asked him to accuse the president, along with an influential Antioquia businessman and landowner, of involvement in the attempted assassination, in 2003, of a paramilitary leader from Southwestern Antioquia known as "René." In exchange for his testimony, Tasmania said, Velásquez had offered him a sentence reduction, admission to a witness protection program, and the relocation of his family. The letter concluded: "My concern, Mr. President, is that Mr. Velásquez, it appears to me, wishes to harm you. It is the only thing that interests him. In exchange for that, he will give anything."

The claim that Uribe would have ordered an assassination seemed, as one of the radio hosts put it, "delusional." But what disturbed him about all of this, Uribe emphasized, was the behavior of the Supreme Court. The court had no jurisdiction to investigate the president, so what was Velásquez doing, trying to get Tasmania to testify against him? The implication seemed clear: Velásquez must be trying to frame the president for murder. And at this point, Uribe said, he felt he had no other choice but to publicly call on the attorney general to conduct a criminal investigation into Velásquez's actions.

Uribe's appearance on La FM that morning went on for nearly an hour and a half. Finally, he hung up to take more calls on the Tasmania letter from other radio stations. Broadcast radio still had a huge following among the nation's more than 45 million inhabitants. People across Colombia—from the northern Caribbean towns of Cartagena and Santa Marta, to the lush coffee-growing regions in the mountains, to the flatlands on the eastern border with Venezuela, and to the Amazon rainforest farther south—listened to Uribe, fascinated and confused, as they started their day.

To most Colombians, the story about Tasmania's letter came out of nowhere. They had never heard of René or Tasmania. It seemed odd for the president to devote so much energy to what a low-level criminal wrote from prison. On the other hand, to many, it made sense for Uribe to fight back. After all, Uribe's enemies—the people who would like to sabotage his achievements, weaken the military, and keep the country living behind bulletproof glass—might lurk anywhere, even in the country's highest courts.

By contrast, few Colombians knew much about Velásquez. The media had already identified him as the coordinator of the parapolitics investigations, in some cases calling him the "star judge" of parapolitics, but before he, too, went on the radio that morning to deny Uribe's accusations, Velásquez had never been at the center of the national spotlight.

"It's absolutely false," Velásquez retorted, when La FM's hosts asked about Tasmania's letter. "The country can be certain that the court does not use such methods to investigate, and that it does not have jurisdiction to investigate the president—that alone is enough to thoroughly undermine those claims." So what was behind all this? Velásquez went on: "I have always acted with a great deal of loyalty and probity, keeping the justices constantly informed. I do not hide myself to conduct investigations. The only purpose that can be seen in all this is to discredit the investigation."

And then Velásquez added his own bombshell to the story: "Last week I informed the criminal chamber of the court of what I could see was coming, as I had been warned that an investigation or intelligence activity of some sort had been started against me. In light of that, the court summoned the attorney general and inspector general to hear in person and in detail what had happened [and] formally filed a criminal complaint with the attorney general."

Over the course of many more interviews, Velásquez would explain his version of events in detail: several weeks earlier, a couple of investigators who were working with the court and charged with looking into the situation in Antioquia had been asking around about potential witnesses who knew about links between paramilitaries and several Antioquia congressmen—including the president's second cousin, Senator Mario Uribe. In the process, they had received reports that Tasmania might have some relevant information, so they met with him. Tasmania asked them whether he would get any benefits if he cooperated, and they explained that any discussion of benefits had to be conducted directly by the assistant justices. They put Tasmania's lawyer, Sergio González, in touch with the court. As a result, on September 10, 2007, Velásquez and another assistant justice who was looking into Antioquia, Luz Adriana Camargo, had traveled to Medellín to meet with Tasmania.

Tasmania wanted to be included in the Justice and Peace process, so he could have his sentence reduced to the five to eight years available to the paramilitary leaders, but the justices explained that that was not in their hands: it was up to the government to decide who went on the list of paramilitaries who could benefit from that process. Instead, the two justices explained the standard benefits available to witnesses who cooperated, which included a reduction of about one-sixth to one-quarter of the sentence they were serving. But Tasmania, who only had a third-grade education and was clearly a low-level paramilitary, struck Velásquez as unlikely to have much valuable information. Velásquez asked him whether he knew of Juan Carlos "El Tuso" Sierra, a major drug trafficker who had been allowed to demobilize along with the paramilitary leaders. El Tuso was from the town of Andes, where Tasmania said he operated, and yet Tasmania denied knowing about him—a statement that was so absurd that Velásquez immediately concluded Tasmania was lying. Tasmania said that he could talk about murders and other activities of the Southwestern Antioquia Block of the paramilitaries, but the justices said they were not interested in that: they were only investigating links with members of Congress—for example, Senator Mario Uribe, who was also from Andes. Tasmania said he didn't know anything about congressmen, and that he had only seen Mario Uribe driving around once. He did volunteer that he knew something about "a problem" that President Uribe had had with René, but Velásquez told him that the court didn't investigate the president, and did not pursue the matter further. In light of Tasmania's apparent lack of knowledge, or recalcitrance to share what he knew, Velásquez decided to cut the interview short and leave. But then González asked him to wait. The lawyer pulled Tasmania aside, and after a few minutes came back and said they needed some time for Tasmania to organize his thoughts. If Velásquez left them his cellphone number, they would get in touch soon. Velásquez agreed, and then he left. The meeting was unremarkable—like many meetings Velásquez and other justices had held with prisoners or potential witnesses over the course of their investigations. Velásquez would not have given it a second thought were it not for what happened the very next day.

Velásquez had finished his workday and was catching a ride home with his son Víctor—Velásquez still did not drive—when his cellphone rang. It was a call from the president, the operator told him. The president? Velásquez had not spoken to Uribe in many years. Why would he be calling? Uribe's unmistakable voice came on the line, very friendly, asking how Velásquez was doing. But the president quickly got to the point: Uribe wanted to know whether there was some kind of investigation in the court against him. There was a great deal of concern in the presidency, he said, because someone called Tasmania was saying that Uribe had provided him with weapons to carry out an attack against the paramilitary leader René. Did Velásquez know anything about that? That was strange, Velásquez replied, because he had just been with Tasmania the day before. He assured Uribe that they had not discussed anything related to such an attack, and in any case, Velásquez recalled telling the president, "the court has no jurisdiction to investigate you, I know of no information against you, and if there were any, the court would immediately transfer it to the appropriate authorities." Uribe said, of course, that that was what he would expect, and they ended the call on a cordial note.

Velásquez thought the call was strange, but he was not too concerned. When Velásquez's wife, María Victoria, heard about it, however, she was horrified: she had never believed in Uribe, and now she tried to explain to Velásquez that she had an awful feeling about the call. "There's nothing good in that call, Iván," she told him in the kitchen, tears welling up. Velásquez, seated at the table, tapped his fingers together and asked her not to make things out to be bigger problems than they were—she was reading too much into it; the president was being generous by calling him to clear things up. Still, the next day he informed the president of the criminal chamber of the court, Alfredo Gómez, as well as a couple of other justices about the call.

THROUGHOUT THE YEAR, the court had been slowly making progress in its investigations into members of Congress from Antioquia, including Senator Mario Uribe. Mancuso had testified that he had met with Mario Uribe and Representative Eleonora Pineda—who had already admitted to having signed the Ralito Pact with the paramilitaries, and was under investigation—ahead of the 2002 elections. According to Mancuso, the paramilitaries had agreed to support Mario Uribe and Pineda in part of Córdoba. Pineda said that the meetings happened after the elections, but the voting patterns in the area Mancuso mentioned were highly irregular, favoring Mario Uribe.

With his beady eyes, full mane of white hair, and thick neck firmly set into expensive-looking suits, Mario Uribe appeared eminently comfortable in his role as one of Colombia's most prominent and influential politicians. Not only had he served as president of the Senate, but he had also been a close political ally of President Uribe for over two decades. In the 1980s, the cousins had jointly founded an offshoot of the Liberal Party, called the Democratic Sector (Sector Democrático), and they had been elected to Congress together in 1986—Álvaro to the Senate and Mario to the House. Their movement eventually morphed into the Democratic Colombia Party (Partido Colombia Democrática), which Mario now led, and which was a key part of the president's coalition in Congress, often leading congressional debate on the president's initiatives.

Velásquez also knew Mario Uribe a bit and had a cordial relationship with him. In the 1980s, when Velásquez had joined his brother's private legal practice, his office had been in the El Café building in Medellín, one floor below Mario's office, and they would often see each other on the elevator. Mario Uribe's office messenger had also been a former student of Velásquez's. And Mario Uribe's sister was the dentist for Velásquez's children for years. "She was a very pleasant, professional person, who treated the kids very well, and we liked her a lot," Velásquez said. But as an investigator, Velásquez had to follow the evidence.

On September 26, 2007, at around 5 p.m., the Supreme Court announced Senator Mario Uribe's indictment. The president was attending the UN General Assembly in New York at the time, and when journalists called him, he made only a very simple statement: "As president, I have to support the justice system. As a person, I feel sadness."

A couple of days later, Velásquez was approached by a former colleague from Antioquia, who was close to Mario Uribe. After the usual pleasantries, the man expressed concern about the investigation of Mario Uribe, telling Velásquez that the investigation was part of a fight between the court and the president, and that he was concerned about what could happen to Velásquez. Mario, he said, was very mad, and Velásquez should be careful. The man asked whether Velásquez had ever considered leaving the court: if he wanted to, he could ensure that the government would nominate him to be a justice on another high court. Velásquez expressed disbelief that such a thing was possible, given how upset members of Congress were about his investigations, and the man said not to worry, that it could be arranged. In fact, he said, Mario would like to talk to him—he was just two blocks away. Velásquez cut him short: "I have nothing to say to him." But the man insisted, warning him that there could always be smear campaigns against him, and remarking that Velásquez would not want to be in Mario Uribe's shoes. Eventually, he asked Velásquez if there was anything that could be done to postpone the date on which Mario Uribe was supposed to give his statement to the court. Velásquez said he should file a formal request with the court, and left it at that.

FIVE DAYS BEFORE Uribe's announcement about Tasmania, on October 3, Velásquez attended the regularly scheduled Wednesday meeting of the justices of the criminal chamber to brief them on his work. At the end of the briefing, he paused and shifted gears, saying, "If I may, I would like to discuss a personal problem." The night before, he explained, a contact from the attorney general's office had reached out to him, saying he needed to speak to him urgently. Velásquez had suggested they wait until the next day, but his contact insisted: "No, doctor, it has to be now." So the contact visited Velásquez at his home and told him what he had learned: that in the past few days there had been a secret, high-level meeting at the DAS, at which officials had discussed something about Velásquez and "someone called Tasmania, or Tanzania, something like that," who was trying to do something against the president. The goal of the meeting—which was framed as a matter of national security—was to ask for an investigation to be opened against Velásquez for allegedly trying to frame the president. During the meeting, DAS officials had also displayed some files involving Velásquez, including photos of him and some of his family, as well as all their phone numbers, full names, and addresses, which suggested that the intelligence agency had been spying on the justice. Something had to be done right away, said the contact, or it would be too late to head off what seemed to be an attempt to harm Velásquez's credibility and possibly get him thrown off the court and into prison.

Velásquez was surprised, he told the justices, but he trusted this contact and believed his story: it made sense of Uribe's strange call to Velásquez—and this contact had no reason to know about that, or about the meeting with Tasmania. "This means that the DAS is conducting intelligence operations against me," he said. "They're following me, and my communications are under surveillance."

The justices were alarmed: if this was true, they concluded, the DAS was engaging in obstruction of justice. So they decided to convene meetings with Attorney General Mario Iguarán and Inspector General Edgardo Maya the next day, October 4. At those meetings, the justices asked Velásquez to repeat the story to the other officials, and then they formally filed a criminal complaint over the DAS's surveillance of Velásquez. The following Monday, the president issued his press release about Tasmania's letter.

THE PUBLIC FOCUS on the Tasmania scandal continued for days. News outlets ran interview after interview with the president and members of his administration, as well as with Tasmania himself. Velásquez felt like his phone never stopped ringing—journalists wanted to know why he was trying to frame the best president in the history of Colombia for murder. At Uribe's request, Attorney General Iguarán opened an investigation against Velásquez for the alleged attempt to frame the president. This investigation would run concurrently with the investigation into the court's complaint over the DAS's alleged surveillance of the assistant justice. In all his time working on the parapolitics cases, Velásquez had never felt so much pressure.

Velásquez was convinced that, had it not been for the tip he had received about the meeting at the DAS, and his quick action to inform the Supreme Court, Uribe's onslaught against him in the media might have gotten him fired. Getting rid of him was probably the objective behind the entire Tasmania episode, though exactly who was behind it, and why, remained hazy. Even though the whole criminal chamber was involved in the investigations, the media had identified Velásquez as the main force pushing the cases forward, and so he was an obvious target for people who wanted to discredit the endeavor.

Other members of the court, however, may have been inclined to believe Velásquez, because they had themselves already felt the effects of Uribe's frustration—including through the president's attacks on the court over the preceding months. The Supreme Court president, César Julio Valencia, also said he had had a troubling phone call with President Uribe. He had received his call on September 26, just a couple of hours after the court announced that it had indicted Senator Mario Uribe. According to Valencia, early that evening he was at a meeting with the head of the office of the UN High Commissioner for Human Rights when a secretary pulled him out of the meeting because the president was looking for him. Valencia remembered that when he got on the phone, the president sounded "furious." Uribe spent about half an hour complaining to the justice about Tasmania and Velásquez— this was many days before the October 6 press release about Tasmania's letter. Much later, Valencia would tell a journalist that President Uribe also touched upon the Mario Uribe case, though Valencia refused to elaborate on what Uribe had said. Surprised and shaken, Valencia said little on the phone call with Uribe—as he later remembered it, most of his answers had been monosyllabic. But the next day, September 27, Valencia briefed several other justices who worked with him on the civil chamber of the court about the call. He also informed Sigifredo Espinosa, who was then acting president of the criminal chamber. Valencia did not know Velásquez well, as they were on different chambers of the court, so he didn't tell Velásquez about the call at the time.

Once President Uribe made his public accusations against Velásquez in connection with the Tasmania letter, Valencia and the rest of the court decided to back up the assistant justice. On a radio show, Valencia warned that what Uribe had stated was not only incorrect, but also posed a threat to Velásquez's security. Moreover, he said, it amounted to obstruction of the parapolitics investigations. Sigifredo Espinosa also spoke out in defense of Velásquez.

But the justices were courting Uribe's ire. On some news shows, Uribe insulted the justices, calling Valencia a fraud. On La FM radio, the president said that the last time he had seen Justice Espinosa, Espinosa had asked him for help getting one of his relatives into college. Uribe said he had not been able to help because the person didn't meet the requirements, but that he "hoped that wasn't why" Espinosa was mad at him. Uribe added that Espinosa had asked him to his house to eat some beans, but that Uribe had been unable to attend.

To most of the justices, who were not used to working in the public spotlight—much less to being subjected to personal attacks by the president—Uribe's comments were highly intimidating. Still, the court as a whole remained consistent in its response. On October 9 it issued a formal statement noting that Velásquez and assistant justice Luz Adriana Camargo had interviewed Tasmania on September 10 as part of their regular work and at Tasmania's request. The next day, the court said, Uribe had called Velásquez, and the court had informed the attorney general and the inspector general of these events. Without specifically referencing Uribe's attacks, the court then called on government officials to "respect the autonomy and independence" of the judges; it "emphatically rejected" as false the suggestion that the court was engaging in any kind of conspiracy. It emphasized that all of its decisions were the result of joint discussion, rather than any one individual's preferences, and, moreover, that it strongly supported the statements of Valencia and Espinosa: they had "acted faithfully as spokespersons" of the court.

A COUPLE OF days after the initial round of interviews, the media reported on yet another allegation against Velásquez, this time coming
from a former paramilitary and retired member of the military, Edwin
Guzmán, who was now living in the United States. The news stories said
that, after seeing the Tasmania story, he had decided to approach the
Colombian consulate in New York to report that Velásquez and another
justice had done the same thing with him: "They said that if I had anything against the president, if I had seen or heard him, no matter what it
was, that I should report it and that they would help me leave the country along with my family." Uribe's supporters immediately seized on Guzmán's claims as further proof that Velásquez was obsessed with trying to
frame the president for something—anything—and would go to great
lengths to do so. To Velásquez's supporters on the court and elsewhere, it
seemed evident that Guzmán's claims were just part of a larger plot to
discredit him, though there was no way to prove it.

URIBE'S PRESS RELEASE and subsequent attacks on him and on the
court initially surprised and disappointed Velásquez. He knew the intelligence service was up to no good, and, of course, he disagreed with
many of the president's policies. But he had always believed that Uribe
was a straight shooter—someone who would confront him directly if
anything was wrong. In Antioquia, when Uribe had backed the establishment of the Convivirs, Velásquez recalled, he did so openly, even
vociferously, despite the fact that many people opposed him. Given
that the president had already called him on September 11 to ask
about the Tasmania meeting, why wouldn't he just call Velásquez directly again after receiving the letter? Why issue a press release and
then go on this media rampage?

To María Victoria, Uribe's actions simply confirmed her suspicions
about his call to Velásquez a month earlier: "Do you now see that there
was nothing good in that call he made to you?" she had asked Velásquez
when he had told her of the secret DAS meeting. It was partly at María
Victoria's insistence that Velásquez had informed the court about it
before Uribe's press conference. "That man can do everything against
you, you have to understand," she had told him. "You're a nobody, and
it's so easy to build up something against you, and then what are we
going to do?"

As the days passed and the attacks continued, Velásquez also started to develop a darker view of what was happening. The Tasmania letter was dated September 11—the same day that Uribe had called Velásquez—but the whole story of how the letter got to Uribe was murky, and in interviews Uribe seemed evasive about it. At first, Uribe had said that by the time he called Velásquez, he had only "heard" about the Tasmania interview from "several sources," which he did not name. He said that after he called Velásquez, he trusted what the assistant justice told him, and "forgot about" the issue. It was only later, Uribe said, that he received the Tasmania letter—he didn't say how. But Uribe claimed he had waited to go public until the DAS had confirmed the authenticity of the letter, and until Tasmania had reiterated his allegations in an interview with the attorney general's office. Once he received that confirmation, he said, he asked the attorney general—both in private and in public—to investigate. But on October 14, the newspaper El Tiempo reported that Uribe's brother, Santiago, had informed the president of Velásquez's supposed offer to Tasmania on the very same day that Velásquez met with the paramilitary. It turned out that Santiago Uribe was a neighbor of Sergio González, Tasmania's lawyer, who told Santiago about the meeting right away.

The connection between Santiago Uribe and Sergio González was in itself suspicious. But Velásquez also wondered why, if Uribe had known about the meeting as early as September 10, he had waited nearly a month to go public. The explanation about waiting for the DAS to confirm the authenticity of the letter did not add up: Why would the DAS take so long to confirm something so simple? And it was still unclear how the actual letter got into Uribe's hands.

And then there was Tasmania's behavior: the day after Uribe's press release about the Tasmania letter, Velásquez listened to an interview that La FM conducted with him, and he was surprised at the ease with which Tasmania spoke. The illiterate paramilitary had barely said a word when Velásquez had interviewed him, and had used fairly basic language when he did speak. Somebody must have coached him on what to say on the radio.

Velásquez also soon learned that on October 1, Tasmania had been transferred from Patio 2, the maximum-security section of Itagüí prison, where he was among the general population, to Patio 1, which held only a few dozen senior AUC leaders, who were participating in the Justice and Peace process. The transfer had major implications for Tasmania's quality of life: In Patio 2, family visits and a prisoner's ability to receive packages were tightly restricted, and the prisoners had no access to televisions, phones, or computers. Now, in Patio 1, this low-level paramilitary could enjoy much more frequent visits from his four children; he could watch TV and use a cellphone and a computer; and instead of regular prison food, he could eat food that was specially prepared for the paramilitary leaders in a separate kitchen.

All these facts, combined with the intensity and persistence of the attacks against him, led Velásquez to conclude that he had been the target of a coordinated operation to undermine the parapolitics investigations and discredit him personally—maybe even get him kicked off the court. It was sheer luck that he had learned about the DAS's actions beforehand, and had been able to warn the court and get it on his side.

But Velásquez was now constantly wondering: What other attacks might be in the works?

CHAPTER 14

BETRAYAL

RICARDO CALDERÓN WOKE UP AT 1 a.m. on May 13, 2008, to a call from Antonio López, the paramilitary known as "Job" who had contacted him in 2007 with accusations about the Supreme Court: "They're taking my papa away." He was referring to his boss, Diego Murillo Bejarano, or "Don Berna," who had headed up the Envigado Office and the Cacique Nutibara Block of the AUC. "Do you know what's going on?"

Calderón had no idea what Job was talking about, but the story was soon all over the news: shortly after midnight, hundreds of police officers had surrounded prisons in three different cities and taken fourteen men out, including most of the top paramilitary leaders—Don Berna, Salvatore Mancuso, Rodrigo Tovar Pupo ("Jorge 40"), and others, including drug trafficker Juan Carlos "El Tuso" Sierra—and transported them to a major military air base outside of Bogotá, the Military Transport Air Command (Comando Aéreo de Transporte Militar, or CATAM). There, police handed them over to officials from the US Drug Enforcement Agency, who loaded them onto an airplane bound for the United States, where indictments were pending against them.

In a press conference, flanked by his defense minister, Juan Manuel Santos, and his minister of interior, Carlos Holguín, and surrounded by multiple cabinet members, National Police Chief Óscar Naranjo, and Peace Commissioner Luis Carlos Restrepo, President Álvaro Uribe read a statement explaining the extraditions: "Today at dawn, a group of citizens was extradited because some of them had committed new crimes after subjecting themselves to the Justice and Peace Law, others were not cooperating as they should with the justice system, and all were failing to meet their obligations to provide reparation to victims by hiding assets or delaying their turnover." Uribe pointed out that the government had retained the capacity to decide whether someone should be included on the list to receive Justice and Peace benefits, as well as to decide on suspension of extraditions. The paramilitaries' demobilization process was the first time, he said, that persons in a peace process had been required to tell the truth and provide reparation. But the truth had to be "simple and timely" and could not be "manipulated." The United States, he said, was still committed to allowing the extradited paramilitaries to continue participating remotely in judicial proceedings in Colombia; any assets turned over to US authorities would be transferred to Colombia for the reparation of victims. This arrangement, Uribe said, would contribute to a telling of "the truth without distortion."

A week before, the government had extradited another paramilitary leader, Carlos Mario Jiménez, aka "Macaco," who commanded the "Central Bolívar Block" of the AUC, which operated in multiple regions scattered throughout Colombia. But that extradition was no surprise: in August 2007, the United States had filed an extradition request for Macaco, citing evidence that the paramilitary had engaged in extensive trafficking of cocaine to the United States as recently as 2007. Because the US indictments involved criminal activity that continued well past the passage of the Justice and Peace Law—in fact, the indictment specifically referenced bank transactions dated the same day of and the day after the passage of the law—it would have been very difficult for the Uribe government to justify ignoring the request and letting Macaco stay in the Justice and Peace process. Instead, on August 24, 2007, a few days before the request was made public, the government transferred Macaco from Itagüí prison to a more secure facility in Cómbita, claiming that it had become aware of ongoing criminal activity by the paramilitary. It did the same to Don Berna. Then, in September, the government transferred Macaco to a navy brig in the Atlantic Ocean, citing security reasons. The extradition had been delayed while the Supreme Court reviewed the extradition request; once the Supreme Court approved the extradition, in April 2008, and after the High Council of the

Judiciary lifted a stay, in May, the government moved quickly to ship Macaco away.

The extradition of the other paramilitary leaders, however, seemed to have come out of nowhere. A year had passed since Calderón had published his blockbuster stories about how the supposedly demobilized paramilitaries were committing crimes from prison, and—with the exception of Macaco—the government had not even tried to expel them from the Justice and Peace process, much less extradite them. For Uribe to claim, all of a sudden, that he was extraditing them because of their crimes made no sense: Why do this now?

Years later, people involved in the decision would offer slightly different explanations. Presidential adviser José Obdulio Gaviria would say that the paramilitaries were surprised by their extradition: they had bought the line of the government's critics, who said that the Justice and Peace Law was meant to secure their impunity. But Gaviria insisted that that had never been the case. The law clearly stated that they could not commit more crimes, and they had been warned. Once reports started to trickle in from the United States indicating that the paramilitaries were still involved in arms and drug trafficking, Gaviria explained, Uribe decided that he had no choice but to activate the extradition orders.

General Óscar Naranjo, the chief of police, said that—at least with regard to Macaco and Don Berna—the decision to extradite them was based on information that the police had been collecting. He said that from the time he was appointed, Defense Minister Juan Manuel Santos had asked him to bring him any evidence of paramilitaries committing crimes from prison; if there was such evidence, he would talk to the president about extraditing those who were involved. Naranjo said the police then did legally collect recordings showing that Macaco and Don Berna were giving orders from prison, and he brought that evidence to the government, prompting the security meeting at which Uribe decided to proceed with the extraditions. Asked why the president decided to extradite all of them, rather than just Macaco and Don Berna, Naranjo simply said, "That was a decision the president made."

In his own autobiography, Uribe recounted simply that it became obvious over time that the paramilitaries were still committing crimes and were not going to turn over their wealth, and that Colombia's prisons were not strong enough to contain them. "I had one reason, and one reason alone, for extraditing these men," he wrote. "I thought it would improve Colombia's security. I believed that by removing these individuals from our country, we could not only prevent them from committing further crimes, but also show other individuals that they would face dire consequences if they did not cooperate with us. . . . [T]he decision was in fact not abrupt at all; it was the culmination of a years-long, painstakingly incremental process of trying to convince these men to cooperate."

AT THE TIME, Calderón was particularly intrigued by the decision to extradite Don Berna. On the surface, his extradition made sense, as it was well known that Don Berna was one of the paramilitary leaders most wanted by the United States: the United States had issued a provisional arrest warrant for him as early as July 2004, for trafficking millions of dollars' worth of cocaine into the states. In fact, cables later made public revealed that in meeting after meeting, the US embassy in Colombia had raised Don Berna's case with the Colombian authorities, pressing for his extradition. The DEA considered him not only a major drug trafficker, but "the de facto leader" of the AUC, "in charge of its narcotics-trafficking activities, including all of its cocaine transportation and financial operations." Berna, the DEA charged, "maintained his power in the AUC in part from the proceeds of his drug-trafficking activities."

But the Colombian government's treatment of Don Berna had swung back and forth repeatedly over the years, sometimes seeming tough, and other times inexplicably lenient. Berna's inclusion among the paramilitaries at the negotiating table was controversial from the start, as he was known primarily as a criminal and drug trafficker (though Berna's claims to being a paramilitary were arguably stronger than those of drug trafficker "El Tuso" Sierra and some others whom the government had allowed to participate in the demobilizations).

In fact, Berna had a long and sordid history: It was said that in his youth he had been a member of the Popular Liberation Army, a guerrilla group that had demobilized in 1991. By his own account, he had become the right-hand man for the Galeano brothers, close associates of Pablo Escobar, by the mid-1980s. When Escobar had the Galeano brothers murdered in a dispute over money, Don Berna joined forces with the Castaño brothers and the Cali cartel to form Los Pepes, the group that focused on hunting down Escobar and his associates. According to a book that Berna later published, his own little brother, Rodolfo—rather than members of the police's Search Bloc—was the person who finally shot Escobar to death on a Medellín rooftop in 1993, though this claim contradicts the official version of events. After Escobar's killing, Berna gradually rose to power in Medellín's underworld, eventually running the Envigado Office and exerting control over the La Terraza gang, both of which were behind many of the worst murders in the city. He had maintained close ties to the Castaño brothers, however, and by the time the demobilization negotiations with the Uribe government started, he was claiming that he was a member of the AUC.

Despite Berna's shaky claims to membership in the paramilitaries, he was the first commander to "demobilize" troops. The demobilization of paramilitaries under his control began with the Cacique Nutibara Block of the AUC in 2004, and it had been widely criticized as a sham. Observers claimed that, at the last minute, members of Don Berna's group had gone through Medellín's low-income neighborhoods recruiting young men to pass themselves off as paramilitaries. Berna, it was said, had wanted to put on a big show of demobilizing a lot of men without really giving up any power.

Then, in May 2005, while the paramilitary leaders were negotiating in Santa Fe de Ralito, the government entered the negotiation zone to arrest Don Berna for allegedly ordering the murder of Córdoba state congressman Orlando Benítez, his driver, and his sister alongside a road near Ralito—news reports said Benítez had disobeyed Berna's orders not to campaign in the region. That afternoon, the government mounted a massive and showy manhunt, involving hundreds of police officers, while Uribe announced that he was not going to allow the negotiation zone in Ralito to become a "paradise of impunity." In Medellín, Berna's base of operations, transportation ground to a halt as Berna's associates threatened bus and taxi drivers to make them go on a forced strike to protest the manhunt, and perhaps as a show of strength. Berna managed to escape Ralito, but a couple of days later, he turned himself in.

Then the government seemed to soften its stance: it did not take Berna out of the demobilization process despite his violation of the paramilitaries' cease-fire, and for several months it held him at a ranch in Valencia, Córdoba, instead of a regular prison. In June 2005, the US chargé d'affaires, Milton Drucker, told Uribe and his advisers that the credibility of the entire demobilization process was at stake: Don Berna needed to be brought to justice for his crimes, and he needed to be taken out of the demobilization process. According to US cables, the Colombian officials insisted that Uribe had taken a tough line on Berna by arresting him, but they resisted taking him out of the demobilization process because he had promised to demobilize the remainder of his troops. A couple of months later, the government held another demobilization ceremony for 2,033 members of the "Heroes de Granada Block" of the paramilitaries, which Don Berna claimed included the last of his troops. However, for years people in Medellín would claim that Don Berna and his men—including Job and other members of the Democracy Corporation—continued to exert tight control over crime in Medellín and surrounding areas.

The government did eventually move Don Berna to a higher security prison in Cómbita, where he was kept separate from other paramilitary leaders for a couple of years. That changed in September 2007: when the government transferred Macaco to the navy brig, it also started to transfer Don Berna to another brig in the Pacific Ocean. But shortly afterward, it announced that Berna's transfer had been a mistake, the result of an outlandish miscommunication between the Ministry of Interior and the National Prisons Institute. Berna's real name was Diego Murillo; the person they meant to transfer was the infamous drug kingpin Diego Montoya.

By the end of the botched transfer operation, one of Calderón's colleagues at *Semana* reported, the government had used more than a thousand men, three armed helicopters, multiple vehicles and motorcycles, and the two brigs. *Semana* noted that it was "worrying, that having in its hands the drug lord most wanted by the US and Colombia, and two of the former 'para' chiefs who may have continued committing crimes from prison, there was not the least bit of care to avoid errors like this one."

Perhaps even more oddly, after the transfer, rather than leaving Don Berna in the maximum-security prison in Cómbita, the government placed him in La Picota, a prison in Bogotá that housed most of the politicians in detention for links to paramilitaries. La Picota had a reputation for being much more comfortable than most of the prisons in the country. Far from being treated as someone the government was readying for extradition, Berna seemed to be getting special treatment.

No wonder, then, that Job was astounded at his "papa's" extradition.

TO VELÁSQUEZ, the extraditions came as a shock. Despite Uribe's attacks on him, he had kept his investigations into Congress moving forward, and he had high hopes that, since they were required to tell the truth about their crimes, some of the paramilitary leaders might begin talking to him about their links to politicians, as Mancuso had already started to do. But by extraditing the paramilitary leaders, Uribe had sent away the witnesses who might have the most to say about their links to politicians. As a result, the extraditions felt like yet another chapter in the government's attacks on the court.

In fact, what the media described as the "train collision" between the court and the president had continued ever since the Tasmania episode. On January 14, 2008, the newspaper El Espectador published an interview by the journalist Cecilia Orozco with Supreme Court President César Julio Valencia that led to yet another blow-up with Uribe: In response to Orozco's question about the phone call he had received from Uribe on September 26, 2007, Valencia said that "the call by the head of state deeply surprised me. The criminal chamber had just indicted Dr. Mario Uribe. In that moment, in an angry tone, he expressed his unhappiness over some decisions that the chamber was taking and, in not very clear terms, made reference to other facts related to the actions of an assistant justice." Orozco interrupted Valencia: Did Uribe specifically refer to his cousin's case? Valencia replied: "Yes." The journalist pressed him further: Did Valencia believe that the president was angry not only because of the Tasmania case, but also because of the Mario Uribe indictment? Valencia responded vaguely, saying only, "I don't think things are the way you're describing them. I do get the impression, yes, that the president acted too quickly to call me, even though he had, as I understand it, previously spoken with other officials about the Tasmania issue." Orozco asked Valencia to describe exactly what Uribe had said to him about the Mario Uribe case, but Valencia refused to say anything further.

Valencia was in Paris attending a conference when *El Espectador* ran the interview, and he was stunned to receive a fax from the president the very next day. It consisted of two lines: "I have never spoken with you or any member of the Honorable Supreme Court of Justice about subjects that refer to political figures investigated for alleged links with paramilitaries. I ask you to remember and make a correction to El Espectador." Valencia wrote back that he had no reason to make a correction, as Uribe had, in fact, called him on September 26 and expressed in an angry tone his concern over the indictment of Senator Mario Uribe, as well as over the Tasmania issue. A couple of days later, President Uribe issued a press release recognizing that he had called Valencia on September 26, but insisting that the sole purpose of the call was to discuss the Tasmania case. He claimed that he had witnesses who could confirm that he had not discussed the Mario Uribe case, including the Colombian ambassador to the United Nations, Claudia Blum, and the Colombian ambassador to the United States, Carolina Barco. The president announced that he was pressing criminal charges against Valencia for slander.

"I was not concerned," said Valencia about the charges later on. He felt comfortable that he had told the truth. But the charges were alarming: the entity charged with investigating members of the Supreme Court was the Accusations Committee of the Colombian Congress, which at the time was packed with pro-Uribe parliamentarians. No matter how well he defended himself—and Valencia was represented by a top lawyer, Ramiro Bejarano—he had to worry that the investigators would be biased. As the case moved forward over the following months, Valencia also had to deal with frequent insults from people on the street. Many people recognized him and called him names, including "a son of a bitch," for his supposed actions against the president.

MEANWHILE, the government was scrambling to deal with a number of new scandals. In February 2008, Francisco Villalba, the paramilitary witness who years before had provided testimony to Velásquez's friend Amelia Pérez in connection with the El Aro and Pichilín massacres, had given new statements to prosecutors about El Aro. Villalba, who was then serving thirty-three years in prison for his involvement in the El Aro massacre, claimed that the brothers Santiago and Álvaro Uribe had participated in a meeting along with military officers and paramilitary leaders Carlos Castaño and Mancuso a few days before the El Aro massacre. According to Villalba, the El Aro massacre had been committed as part of an operation to rescue some hostages, and after the massacre, Álvaro Uribe, who was then the governor of Antioquia, had once again met with the paramilitaries to congratulate them, because the hostages were now safe and sound. There was no record of Villalba making these accusations before, but he claimed that he had told some of the CTI investigators in the late 1990s about it—and that they had later been killed by members of the paramilitaries working with the Fourth Brigade of the army.

The testimony got ample media coverage, even though there were good reasons to believe that Villalba was at least partly lying. Prosecutor Amelia Pérez had never trusted Villalba, ever since she had first interviewed him; there had always been parts of his testimony that were inaccurate. And this new testimony had serious inconsistencies: for example, he claimed that General Alfonso Manosalva had been present at the meeting three days before the massacre, but Manosalva was dead by then. Nor did any other paramilitaries corroborate his testimony about Uribe—though Mancuso later did allege that the Fourth Brigade, under General Carlos Alberto Ospina (who replaced Manosalva), had provided logistical support to the paramilitaries. He also claimed that a helicopter belonging to the Antioquia governor's office had flown overhead during the massacre.

On April 20, 2008, the TV program *Noticias Uno* released an explosive interview by journalist Daniel Coronell. On the screen, Coronell made clear that this was a recording from August 8, 2004. The subject of the interview was Yidis Medina, a brown-haired, still young, round-faced former congresswoman who was initially seen nervously picking lint from her thick red, brown, and beige sweater. Then she crossed her arms and began to speak: She was the only person, she said, who could confirm what happened, and so she feared for her life—one of her colleagues, she claimed, had told her to be careful about speaking because the government would not fulfill its commitments to her. "It would be very easy," she said the colleague warned her, for her to appear murdered, or for her to have an accident and for them to say that she was hit by a car and died.

Medina had surprised many observers in 2004 when, after giving the impression that she would vote against a bill to allow Uribe to run for a second term, she had changed her vote at the last minute. Another member of Congress, Teodolindo Avendaño, who had originally opposed the bill, never showed up to vote. In the Noticias Uno interview, Medina claimed that shortly before the vote, she had attended a meeting with Uribe's chief of staff at the time, Alberto Velásquez, who had tried to persuade her to be "patriotic" and vote for reelection. In the middle of the meeting, she said, Uribe himself had made an appearance and repeated the same thing, saying that whatever she wanted, whatever agreements she discussed with his adviser, he would fulfill them, because he was a man of his word. She claimed that Uribe had said he wanted to save the country, and he wanted more time to finish his plan for the government. He had also promised, she said, that later on, once the noise around the bill had died down, he would allow her to name someone to a foreign consulate. After the president left, she told the interviewer, Velásquez and the minister of the interior, Sabas Pretelt, continued negotiating with her, on Uribe's orders. They promised that she would be allowed to fill three positions in the Middle Magdalena region. She claimed that she also spoke with the minister of social protection, and the minister of social protection also spoke with Teodolindo Avendaño, the other member of Congress whose position on the bill changed. The day after she voted in favor of reelection, Medina said, Uribe called her to thank her and repeat his commitments. But later on, according to Medina, the government seemed to be backtracking on its promises. As a result, she decided to record the interview with Noticias Uno, but on one condition: that they not publish it unless she was killed or the government failed to deliver on its promises. Medina received her own copy of the recorded interview and also agreed not to share it with others. Four years later, Coronell found out that Medina had been talking to another journalist about what had happened and had revealed the existence of the video. Their agreement was now breached, and so, with Medina's explicit permission, Coronell published the interview.

Uribe immediately denied Medina's allegations, but the Supreme Court opened an investigation into her actions. On June 28, 2008, she was convicted of bribery. The court notified both the Accusations Committee of Congress and the attorney general's office of its ruling so they could also open investigations into other officials who might be implicated.

At the same time, the investigation into Senator Mario Uribe was ramping up. He had resigned from the Senate after his indictment, so his case had been transferred from the Supreme Court to the attorney general's office, which now had jurisdiction over it. Two days after *Noticias Uno* published Medina's interview, on April 22, a prosecutor ordered Senator Uribe's arrest.

Attorney General Mario Iguarán recalled that ordering the arrest was a difficult decision for him: "I would have preferred not to take a decision against him," he said. "I knew him well." When Ramiro Marín, the prosecutor handling the case, told him he was ready to issue an arrest warrant, Iguarán said, he sat with the prosecutor for hours, playing devil's advocate, to test Marín's arguments for any weaknesses. The arrest warrant was based in part on Mancuso's statements about meeting with Mario Uribe and Congresswoman Eleonora Pineda to arrange the distribution of votes in Córdoba—according to the prosecutor, Uribe went from getting 3,985 votes in the 1998 elections to nearly triple that amount—11,136 votes—in the 2002 elections, perhaps as a result of the arrangement. The voting patterns in the state had also been highly atypical in ways the prosecutor considered consistent with fraud.

After five hours of arguing with the prosecutor, Iguarán said, he was convinced that Marín was right and they had to move forward. However, he asked Marín to hold off on the arrest for a little longer, so he could go and talk to President Uribe himself—he thought it was appropriate to give him some warning that this was coming. That night, he said, Uribe argued in his cousin's defense, like anyone would who saw a loved one in that situation. But Uribe seemed to accept the decision.

The next morning, Mario Uribe was at the Costa Rican embassy, claiming that he was the victim of political persecution. It seemed as if he had learned about the arrest warrant before it could be carried out, and he had decided to seek asylum. But by the end of the day, Costa Rica had denied his application, and the CTI took him into custody.

IN THE MIDST of these scandals, Uribe administration officials found another subject to discuss in the media: at a public event with members of Congress and various administration officials in the Urabá region of Antioquia, Ferney Suaza, a demobilized paramilitary from

Urabá, stood up and asked the officials to give President Uribe a message. A group of nongovernmental organizations and other people had tried to bribe Suaza, urging him to testify as to links between the president and paramilitary groups. Immediately, one of the congressmen present put Suaza on the phone with Uribe, and soon, Uribe and people from his inner circle were again taking to the airwaves to complain about what one presidential adviser, Fabio Valencia Cossio, called an "international plot" involving a "cartel of witnesses" against the government.

Meanwhile, another scandal had erupted in the media over a couple of trips by justices of the Supreme Court that had supposedly been paid for by a man named Ascencio Reyes, who was rumored to have "links" to persons involved in drug trafficking. Reports also said that Reyes was influential in the attorney general's office, and that he was so close to Attorney General Iguarán that he had attended Iguarán's swearing-in celebration. In a story written by one of Calderón's colleagues, *Semana* posted a photo of Iguarán and a man it identified as Reyes, supposedly at the swearing-in. The photo would later turn out to be of someone else, not Reyes, but officials and pro-government commentators immediately seized on the Ascencio Reyes story. According to them, it was evidence that the court was corrupt. They revived their attacks on Velásquez's investigations.

EVER SINCE PRESIDENT URIBE had made his announcements about the Tasmania letter in October 2007, Iván Velásquez's life had been upended. On the court, Velásquez found that many of his colleagues were suddenly afraid of conducting investigations in the way they had done before—every time they interviewed a witness, they had to wonder whether that witness would later do a "Tasmania" on them, claiming that the justices had solicited false testimony. "With Tasmania, the government got many members of the investigative commission to practically stop working," Velásquez would later recall.

And although Velásquez attempted to forge ahead, many of his contacts—prosecutors, judges, investigators—who would ordinarily have chatted with him and shared information, were now reluctant to be seen with him. One woman at the inspector general's office, someone he had once considered a friend, flatly told him that even though she thought highly of him, she could no longer speak with him; if people knew they were friends, she could be fired. So Velásquez never spoke to her again. But at least, he thought, she had told him what she was doing. Many other contacts simply vanished. "It was like when someone knows there is a death threat against him, and nobody will enter the car with him for fear that a bomb will go off," he would later explain. His wife, María Victoria, also later recalled that she tried to organize a party in those days, and ended up having to cancel it, because so many of their former friends said they could not attend. Velásquez had aspired to become a full justice on one of Colombia's high courts, but now the other Supreme Court judges, whose support he would need to get confirmed, gave him the cold shoulder. His future in the judiciary, it seemed, was now over.

The Tasmania episode also affected Velásquez's children: Velásquez's youngest daughter, Laura, who was starting university, was so upset by the attacks on her father over the Tasmania letter that she missed a couple of weeks of school. By the time she went back, word had spread about who her father was, and many of her classmates refused to talk to her.

Even going out could be stressful: on one occasion, Velásquez and María Victoria were at a shopping mall when a woman stopped them to angrily ask why Velásquez was trying to harm the president. His daughter Catalina noticed that when they entered restaurants together, the entire room would go silent as people stared at him. They also had to worry about security: One day, Laura was on her way to take the public bus to school when she noticed men photographing her. A few days later, Catalina and her husband were in their car on their way to her job when she noticed a group of people taking photos of her from another car; she pretended not to see them, and they made a point of driving next to her. The family took it as a warning.

Shortly after Uribe's accusations against Velásquez, and the Supreme Court's complaints, the police assigned the assistant justice a bulletproof car, a driver, and two armed guards. But in late November, the family was rattled when they received a letter from a senior police official saying that he had determined that Velásquez did not need the guards, because he had the same level of risk as any other Colombian. The Supreme Court complained publicly, and Chief of Police Óscar Naranjo intervened. He immediately reinstated the security detail; the officer who had removed it had not consulted with anyone, he said, and had disobeyed written instructions.

Regardless of the level of protection her husband had, María Victoria was terrified that someone would try to kill him. Certainly, an attack on Velásquez would carry political costs, but you could never be sure how far some people would be willing to go to stop his investigations. On April 22, 2008, the Protection Directorate of the attorney general's office sent a letter to Jairo Castillo Peralta, known as "Pitirri," the Canada-based witness who had been testifying against the Sucre congressmen and Mario Uribe: "Through intelligence information, this directorate has become aware that two persons may be traveling as tourists to that country to assassinate you," the letter said. The officials asked Pitirri to inform the Canadian authorities to ensure that his security measures were strengthened "in the extreme." Although the letter was marked secret, Pitirri immediately made it public: he had no formal security measures in place, and found it odd that the Colombian authorities were writing to him, instead of coordinating directly with Canada to ensure his protection.

Velásquez tried to calm María Victoria down, but he, too, was now on high alert. Deep, dark circles hung from his brown eyes, and he was constantly on the lookout for threats: he went quiet whenever a waiter approached his table at a café, and he removed the battery from his phone whenever he had a sensitive conversation, to keep the intelligence service or other unknown enemies from tapping it as a surveillance device against him.

And yet Velásquez also had encounters that encouraged him to keep going: people he didn't know stopped him on the street to say things like, "You're very brave," "Keep going," and "Don't let the president stop you." In a society that rarely tolerated different points of view, and where there was overwhelming pressure to support the president, at least some people saw the court's willingness to go after powerful members of Congress as a reason for hope—a sign that it was possible to go against the current and stand on principle.

WHEREAS VELÁSQUEZ VIEWED the extraditions as a blow to his investigations, and Calderón viewed them as a way to silence the extradited paramilitaries and intimidate the ones who were left behind, the George W. Bush administration in the United States welcomed them. To the US government, the extraditions were valuable for at least two reasons: the Justice Department wanted to prosecute the drug kingpins, and, as noted by White House spokesperson Dana Perino, the extraditions might help "persuade" Democratic members of Congress to finally move on the pending free trade agreement with Colombia. Over the preceding year, opposition to the deal seemed to have hardened, despite the Colombian government's aggressive lobbying in DC—which had even included trying to enlist former president Bill Clinton's help. In October 2007, the *New York Times* ran an editorial urging members of Congress to hold off on a deal: "President Álvaro Uribe and his government have not done enough to bring to justice the paramilitary thugs and their political backers responsible for widespread human rights violations. . . . [W]ithholding ratification can still be used as a lever to change Mr. Uribe's behavior." The two leading Democratic presidential candidates in US elections that year, Barack Obama and Hillary Clinton, had also expressed opposition to the deal. But Bush viewed the trade pact as a high priority, and in April 2008, in a move that many Democrats viewed as aggressive grandstanding, he announced that he was submitting the deal to Congress to force a vote. Regardless of their effect on investigations in Colombia, the extraditions now made it very hard to argue that the Uribe administration was being soft on the paramilitaries.

Part IV

TRUTH

Bogotá, 2008–2010

CHAPTER 15

CONFESSIONS

"IS THIS A TRAP?" IVÁN Velásquez asked himself as he read the letter from Iván Roberto Duque.

Duque, also known as "Ernesto Báez," was one of Colombia's longest-running paramilitary leaders: a lawyer and politician, Duque had been a senior member of one of Colombia's first "self-defense" groups, the Association of Middle Magdalena Ranchers and Farmers (Asociación Campesina de Ganaderos y Agricultores del Magdalena Medio, or ACDEGAM), which in the 1980s was already committing large numbers of killings and "disappearances" of community leaders, trade unionists, and others they associated with the left. Later on, Duque was said to have become one of Carlos Castaño's closest advisers, and then, when Castaño lost influence within the AUC, Duque joined the Central Bolívar Block as a close adviser to its leader, Carlos Mario Jiménez, aka "Macaco," whom President Álvaro Uribe had extradited in May 2008. The articulate and sharp Duque often portrayed himself as an intellectual leader for the AUC—a political representative and a true believer in the group's far-right-wing views, who was not involved in the "military" or operational side of the group's activities, though reports suggested otherwise. The paramilitaries from the Middle Magdalena had always been close to drug traffickers, including Gonzalo Rodríguez Gacha, known as "The Mexican," a Medellín cartel member who had bought land in the Middle Magdalena region and provided substantial funding to the group. But the United States had never requested Duque's extradition, and so Duque was still in

Colombia, participating in the Justice and Peace process and serving a reduced sentence in Itagüí prison on the outskirts of Medellín.

In June 2008, Duque sent a letter to Velásquez, writing that he had learned of supremely serious matters that he wanted to report to him immediately. He asked that Velásquez meet with him and José Orlando Moncada, that is, "Tasmania," as soon as possible. Tasmania had in fact cosigned the letter—proof, Duque said, of the younger man's goodwill.

Velásquez had interviewed Duque at length as part of the parapolitics investigations, and he had a good rapport with the paramilitary leader, who seemed eager to talk. With his loud, raspy voice, dramatic storytelling style, and prodigious memory, Duque was a surprisingly magnetic witness, and so far, his testimony about politicians' links with his group seemed fairly credible. Still, Velásquez had every reason to question the motives behind this letter, especially with Tasmania involved. Was this part of yet another elaborate attempt to get him in trouble by manufacturing "evidence" against him? Thanks to the court's backing, Velásquez had been able to hold onto his job, for now, but he was well aware that another flurry of attacks could be in the works. And yet, if this was a genuine offer to talk, Velásquez could not ignore it.

So, as soon as he obtained permission from the justices, Velásquez slipped an audio recorder into his suit-jacket pocket and traveled to Itagüí.

"OH JUDGE, I'm so ashamed, forgive me judge!" Tasmania finally said. He had looked flustered when he first came into the large prison meeting room where Velásquez—after negotiating an unusually difficult amount of paperwork to access the prison—was waiting to interview him. "Calm down," Velásquez had greeted him, making clear he was turning on his audio recorder. "Have a seat." But almost immediately, the strong-looking, still-young Tasmania launched into an apology for the letter to Uribe. Then he began to tell Velásquez his version of events, which he would later repeat under oath.

According to Tasmania, it was "totally false" that Velásquez or any of the investigators who came to talk to him had ever asked him to speak about President Uribe. He recalled that Velásquez had asked him about Mario Uribe—which was to be expected, because Tasmania had come from Mario Uribe's hometown, Andes—and that Velásquez had asked him about a drug trafficker, Juan Carlos "El Tuso" Sierra, who was also from Andes and had demobilized with the AUC. But what was in the letter to the president was simply false.

In fact, Tasmania said, he never wrote the letter to Uribe—he only went to school up to third or fourth grade, and could not have written it. Rather, he had signed the letter without reading it, because it was among several documents he was signing to apply to enter the Justice and Peace process—he thought his lawyer, Sergio González (whose office was in the same building as Mario Uribe's), had written the letter. It was only after he signed it that El Tuso, who was also in Itagüí prison, and who had secured González's representation of Tasmania a couple of months earlier, told him what he had signed. According to Tasmania, El Tuso said the letter was needed "to help some friends." Tasmania expressed concern about the letter—he didn't want to get into trouble. But El Tuso said it was no big deal—he had to go along with the plan, because "his family" was at stake. According to Tasmania, El Tuso had used a threatening tone; at the same time, the drug trafficker had offered him benefits, such as "money and a house for my mom." Tasmania had many children, so the money was appealing. Also, El Tuso promised to get Tasmania moved to Patio 1 in Itagüí, where the paramilitary leaders participating in the Justice and Peace process were staying. There, he would enjoy many more comforts, including better food, a television, and frequent visits from family. In fact, Tasmania said, El Tuso and González had delivered on the transfer promise almost immediately; on October 1, 2007, he had been informed that by presidential order he was being transferred to Patio 1. Then, soon after the letter was made public, González and El Tuso arranged to have his mother relocated from her little plot of land to a new house. They began to pay her rent and utilities.

Once President Uribe made the letter public, on October 7, Tasmania was flooded with calls from the media, and El Tuso helped him respond. Tasmania claimed that El Tuso and González even drafted a script for him to read from for his interview with Vicky Dávila of La FM radio. The goal, El Tuso told him, was to "attack justices." Tasmania said he didn't even know what a justice was—"I'm a peasant," he said. But El Tuso told him that a justice was a lawyer, and that

Tasmania shouldn't worry about any of that because they would get lawyers to defend him.

According to Tasmania, El Tuso told him that the "friends" they were trying to help were Mario Uribe, the president's second cousin, and Santiago Uribe, the president's brother. After one interview, Tasmania said, El Tuso even showed him a letter in which—according to El Tuso—Mario was congratulating Tasmania for his work. He said he was told that letters had come from both Mario and Santiago, though he didn't know them or their handwriting, so he couldn't confirm that.

Later on, Tasmania told Velásquez, El Tuso and González abandoned him. El Tuso stopped talking to him, and after six months they stopped paying his mother's rent. He never received the money he had been promised. After President Uribe extradited the paramilitary leaders, including El Tuso, Tasmania managed to get ahold of González to ask what had happened to all their promises, but the lawyer told him that that was old news. Tasmania wasn't going to get any help anymore because the paramilitary leaders were gone.

"I became very sad," Tasmania later said. "I like music, I like to play the guitar and sing. I used to always get together with Báez [Iván Roberto Duque] in a library office to play guitar. He saw I was worried and asked, 'What's wrong with you? Why are you like that?' I told him about the frame job against Iván Velásquez in which they had involved me, and said look at the problem I had now, that I had to give statements but didn't even have a lawyer to do anything, that they dumped me along with my family. . . . [Duque] said, 'You need to communicate with the court, with that justice, to explain.'"

So, according to Tasmania, Duque drafted the letter that Velásquez later received. Tasmania just wanted to clear things up, he said. Now that he knew what a justice was, he was sorry. He was also scared.

Once Tasmania had finished, Velásquez spoke to Duque, who confirmed what Tasmania had said. Both men said they would be willing to repeat their statements to investigators.

Although Velásquez wasn't sure if he was getting the full story, a lot of what Tasmania and Duque said made sense to him. At a minimum, their statements should finally be enough to put President Uribe's accusations against him to rest. Not only that, but Tasmania's allegations against González, Santiago Uribe, and Mario Uribe should give investigators solid leads to pursue.

MEANWHILE, RICARDO CALDERÓN was actively pursuing what he now viewed as the larger story behind the Tasmania scandal: the existence of an ongoing plot, involving people at the highest levels of the government, to discredit and undermine the Supreme Court, particularly Velásquez. In April 2008, he had a conversation with Edwin Guzmán, the former paramilitary in Washington, DC, who, shortly after the Tasmania scandal broke, had stated that Velásquez had offered him benefits in exchange for testifying against the president. Like Tasmania, Guzmán also took his statement back. According to Guzmán, he had made the accusation against Velásquez because an official had offered to help him get visas to bring his family to the United States. "And because I was desperate, well, I said what they told me to say. The bad thing is that after they had me talk to journalists and I gave the statement, they never even answered my calls again, and obviously didn't do anything they promised." In an interview with Calderón, the official Guzmán had mentioned strongly denied the former paramilitary's new claims. Combined with Tasmania's retraction, however, these new statements suggested that there had been a much larger plot. Calderón would keep trying to piece it together.

WITHIN A MATTER of weeks, thanks to Tasmania's and Guzmán's retractions, the attorney general's office closed its investigation of President Uribe's allegations against Velásquez. Instead, it ordered the investigation of Sergio González, Tasmania, and Edwin Guzmán for their involvement in the plot against the assistant justice. But Velásquez was dissatisfied: the prosecutors did not even mention the names of Mario or Santiago Uribe, apparently having decided not to investigate their potential roles in the plot. Years later, then attorney general Mario Iguarán said that such an investigation "should have moved forward."

Velásquez's suspicions were further stoked when, in August 2008, additional facts came to light that raised questions about how the Tasmania plot had come about. Ramiro Bejarano, a prominent law professor and attorney—and frequent critic of President Uribe through a regular op-ed column in El Espectador—who represented César Julio Valencia in the defamation case Uribe had brought against the Supreme Court president, had filed a public records request with the government to find out how Uribe had received the letter. The Uribe administration replied that it had obtained the letter from the head of the DAS, María del Pilar Hurtado. Bejarano filed another public records request with the DAS to find out how Hurtado had learned of the Tasmania case. She replied in writing that the information had come from Bernardo Moreno, President Uribe's chief of staff, who had asked her to send detectives to Itagüí prison to pick up some documents in the national interest. Bejarano followed up with a records request to Moreno, asking how he learned about the Tasmania letter. Moreno replied that he had learned about it through an anonymous call on September 29, 2007—he could not identify the caller—and so that day he had asked the head of the DAS to look into it.

In an op-ed in *El Espectador*, Bejarano highlighted some of the strange facts in the case: it was odd, to begin with, that Moreno "could not recall who called his exclusive phone number to discuss this issue." It was stranger still, he noted, that in an interview, Santiago Uribe had insisted that "on September 10, 2007, Mario Uribe called me and said that . . . Sergio González was going to bring me a very serious letter. The next day, he showed up and brought me the letter." According to Santiago, however, it was Mario Uribe who delivered the letter to the president. "I don't know if he did it in person or through José Obdulio [Gaviria, presumably]. The president's accusation came after that." Not only did Moreno's account about the presidency first learning about the letter through an anonymous call in late September make no sense, since Santiago was claiming that Mario delivered it to the president, but there was also nearly a month-long gap between the day Santiago Uribe said he received the letter, September 11, and the day President Uribe made it public, October 7.

Velásquez had always wondered about the origins of the Tasmania letter, and he had repeatedly urged the prosecutors to find out more about how the letter got to the presidency, but the attorney general's office had failed to dig into the issue. Bejarano's findings only underscored his concerns. In a lengthy interview in *El Espectador* a few days after Bejarano's column, he flagged another inconsistency in the official version of events: "The director of the DAS has admitted that on September 30 she sent for the document in the morning, and that afternoon she took it to the president. That would mean that the president first read the letter on September 30. If that's the true order of events, then how did the president go about asking Justice

Valencia about my supposedly irregular conduct with Tasmania on September 26?"

In addition to all this, Velásquez pointed out in the interview, there seemed to be a number of connections between Mario and Santiago Uribe and Sergio González, the lawyer who represented El Tuso and Tasmania. For example, he said, he had learned that González had an office in the same building as Mario Uribe's, and prosecutors had been able to establish that fact; also, Santiago Uribe had admitted that he shared Mario's office. Santiago had also acknowledged in an interview that he and González had neighboring land. Velásquez couldn't corroborate all of these claims, and he didn't know whether prosecutors had asked Mario and Santiago Uribe or Sergio González about them. But, combined with all the inconsistencies about how the letter got to the presidency, as well as Tasmania's claims about Mario and Santiago, he thought it was clear that somebody was lying. The prosecutors, he said, should have tried harder to get to the bottom of it all.

Ultimately, Velásquez said, "there was a criminal organization behind this plot. And not only involving Sergio González and Tasmania. What was its interest? There's an unfortunate situation in all of this, which is that many of the defendants have directed their hatred toward me, as if I were the source of the parapolitics investigation. . . . There's an evident goal of harming me, on the one hand. On the other, there's also the goal of discrediting the court's investigations."

NEW ALLEGATIONS KEPT surfacing against Velásquez. He felt that people close to the Uribe administration had now undertaken a persistent campaign to discredit him and his investigations. In August 2008, *El Espectador* reported on new allegations by Betty Barreto, who was said to have been the cook for the paramilitary commander Héctor Germán Buitrago (aka "Martín Llanos") for many years. She was claiming that Velásquez and two other investigators had improperly offered alcohol to her and her son—who had reportedly also worked with the paramilitaries—when they were interviewing them in Yopal, in the state of Casanare, at the end of her workday. She told journalists that she felt that the investigators were trying to get her drunk so she would talk. The article also made it sound like Barreto felt they were pushing her to talk specifically about Colombian politician Germán Vargas Lleras. When asked by journalists, Velásquez said that the team had indeed gone out for a drink while they talked to the witness, and that she had talked at length about the history of the paramilitaries in Casanare, which she knew well. But there was no effort to get her drunk, or to get her to talk about any particular member of Congress. "You don't conduct investigations at the desk of a court office," Velásquez would say later on, reflecting on the incident. He had simply been trying to gain the trust of a witness who had important things to say, and that meant spending time talking with her, following her lead. In his view, it was unfortunate that as a result of a groundless scandal, the country "missed out on an important opportunity to get to know an important part of the truth about the relationship of . . . Colombian politicians with Martín Llanos's paramilitaries." Soon afterward, Barreto said she had been misquoted. She essentially confirmed Velásquez's version of events, saying that even though there had been alcohol during her meeting with the investigators, she was never pressed to give any information or to talk about Vargas Lleras.

Around the same time, Senate president Nancy Patricia Gutiérrez, who was then under investigation for paramilitary links, released a recording she had surreptitiously made of a conversation she had had with one of the investigators working with Velásquez's team, Juan Carlos Díaz Rayo. Over the course of the long conversation—which in tone suggested a high degree of familiarity between the investigator and Gutiérrez—Díaz Rayo expressed some concerns about how the parapolitics investigations worked. In particular, he made a comment about a case the court had open, number 26,625, in which he said Velásquez was collecting evidence against multiple members of Congress without notifying them that they were under investigation, as would normally be required. Gutiérrez and others tried to portray this as a grave violation of due process rights, and President Uribe publicly backed Gutiérrez up. In fact, Uribe made new insinuations about the courts, stating that "some senator has told me about feeling that certain sectors of the justice system had asked him or her for money. I've asked, 'Why don't you report them?' But the person told me that it was done in such a subtle way that it would be hard to report, and also that he or she is afraid to do so."

Soon after, Díaz Rayo was reportedly removed from the investigative team. As for the substance of Gutiérrez's complaint, Velásquez explained to the media that, although it was true that there was a general open case, number 26,625, in which the court could receive testimony related to parapolitics, it was not focused on any one individual, and so they had not violated any rights—the minute an investigation did focus on an individual, they opened a new case for that person. In fact, conducting preliminary inquiries about possible paramilitary links with politicians was the mission the court had given him—there was nothing improper about that. After a special meeting to discuss the new allegations against Velásquez, the court ended up "decisively and emphatically" backing Velásquez's work.

BUT COMMENTATORS and politicians continued attacking Velásquez and the court, often referring darkly to a "cartel of witnesses" that Velásquez was supposedly running, or talking about his supposed mismanagement of investigations, without giving much detail. No matter what Velásquez did, or what the evidence showed, it felt as though there would be no end to the efforts to discredit him.

CHAPTER 16

INSIDE THE PRESIDENTIAL PALACE

"**WHAT A WASTE OF TIME,**" Ricardo Calderón thought to himself as he listened to the Democracy Corporation members talk. It was early 2008, months before the paramilitary leaders were extradited, and Calderón was sitting in the lovely terrace of a small hotel in the exclusive Poblado neighborhood of Medellín, surrounded by tropical plants and hummingbirds, as elegantly dressed servers came by with more drinks and food for the group. Calderón had traveled to Medellín for other reasons, but the paramilitary known as "Job" (Antonio López) had urged him to meet with him and some of his associates to listen to what they were doing in the city.

The men from the Democracy Corporation, a nonprofit made up of demobilized paramilitaries in Medellín, had a well-practiced pitch about their work: their association, led by Job and a few other former members of the group that had been led by Don Berna (Diego Murillo Bejarano) who were free and not participating in the Justice and Peace process (because there were no criminal charges against them), was helping demobilized paramilitaries reintegrate into civilian life. In close collaboration with Medellín's office of reintegration, which was headed by Jorge Gaviria, brother to presidential adviser José Obdulio Gaviria, the Democracy Corporation found jobs for demobilized men, helped them get schooling, represented them in negotiations over benefits with the government, and helped them to participate in an organized way in local politics—peacefully rather than through the use of force. They also organized the demobilized men, naming "coordinators" for different groups, which mirrored some of the original structure of the armed groups in various neighborhoods in the city.

Medellín had experienced a dramatic drop in homicides in the past few years—after a peak of 184 murders per 100,000 residents in 2002, the number of killings dropped by half in 2003, and now stood at 28.7 per 100,000. As a result, both US and Colombian officials were talking about a sort of Medellín "miracle" and a "revolution" in violence reduction. Bush administration officials, who were aggressively pushing Democratic legislators in Washington to approve the pending free trade deal, had been particularly effusive in holding Medellín out as a model, not only for violence reduction but for President Uribe's security and demobilization policies. The Democracy Corporation had capitalized on this narrative, and a meeting with leaders like Job, Giovanni Marín, William López (aka "Memín"), and Fabio Acevedo—all tough-looking but smooth-talking associates of Don Berna—had become almost a required stop for delegations of foreign officials visiting Colombia.

Calderón had few illusions about what the Democracy Corporation really was. To him, it was clear that this was a mechanism through which Don Berna, and perhaps other, new leaders, could continue exerting control in the city with a veneer of legality. There had already been reporting in the media about the fear Medellín residents were living with because of the ongoing threats by demobilized paramilitaries. Democracy Corporation members had been trying to take over local community councils—and their access to state resources—through intimidation. It was said that they killed community leaders, "coordinators" of the demobilized, or others who didn't follow the orders of Berna's men. The Democracy Corporation members themselves had acknowledged that the drop in homicides had more to do with the fact that Don Berna's group had vanquished most of its rivals in 2002 than with the demobilization process. So listening to Job and his buddies talk about their social work was frustrating and mind-numbingly boring to Calderón. He was only doing it on the off-chance that he would gain some insight into what Job was really up to behind the scenes.

Calderón had never believed Job's vague claims to have evidence against Iván Velásquez, but he had been intrigued enough to keep meeting with Berna's associate. As luck would have it, soon after they first met, in mid-2007, Job had started to spend much of his day in meetings and taking calls from the terrace of a steak restaurant very close to Calderón's office in Bogotá. When Job got close to the corner of the terrace, Calderón could even take photos of him and the people accompanying him from his office window. Soon, he was regularly photographing Job in different parts of the restaurant, not only from the window, but also from *Semana*'s rooftop, and even from a car with tinted windows that he borrowed from a friend—this went on for eight months or more. Calderón's mother passed away in August 2007, and Calderón threw himself into his work even more than in the past as a way to deal with his grief. Calderón's schedule was highly irregular, but it seemed like Job was spending virtually all his time at the restaurant—arriving at 11 a.m. and staying until 11 p.m. Sometimes Calderón would join Job for lunch, and Job began introducing him to some of his associates, which even included a former police officer who now seemed to be working as Job's assistant. On those occasions, Calderón would convince some of his colleagues to help him film the meetings from afar.

The Medellín Democracy Corporation meeting was just part of Calderón's ongoing cultivation and monitoring of Job. Months later, it would turn out to be critically important to Calderón in showing the lengths to which the paramilitaries were going to help the government discredit the parapolitics investigations.

THE OFFICES OF THE governmental National Learning Service (Servicio Nacional de Aprendizaje, or SENA) in Apartadó were packed—and, as was always the case in the main town in the tropical Urabá region of Antioquia, muggy. It was April 24, 2008—two days after Mario Uribe's arrest, and four days after *Noticias Uno* published the video of Yidis Medina saying that she had been bribed to vote for Uribe's reelection. Several high-level officials from Bogotá had descended upon the SENA offices for a meeting about "productive projects" that the government was supposed to put in place to create jobs for demobilized men.

As the meeting, which was being streamed live on the public TV channel, came to a close, one of the local demobilized leaders asked to speak: he wanted to inform President Uribe of something that had happened to him. He went on to say that he had recently been

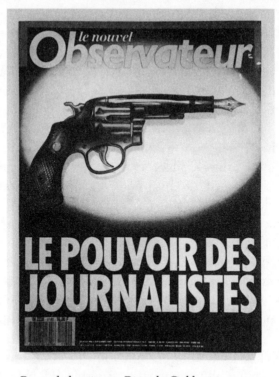

Poster belonging to Ricardo Calderón,
Bogotá, October 2016. It used to hang in his
office at Semana *when he was investigating*
the 2009 DAS scandal. © Maria McFarland
Sánchez-Moreno.

approached by someone who offered him 200 million pesos (around US$100,000) if he would say that President Uribe and other members of the region's political class had connections to the paramilitaries in the Urabá region. The statement led to another storm of media coverage, with the man who had spoken appearing in multiple news outlets repeating his claim about the attempted bribe. He added that he had been offered potential asylum in Canada or another country, with the help of a nongovernmental organization, and that he was worried, because this was "a clear effort to destabilize" the country's democratic institutions, and he didn't want to participate in that. He refused to identify the people who had approached him, stating that he would do so in a longer conversation with the president. He did not agree with many of the president's policies, and had never voted for him, he added, so this was not a situation in which he was trying to do the president a favor.

Uribe administration officials immediately seized upon the demobilized man's statements as further proof that people were plotting against the president. Presidential adviser Fabio Valencia Cossio spoke of "an international plot" against Uribe and told the media that the man's claims were proof that there was a "cartel of witnesses" against the government—an implicit attack on Velásquez. "One week they set something up from one prison, and the following week, they do it from outside the country," said Valencia Cossio.

Calderón could not believe his eyes when he saw footage of the demobilized paramilitary making these statements: it was Ferney Suaza, one of Job's associates, who had participated in the hotel meeting with Democracy Corporation members a few months earlier in Medellín. There was no way, thought Calderón, that this was a mere coincidence. In the preceding months, Job had kept hammering away at his claim that Velásquez was corrupt, though for a long time he offered nothing concrete to back up those claims. Now one of Job's associates was giving further ammunition to those who were claiming that the court was persecuting the president.

Calderón finally confronted Job directly: What was going on? It was all very simple, Job told Calderón: There was a battle between the court and the president, and the paramilitaries had to pick a side. They had decided to help Uribe by gathering evidence against the court. But, Calderón was starting to understand, the paramilitaries' activities were going well beyond "gathering" evidence.

Soon after, Job finally brought Calderón material that he described as evidence of Velásquez's corruption: it was a video recording taken in an office of a round man in a suit and glasses, named Henry Anaya, who was talking in an animated manner with Diego Álvarez, the dry, wiry, bearded lawyer who represented Don Berna. On the video, Anaya seemed to hold himself out as a representative of the Supreme Court, and to be asking Álvarez for US$15,000 in exchange for, apparently, getting "improvements" in Don Berna's prison conditions. Job urged Calderón to publish the video, but to Calderón it was absurd: Anaya might well be trying to scam Don Berna's lawyers, but it was clear that he didn't work for the court, and the video didn't show any misbehavior by the court itself. Job later shared another video with Calderón of Velásquez meeting with Don Berna's lawyer, but the video showed nothing out of the ordinary or inappropriate. And he shared audio recordings of prison conversations between Don Berna and the former IT chief from the DAS, Rafael García, apparently with the goal of discrediting García, whose testimony was important in several of the parapolitics cases—though the recordings didn't really do that.

Meanwhile, Calderón discovered that one of his *Semana* colleagues, whom he considered very close to the Uribe administration, had obtained a copy of the Anaya video and the García audio recordings from senior officials. That was interesting: How did the administration get the material? Clearly, there was some channel of communication between Don Berna's people and the administration. Calderón persuaded the magazine to hold off on publishing the recordings—he wanted to nail down the full story.

Calderón was not surprised that Job was involved in some kind of effort to smear Velásquez. After all, Job had admitted as much. But if the administration was sharing these recordings, that suggested it was actively working with Job and Don Berna.

"I JUST CAME out of the Casa de Nari," a deep male voice, with a thick Antioquia accent, said on a never before published audio recording, referring informally to the Casa de Nariño, as the presidential palace is known. Calderón recognized the voice—he knew it well—and sat back, satisfied. This was the last piece of evidence he needed to write the story.

On August 25, 2008, Calderón revealed to the public just how close Job had gotten to the highest circles of political power in the country. With new audio and video recordings that he obtained from various sources that had been monitoring Job's activities, Calderón reported in *Semana* that four months earlier, on April 23, Job and Don Berna's lawyer, Diego Álvarez, had entered the Casa de Nariño and met with some of Uribe's closest advisers. They included the president's legal counsel, Edmundo del Castillo, and his press secretary, César Mauricio Velásquez, as well as a couple of other individuals. There, Álvarez and Job had offered supposed "evidence" against the Supreme Court—in particular, the Anaya video and the recording of

Iván Velásquez meeting with Álvarez. The meeting happened the same week that *Noticias Uno* made the video of Yidis Medina public, in which she accused the administration of buying her vote, and just a couple of days after Mario Uribe's arrest. It was also the day before Job's associate Ferney Suaza made his explosive statements in the media about how mysterious people had been offering him benefits in exchange for testifying against Uribe.

Don Berna and his men had come up with a "Machiavellian" plan, Calderón wrote, to surreptitiously record members of the Supreme Court and other persons and take those recordings to the government in exchange for benefits. This behavior by the paramilitaries was unremarkable, since, after all, they were "criminals with a mafia-like modus operandi." But what was surprising, Calderón wrote, was that "in the heart of the Casa de Nariño, just a few meters from the office of president Álvaro Uribe, the legal counsel and press chief would meet with envoys of 'Don Berna' to receive information against the court. And what did the paras want in exchange? To delay the extradition of 'Don Berna,' as the paramilitaries themselves acknowledged to *Semana*."

Calderón explained that Don Berna and his men had started to develop their plot soon after President Uribe launched his first attacks on the court over the Tasmania letter, when they realized the depth of the animus the government had toward the Supreme Court. They had seen an opportunity to make themselves useful to the administration by collecting or manufacturing material that the administration could use to harm the court, and particularly Velásquez. So they decided to secretly record several people with the goal of collecting material that might be useful to them. Don Berna's men knew that Anaya didn't work for the Supreme Court, but even so, he did have contacts in the court, including Iván Velásquez himself, because he had been an intermediary with witnesses in some of the court's cases. That's why Berna's people had specifically reached out to Anaya: they hoped they could get him to say something they could use to smear the court. Anaya had apparently seen an opportunity to make some money by boasting of his connections in the court and offering to use them on Don Berna's behalf—as revealed in the video. Anaya had also, Calderón noted, managed to arrange meetings between Velásquez and Álvarez, which the paramilitaries had also recorded, in an effort to get Velásquez to say something they could use against him. But, as Calderón had already seen in the videos that Job had given him, Velásquez had said nothing in any way problematic in these meetings. Still, Don Berna's people had tried to make the most of what they had, and had offered the videos to the administration.

But, Calderón noted, "like any good *mafioso*," Don Berna had covered all his bases. So, in addition to collecting material that would implicate the court, he also sought material that he could use as a sort of "insurance policy" against the government. Once the government transferred him to La Picota prison (after the bizarre episode in which it put him on the navy brig), Don Berna had shared a cell for a while with Rafael García, the former IT chief for the DAS, who had implicated the DAS director, Jorge Noguera, years before. He had spent hours talking to García, secretly recording his conversations. On the recordings, Berna could be heard trying to goad García into saying things that would undermine the parapolitics cases. But Calderón also noticed that, on some of the recordings, Berna repeatedly tried to get García to tell him information that might be harmful to President Uribe.

All of these efforts came to a head on April 3, 2008, when the Uribe administration extradited "Macaco" (Carlos Mario Jiménez), the former leader of the AUC's Central Bolívar Block, to the United States. Don Berna was sure that he would be next, because of the United States' intense interest in his extradition. Don Berna knew, Calderón wrote, that there was no way he could avoid ending up in a US prison. But he wanted to buy time so his lawyers could negotiate with US officials, and so he could get his criminal organization in Medellín in order. So Berna's men had ramped up their efforts to persuade the Uribe administration to delay their commander's extradition.

Before writing the article, Calderón had spoken to Edmundo del Castillo, Uribe's general counsel, as well as César Mauricio Velásquez, the press secretary. Both had confirmed that they had been at the April 23 meeting with Job and Álvarez. Del Castillo said he had also met on two other occasions with Berna's lawyer, Álvarez. It later became clear that they had been joined in the meeting by a representative of the DAS, as well as two other individuals. According to Del Castillo, he had agreed to meet with Job because Job had said that he had evidence of a plot by the court against the president, but Job had not asked for anything in exchange. In other words, Calderón wrote, criminals had secretly recorded the Supreme Court's top investigator in an effort to smear him, and had then given the recordings to high officials from the president's office. And then, instead of reporting them, those officials "had decided to maintain a complicit silence."

Worse yet, as Calderón already knew, someone in the Casa de Nariño had tried to distribute some of the paramilitaries' recordings to the press to smear the court. "As if that weren't enough," Calderón wrote, they then tried to cover it up. "To avoid leaving behind evidence that the paramilitaries were the ones who collected the secret recordings," Calderón reported, based on statements by senior intelligence officials, "an official from the Casa de Nariño called the DAS to ask it to install hidden microphones and tap certain phone lines, including that of Assistant Justice Iván Velásquez and the man in the video, Anaya."

Don Berna's plan did not work out: a little over two weeks after the meeting, Uribe extradited him to the United States along with the other paramilitary leaders. And on July 28, as Job ate lunch at Angus Brangus, a steak and seafood restaurant in the El Poblado neighborhood in Medellín, two men with guns interrupted him, shooting the paramilitary to death for reasons that would never be entirely clear.

STANDING STRAIGHT IN front of a background of blue curtains, next to the Colombian flag, President Uribe read a carefully worded statement, responding to Semana's report. He had, Uribe acknowledged with a poker face, learned of Del Castillo's meeting with Job beforehand, and he did "not disallow it," as it was policy in the presidential palace to "meet with all people who might bring relevant information about public order." The paramilitaries, he said, had told his staff that they had evidence that Supreme Court investigators were manipulating witnesses so they could accuse the president of something. And that, Uribe said, was "serious." To explain further, he said, "Because you know, we have had many difficulties in that regard. In Colombia today there is a trafficking in witnesses, in testimony, and that is corruption and we have to eliminate it too." Ultimately, he said, the presidency had decided not to report anything to prosecutors because they had found the information that the paramilitaries gave them to be "irrelevant," and they had thought it would be irresponsible to make accusations against the court based on the videos they had seen. However, they had turned the material over to the DAS to be transcribed, though the DAS was still working on that because parts of the recordings were "inaudible."

Uribe's statement raised far more questions than it answered, as Calderón and one of his colleagues noted in *Semana*: Why would the presidency have a policy of meeting with all people who had information about public order, when there were entire state agencies, including the police and the armed forces, devoted to that? Was the Supreme Court a threat to "public order," in his mind? Why would the press secretary and the general counsel be charged with meeting with paramilitaries, when it wasn't within their job descriptions? Why had Job been given permission (as Calderón discovered) to enter the presidential palace with his car, through the basement, when all official visitors had to go through the front door? And if the whole meeting was aboveboard, why was there no official record, as there would be for any other visit, of Job having entered the Casa de Nariño? Rather, Calderón had discovered, there was only a record of Berna's lawyer, Diego Álvarez, coming in in his car—and Job was not listed as a passenger. Finally, Calderón asked: "If, as the president said, the information was 'irrelevant,' . . . what was the point of leaking some of the recordings and transcripts to a media outlet?" Here, Calderón was referring to the material he assumed someone in the presidential palace had given to one of his colleagues at *Semana*. He went on to note that it was equally curious that even though the recordings had inaudible portions, the transcripts made in the Casa de Nariño and shared with the media included language that wasn't even in the recordings.

Calderón's article—combined with what many in the public perceived as a disturbing response by the president—caused a massive national scandal, with virtually all other media outlets in the country covering his findings. Iván Velásquez had had some sense of what was coming: he and Calderón had recently reconnected after a long period of not speaking, and Calderón had asked him a number of questions to cross-check information in the article. But it was a relief to have more evidence supporting his own belief that he had been the target of a coordinated smear operation.

Calderón was convinced that, ultimately, the decision to extradite the paramilitaries came down to the simple fact that keeping them in Colombia had become more risky to the administration than sending them away. Berna, hoping to avoid extradition to the United States, had followed two paths simultaneously: on the one hand, offering to help the government, by collecting an array of recordings that could harm the court or the parapolitics investigations, and, on the other, trying to get ahold of information he could use to blackmail the Uribe administration. It was clear to Calderón that the paramilitaries were getting out of control—not just because of their continued criminal activity, which Calderón had reported more than a year before—but because they might turn on the administration.

In December 2008, another journalist, Félix de Bedout, added further fuel to this theory, when his W Radio show published audio recordings of a meeting the paramilitary leader Salvatore Mancuso had had with politicians Eleonora Pineda and Miguel de la Espriella, while Mancuso was still in Colombia and participating in the Justice and Peace process. In the recordings, Mancuso could be heard telling the two politicians that they needed to remember every name of any politician who had collaborated with the paramilitaries, and start disclosing them—his idea, apparently, was to overwhelm the system. "The more people are involved, the faster there will be a solution," Mancuso had said. "Uribe can't imprison 20,000 people, and he can't imprison the 100 most important people in this country, he can't. What is he going to do with his ministers, with his minister of defense? What is he going to do with his vice president?" This effort, it seemed, was partly why in 2006 De la Espriella and Pineda had first revealed the existence of the Ralito Pact, which had involved several politicians. But what else had Mancuso been planning to reveal?

Besides, Calderón was starting to learn, the court's enemies in the government had plenty of other tools at their disposal, without the paramilitaries' help, to go after Iván Velásquez's investigations.

CHAPTER 17

SPIES

AT 11 A.M. ON FEBRUARY 18, 2009, Ricardo Calderón was walking down the street to Hacienda Santa Bárbara, a high-end red-brick shopping mall in Bogotá, when his DAS sources pulled up next to him and dragged him into their car. He had assumed that—as on other occasions—the DAS agents would ask him to climb into the trunk of their car in the basement parking lot, and drive him to an unidentified location to talk. They had good reasons to be paranoid, so he didn't mind following their instructions whenever they met. But this time, they punched him in the brow and knocked him out. When the guard outside his building woke him up the next morning on the front lawn of his apartment building, Calderón could not remember anything that had happened over the past twenty or so hours. He went to the emergency room for stitches on his head wound, and a blood test revealed that he had been administered a drug similar to scopolamine, or "Devil's Breath," which left him able to function but with no awareness or recollection of what he was doing.

Around noon, Calderón pulled up to *Semana*'s offices to tell his editor what had happened. He was taken aback to find the same agents waiting for him by the building's entrance. He took them into his office to talk, and they immediately apologized: "We're so sorry, but you have to understand," Calderón recalls them saying. The agents had been talking with him for so many months, without Calderón writing any articles, that they had become afraid that he was working for the counterintelligence branch of the DAS.

Meanwhile, the word had been getting around within the agency that Calderón was writing something big about them. A counterintelligence agent had spotted Calderón talking to one of his sources, and had alerted the DAS's counterintelligence director, Jorge Lagos. As a result, Calderón's sources said, counterintelligence agents had begun destroying incriminating material and were now conducting a witch hunt within the agency, trying to find out who else might be talking to the media. Calderón's sources were nervous. They didn't understand why he hadn't done anything yet with all the information they had been giving him, so they had decided to dope and interrogate him. "Last night we realized that you were loyal, but we had to be sure that you hadn't been sent by Lagos," they explained. Calderón accepted their apology and said he understood. But the incident changed things: he had kept the lid on his latest investigation for a long time and would have liked to continue investigating. But what if his other sources also grew suspicious? What else might they do to him?

Calderón's wife, Mónica, was having dinner with her mother, who was visiting them, when she saw him walk into their apartment with a huge bruise on his head. He tried to avoid being seen, but she rushed to him, alarmed. What had happened? she wanted to know. Calderón always tried to keep the threats he received from Mónica, as he didn't want to upset her. The only one she had ever directly encountered was a message on their phone's answering machine in 2004, warning Calderón to be quiet or suffer the consequences. The threat, Calderón had believed, was in response to an article he had written about how police officers, apparently working on behalf of paramilitaries, had kidnapped and tortured a young woman they believed had stolen money from the paramilitaries. After that incident, which shook Mónica deeply, the couple had moved, and had gotten rid of their answering machine.

This time, Calderón told Mónica he had slipped and hurt his head by accident. Mónica kept looking him over, to see if he had any other injuries, but she couldn't find any. She didn't believe him, but she also didn't want to upset her mother, so she accepted his explanation and let him go to sleep. Mónica had always known Calderón did dangerous work, and she had never fully understood why he was so passionate about it—she would not choose to do that work herself. But she also knew that it was central to who he was. So the best way for her to deal with it, and not live in a constant state of anxiety, was simply to trust him and try not to know too much about what he was doing.

CALDERÓN HAD STARTED this latest investigation as a result of his monitoring of Job's activities. He had recognized former members of the DAS who were showing up to meet with the paramilitary, and who were clearly passing information on to him. Curious to find out more, Calderón had reached out to some of his DAS sources from the days when he was covering the scandal over paramilitary infiltration of the DAS under its director at the time, Jorge Noguera. Calderón had never revealed their names, so they trusted him. Knowing of Job's efforts to smear the court, Calderón had asked them whether the DAS was spying on political figures—or even the Supreme Court. They confirmed that it was. And so began, especially starting in October 2008, yet another round of surreptitious meetings in which they gave him information. In addition to the basement of Hacienda Santa Bárbara, Calderón would meet them at gas stations, and at various restaurants in the middle of the night, usually on weekends. Initially, they only told him what they were seeing, and explained the structure of the DAS—which operated in cells—and the role of different actors. But Calderón kept pressing them for more.

He also reached out to other people at the DAS, some of whom started to talk. There were DAS agents who didn't agree with what was happening inside the agency, and they wanted Calderón to expose it. Others agreed to talk to him because Calderón figured out that they were angry about the treatment they were getting from their supervisors, or frustrated in some way, and Calderón was able to play on those feelings to get them to open up. With a couple of others, Calderón was able to get them to talk out of fear, because they started to realize that things were getting out of control, and that they could end up in jail for following illegal orders.

By December, Calderón was receiving large quantities of audio recordings and intelligence reports that documented some of the agency's activities. He had already obtained a vast amount of information, but there was more coming, and he wanted to get as much as possible before he essentially shut down his access to the documents by going public.

But at this point, he concluded, continuing his investigation without publishing anything was just not feasible without taking on an unacceptable amount of risk.

ON FEBRUARY 23, 2009, *Semana* ran the first of what would turn into a months-long series of stories, leading with an explosive statement: "The DAS is out of control. It illegally records the calls of judges, journalists, and politicians, and has put itself at the service of drug traffickers, paramilitaries, and guerrillas." This scandal was worse, Calderón wrote, than the one the DAS had faced in 2005, after Noguera's departure and Rafael García's allegations. Based on statements by over thirty witnesses and participants in the events, as well as a vast number of documents and audio recordings, Calderón described an intelligence agency that, instead of focusing on true threats to national security, had poured much of its resources into spying on people perceived as enemies of the Uribe administration. These included opposition politicians, such as Gustavo Petro, as well as journalists, such as *Semana* director Alejandro Santos, and prominent columnists Daniel Coronell and Ramiro Bejarano, who had criticized the government (Bejarano also happened to be the attorney for the Supreme Court president, César Julio Valencia, in the defamation suit brought by Uribe). It also included the Supreme Court itself, and, most importantly, Iván Velásquez.

"Any person or entity that might represent a threat to the government has to be monitored by the DAS. And along those lines, more than a year ago the activities of the [Supreme] Court and some of its members began to be considered and treated as a legitimate 'target,'" Calderón quoted one detective from the Intelligence Directorate of the DAS as saying. Four other DAS officials had corroborated the claim that the DAS was spying on the court. Calderón had reviewed some of the intelligence reports about the court, including one about Velásquez: "Velásquez has been the subject of 'one-on-one tracking' since the Tasmania incident in October 2007," he wrote. "They don't leave Velásquez alone even for a minute, as is evident from the DAS report." The DAS had listened in on more than 2,000 of Velásquez's calls and monitored dozens of his meetings. DAS reports included detailed logs of Velásquez's movements—from the classes he taught at universities to the interviews he conducted with potential witnesses and lunch with his family on weekends. "The risk to judicial investigations is obvious," wrote Calderón. In fact, one of Calderón's DAS sources said, "when the confrontation between the court and the presidency became more acute, about a year and a half ago, the order was to find out as much as possible about all of the justices, by whatever means necessary, from human sources to technical tools. When the confrontation began to slow down, monitoring began to focus only on those that were higher priorities, like Velásquez."

In addition to illegally wiretapping phone calls, the DAS was scooping up emails of their targets—Calderón discovered this by accident, when in early February 2009 a DAS official had called him, alarmed, a few hours after Calderón had an email exchange with fellow journalist Félix de Bedout about some of what he was learning about the DAS. Without thinking, the DAS official said something about the friendship between the two journalists. Calderón asked how the official knew about that, and the official said that Jorge Lagos, the counterintelligence director, had told him. But, Calderón pointed out, the DAS would have had no way of knowing about his contact with De Bedout unless it was monitoring their emails, as Calderón and De Bedout had only recently started to be in touch online. Calderón wasn't able to get a straight answer from the official, but it was clear to him that the DAS was somehow getting access to his or De Bedout's email messages. More broadly, with regard to the media, one of Calderón's sources said that "the priority is to know the information about the ones who worry the government, either because they are too critical, or because, unlike others, the government cannot control them at will."

The DAS conducted its illegal wiretapping through various means. A few years before, the United States had helped Colombia establish what was known as the "Sistema Esperanza" (Hope System), an official wiretapping system formally under the control of the attorney general's office, to strengthen its ability to conduct criminal investigations. The system was operated from several different *salas*, or chambers, including two—the "wine chamber" and the "silver chamber"—within DAS headquarters. In theory, phone calls could only be intercepted through the Esperanza system if there was a judicial warrant for the surveillance. However, Calderón explained, DAS officials had gotten around the warrant requirement by simply getting judicial warrants for phone numbers of criminal suspects, but then—once the order got to the DAS rooms—changing the phone number to that of the target the DAS officials wanted to monitor. Alternatively, Calderón reported, DAS officials had at times manufactured fake warrants, or had tricked prosecutors into issuing warrants based on false information. In addition to the Esperanza system, the DAS had mobile surveillance equipment that it had purchased from the United States. It could use this technology to tap hundreds of phone lines without warrants, and even to track cellphone locations from secret DAS offices.

The story also described several incidents in which DAS information had ended up in the hands of prominent paramilitaries, drug traffickers, and even—in one case—ELN guerrillas, presumably because of corruption within the agency. At times, Calderón wrote, drug traffickers had even been able to get the DAS to carry out wiretapping on their behalf, using its mobile equipment.

In January 2009, Calderón wrote, a small group of DAS officials had been given the order to destroy most of the records of the illegal spying. The word had been spreading internally about Calderón's investigation, and the government had decided to name a new DAS director, Felipe Muñoz, to replace María del Pilar Hurtado. Muñoz was going to take over on January 22, and midlevel officials were nervous about whether their illegal activities would be exposed, especially once *Semana* published. Eventually, investigators from the attorney general's office would uncover video footage from the DAS's security cameras that corroborated Calderón's report: it showed an unusual amount of activity on those dates, with numerous DAS officials exiting the building with what appear to be boxes and briefcases of materials, and even entire desktop computers. Five hours of video from the day Muñoz took over were also missing—supposedly because the cameras stopped working during that period.

In the days after the story broke, Calderón felt like *Semana* was, more than ever, alone. On the radio, on TV, and in the newspapers, commentators were arguing that Calderón's story was false, that it couldn't be trusted, because it was based on anonymous sources, and that there was nothing there. The new DAS director, Muñoz, was also claiming that *Semana* had the facts wrong, and some of the other media outlets seemed to buy Muñoz's line.

Calderón did find one source of support: the national police chief, General Óscar Naranjo, checked in on him, and he made a point of walking with Calderón around the "Parque de la 93," a small, tidy park surrounded by cafés a block from *Semana*'s offices, on a regular basis. Naranjo admired Calderón's courage and humility, and had been impressed by his depth of knowledge about organized crime in the country—on that issue, he said, Calderón "might be the best informed person in Colombia." He couldn't give Calderón armed guards without undermining the journalist's ability to do his work, but by walking with him publicly, he could offer some measure of protection.

Nonetheless, a couple of weeks after breaking the story, Calderón and his wife fled to London, with help from the British embassy. One of Calderón's contacts had warned him that there was an order out to kill him, so Calderón planned to stay outside of Colombia for three months. Mónica recalled that it was extremely difficult for him to leave, not only because he was attached to Colombia, but also because of his phobia of airplanes (apparently caused by a bad flight when he was a child). The entire flight out of the country was a nightmare. But it was good to have a few days of peace in a place where they could walk freely down the street.

Less than two weeks later, however, they were back in Colombia. Administration officials were on the offensive, attacking *Semana* and claiming that the story about the DAS was part of a political plot against the government. Since Calderón had worked alone, there was nobody else at *Semana* who had access to sources and could reply; he could either stay away and let the government kill the story, or he could return and defend it. He chose the latter. Some of his contacts in law enforcement and the intelligence community were also able to at least temporarily halt the plan to have him killed. "After that, we got the funeral announcements and wreaths, but that was a public threat, it was more comforting," Calderón later recalled with a smirk. He kept meeting with his sources, though it became extremely difficult because now he was under surveillance himself: "It was very evident. . . . I would go out for coffee at a bookstore and the guys would be back there holding the books upside down while they watched what we did."

Still, he was able to keep collecting information, often by slipping away in the middle of the night for meetings with sources, and over the following months he published several stories that shed more light on what had happened in the DAS. An investigation by the attorney general's office—including a fairly thorough initial report by the CTI on the files they had found in the DAS—also yielded further details, and the new information started to change the coverage of the story by other news outlets, giving more credibility to *Semana*'s reporting.

The picture that emerged was that, as early as 2004, when Noguera was directing the DAS, the agency had established a group of around sixteen agents called the G-3, led by José Miguel Narváez, who was then the deputy director of the DAS. The G-3 was focused on conducting what Calderón later described as a "dirty war" against human rights groups and members of the labor movement. Narváez had for years held various prominent positions in the Ministry of Defense, in the military, and in military and intelligence training schools, and he was said to have been a teacher of General Rito Alejo del Río, whom former president Andrés Pastrana had cashiered over alleged links to paramilitary groups. Narváez was said to have been close to Pedro Juan Moreno, Uribe's right-hand man in Antioquia, and there were rumors that, early in Uribe's presidency, Moreno had pushed Uribe to set up a new central intelligence agency, with Narváez as its possible head.

The G-3 was the branch of the DAS that—as Calderón had reported during the 2006 scandal enveloping the agency after the former IT chief for the DAS, Rafael García, began making his statements about Noguera—had put together lists of trade unionists and activists and passed those along to paramilitaries. Some of the people listed, including a well-known university professor, Alfredo Correa de Andreis, were later assassinated by paramilitaries under the orders of Jorge 40 (Rodrigo Tovar Pupo), the senior commander of the AUC's Northern Block. But the new documents revealed that the G-3 had also pursued prominent journalists, including Daniel Coronell, the *Semana* columnist and *Noticias Uno* director who later exposed the Yidis Medina scandal; opposition politicians, such as Gustavo Petro; and members of human rights groups. The documentation about Alirio Uribe, the head of a Bogotá-based organization, the José Alvear Restrepo Lawyers' Collective, that litigated human rights cases, included detailed information about his movements and those of his entire family, photos and analyses of his financial transactions, and numerous transcripts of his phone calls.

Another DAS target during that period was Claudia Julieta Duque, a journalist who was then investigating the 1999 assassination of beloved comedian and journalist Jaime Garzón. Some of the DAS files that emerged after Calderón's 2009 story contained detailed notes as well as photos of Duque, and even photos of her small daughter; there was also an instruction manual in the files about how to threaten someone, using Duque as an example. In fact, in November 2004, Duque had received a call that followed the precise formula sketched out in the manual: "Señora, are you the mother of María Alejandra?" they asked her. When she said yes, they went on to say, "Well, I have to tell you that you gave us no other choice. You were told in every possible way and you did not want to listen. Now neither bulletproof trucks nor silly little letters will help you. We're now going to have to go after what you most love. This is what happens to you for being a bitch and getting involved in things that are none of your business." Duque also recalled that the caller said, "Your daughter is going to suffer. We're going to burn her alive, we'll sprinkle her fingers throughout the house." Within weeks, Duque and her daughter fled Colombia. Duque had been working closely with the Lawyers' Collective. A senior official at that organization, Soraya Gutiérrez, also reported threats against her daughter at the time: she received a doll with [drops of] blood on it, and a note saying, "You have a lovely daughter. Don't sacrifice her."

The G-3 was dissolved after 2005, when Noguera resigned, and Narváez was removed from the DAS in the midst of a public fight between the two, in which they traded accusations of paramilitary links. But the illegal spying did not end there: soon afterward, now under the leadership of a new DAS director, the DAS established a new group, the GONI (Grupo de Observación Nacional e Internacional) or National and International Observation Group. According to Calderón, the GONI had many of the same members as the G-3, and it operated under the leadership of Fernando Ovalle, who had previously been coordinating the G-3. In theory, the GONI was divided into subgroups—Falcón, Fénix, and Cóndor—that were supposed to focus on external threats, such as Venezuela, Ecuador, and the supposed Islamic terrorists in Colombia. There was a practical reason for selecting these themes, Calderón later explained: the GONI's interest in getting US assistance, including access to surveillance equipment. In fact,

Calderón said, the GONI did get extensive US support, including mobile surveillance equipment that it used for illegal spying. Calderón reported, for example, that if Senator Gustavo Petro was traveling to Cali, the GONI, which was in theory monitoring a foreign consulate there, would use its mobile surveillance equipment in Cali to spy on Petro. During this time, the GONI surveilled not only opposition politicians but also members of the Colombian Constitutional Court, when in 2005 it was considering a constitutional amendment to allow presidents to serve for two consecutive terms—thus allowing for Uribe's reelection.

Around the same time, the DAS was also restructured a bit, elevating the intelligence and counterintelligence departments to the level of "directorates," supposedly with the goal of making the intelligence-collection process more efficient and transparent. But this status meant that the chiefs of these departments—Fernando Tabares and Jorge Lagos, respectively—now formally had direct communication with the president.

By 2007, according to the information Calderón had collected, the GONI had turned its attention to a new set of targets: Iván Velásquez and other members of the Supreme Court. Initially, the DAS's interest in the court seemed to have been triggered by an interview that Yesid Ramírez, who was then the president of the court, gave to *Semana* in 2006. In the interview, Ramírez—who had previously had a good relationship with President Uribe—sharply criticized the president for having backed the Constitutional Court in a conflict between the two courts over whether the Constitutional Court could review Supreme Court rulings for violations of fundamental rights. It had been widely believed that Uribe would back the Supreme Court on the issue, and so his decision to do otherwise—coming soon after the Constitutional Court approved an amendment allowing him to run for office a second time—had incensed Ramírez. In the interview, he insinuated that Uribe's decision to back the Constitutional Court was a way to repay the court for having approved the amendment. Uribe reportedly called Ramírez to complain about his statements, and it was said that Ramírez hung up on the president. Soon afterward, DAS documents showed, the agency began monitoring Ramírez's movements, examining his financial transactions, and digging into his background. DAS surveillance reports from early 2008 also showed that one of the agency's plans was to look into connections between Ramírez and Ascencio Reyes, the businessman who—according to stories leaked to the press by the presidency—had paid for several justices to take a trip to Neiva.

But it was clear to Calderón that the DAS's surveillance of the court extended well beyond the Neiva trip, and that it was politically motivated. In fact, the surveillance had ramped up significantly in early 2007, after the court indicted Senator Álvaro Araújo, expanding to include many other justices, and focusing in particular on Velásquez.

Calderón started talking to Velásquez much more often, corroborating information and piecing together how different sectors of the government were going after him. "I remember being in his house and talking to [Supreme Court Justices] César Julio Valencia and María del Rosario González and telling them that this was serious," Calderón recalled. "Because Iván had enemies everywhere."

To Velásquez, the DAS scandal was not altogether surprising, as he had received information before the Tasmania scandal broke indicating that the DAS was monitoring him. But seeing the scale of the surveillance still caused him indignation. María Victoria was not surprised either, as she had been saying since the moment Uribe called Velásquez to ask about Tasmania, on September 11, 2007, that she was afraid of what might happen. But she also doubted that Calderón's reports would do much to change the situation: "It's as if you were in quicksand, and somebody threw a broom at you to get you out," when what you needed was something much larger and stronger to fix the problem. What was really needed, she said, was for the justice system to work.

CALDERÓN KEPT PUBLISHING information about what he had found out about the DAS, in part because he was concerned that prosecutors were not following the evidence. After the CTI completed a fairly thorough initial report of the documentation it had found in DAS offices, the prosecutors seemed to be primarily focused on the actions of the G-3, and were ignoring the later behavior of the GONI—including the surveillance of Velásquez and the other justices. Uribe claimed that he was restructuring the DAS, but the government kept minimizing the scandal. Muñoz claimed that there were no recordings of illegal surveillance—essentially stating that *Semana* had no evidence—and at one point stated that Attorney General Mario Iguarán had informed him that there was no evidence against President Uribe or any other official within the administration (Iguarán later said he had been silent on the matter). Other officials would talk about problems in the DAS many years earlier, blame the surveillance on a few bad apples, and deny any involvement by senior administration officials.

In May 2009, La FM radio published some audio recordings of phone calls by opposition politicians and journalists that, the radio station said, the DAS had illegally tapped. Around that time, other outlets reported that Lagos, the counterintelligence chief, had told the attorney general's office that President Uribe's chief of staff, Bernardo Moreno, and close Uribe adviser José Obdulio Gaviria both knew of the DAS's wiretapping of the Supreme Court justices. The inspector general's office also started a disciplinary investigation against several officials within the presidency, including Moreno, though it could not investigate Gaviria because he did not officially have a position within the government.

The Uribe administration replied by announcing a reward for information leading to the arrest of those responsible for the surveillance, while at the same time expressing its surprise at the decision by the inspector general's office to open an investigation. Meanwhile, Gaviria denied any knowledge of surveillance and blamed the entire DAS scandal on a plot against the government, telling a reporter from El Tiempo that there seemed to be "a cell of the most coarse, even criminal, opposition . . . infiltrated within the DAS, because the damage that it has done to Colombian institutions is enormous."

IN AUGUST 2009, Calderón published yet another bombshell story: the DAS was still conducting illegal surveillance. In some cases, DAS sources had told him, they had used hidden mobile surveillance equipment to spy on the members of Congress who were considering the bill allowing for Uribe's third-term reelection. But one of their main "objectives" remained Iván Velásquez. Calderón had obtained recordings of dozens of Velásquez's phone calls from a former DAS official whom Calderón had met through Job. Calderón took them to Velásquez's house, and they sat down together to listen to them: Velásquez confirmed they were recent. Several of them were calls with his family; in others, he talked with his security detail about his movements; in still others, he talked with colleagues about ongoing investigations. This time, Calderón ended up publishing a few of the recordings, including one in which Velásquez could be heard talking to Jim Faulkner, the US embassy's justice attaché. The United States, now under the leadership of President Barack Obama, had been very silent about the DAS scandal so far, and Calderón wondered whether this would force it to speak out more.

One of Calderón's sources explained that after the scandal first broke, the people involved in wiretapping had stopped their activities for a while, "until the storm passed." But once they saw that the criminal investigations were focusing only on the old surveillance, they started their work up again. "Adjustments were made and the difference is that now it's done better and more discreetly," the source said. One of the ways they made their activity more discreet was by working through "external networks," which Calderón described as former DAS agents who had left the agency, but who would still carry out "special jobs" for it.

According to a US cable that was later made public, on August 31, the day Calderón published the story about the DAS's continued spying, the US ambassador to Colombia, Bill Brownfield, convened a meeting of all US government agencies that had any contact with the DAS. At the meeting, Brownfield reported, the agencies agreed that the scandals had made continuing engagement with the DAS "a political liability" for the US government. They each stated that, to the best of their knowledge, their counterparts had not "wittingly participated in any of the DAS's misdeeds, and no assets, equipment, or resources provided by them to DAS were used to commit these acts." Since the scandal had broken, however, embassy agencies had "reduced or eliminated" their contact with the DAS. Soon afterward, embassy officials met with the Colombian vice president, Francisco Santos, who denied any DAS involvement in the new surveillance *Semana* had reported. But, in a sign, perhaps, of Washington's alarm over the extensive surveillance that Calderón was disclosing, embassy officials also met with Calderón himself. Calderón gave them detailed accounts that—as Ambassador Brownfield reported in another cable—"undercut" Santos's claims.

On September 11, the US State Department issued an unusually strong warning to the Colombian government. In a press release announcing the department's certification that Colombia was meeting the human rights conditions attached to military aid, State Department spokesperson Ian Kelly called the allegations about DAS spying—which, he stressed, the media and nongovernmental organizations said were ongoing—"troubling and unacceptable." The recent revelations that the spying continued required that the attorney general's office "conduct a rigorous, thorough and independent investigation in order to determine the extent of these abuses and to hold all perpetrators accountable," said Kelly. A few days later, the *New York Times* published a lengthy article about the DAS scandal, including the latest recordings, along with a quotation from Ramiro Bejarano, who said that President Uribe was "seriously weakening Colombia's democracy."

The day after the *Times* article came out, Uribe gave a statement to the media in which he said, for the first time, that he thought the DAS should be shuttered. DAS chief Muñoz followed up soon afterward, announcing that the government would submit a bill to Congress giving the president the power to dismantle the intelligence agency.

In Calderón's view, the announcement was a way for the government to put an end to the scandal, but it was a poor way of handling the situation. Yes, the DAS needed to be closed down, but in the process, which took two years, a lot of valuable information—records that could have been relevant to the criminal investigations, and even assets—got lost or harder to track down. The agency's 6,000 employees were spread out throughout multiple other government agencies, and it became very difficult to find witnesses to what had happened.

Also, officials continued to try to minimize the scope of the scandal. Soon after Calderón published the August 31 story, officials began to claim that the recordings of Velásquez's calls had not been conducted by the DAS, but rather, by members of the police—even though Calderón knew it was the DAS. During a September 15 meeting with the US embassy, Vice President Santos echoed José Obdulio Gaviria, claiming that a "very dark" anti-Uribe "force," perhaps made up of Venezuelan president Hugo Chavez, the FARC, drug traffickers, or the internal opposition, was behind the attacks on the DAS. Calderón later learned that an associate of Job's who had once worked in the DAS had paid members of the police and army to allow him to use their systems to listen in on and record Velásquez's calls, as a way to cast doubt on the DAS's involvement.

One piece of good news, Calderón reported, was that the attorney general's office had replaced the prosecutors who had first handled the DAS investigation. The first set of prosecutors had focused only on early surveillance; the new ones would be free to look into what happened later. They seemed serious, but they faced tremendous obstacles. The delay in investigating more recent instances of surveillance meant some evidence might have been lost, and it would be harder to reconstruct what had happened.

And still, efforts to confuse and thwart both the investigators and the public continued. All of a sudden, reports were cropping up left and right about alleged surveillance by different government agencies and by private companies. Increasingly, too, investigators who were looking into the DAS scandal were receiving threats. As investigators got closer to the most senior people responsible for the surveillance, Calderón reported, "the dirty war is increasing. And the serious thing is that if this continues, it's very unlikely that we will find out what really happened, and who was behind the *chuzadas* [as the illegal wiretapping was known]."

THE NIGHT OF October 31, 2009, several DAS agents were gathered at a Halloween party in a country house in Chía, on the outskirts of Bogotá. They were relaxed and having a good time, drinking the strong Colombian *aguardiente* and playing music. Even though Uribe had announced that the DAS was going to be shut down, they were fairly confident that that wouldn't happen—after all, the agency had weathered many other scandals over the preceding five decades, and it was still going. But the partying came to an abrupt stop a few hours in, when shots rang out. Hernando Caballero, one of the agents, had gone into the kitchen, and he had now come out with a gun and was shooting at his colleagues. By the time he had emptied his gun, two agents were dead and four others were wounded. Caballero then threw himself into the fireplace, where he burned his face, before some of the agents restrained him and tied him to a tree.

The official version of events was that Caballero had become extremely drunk, lost control, and begun shooting into the crowd. To

Calderón, the story seemed much more sinister. Some of the victims had been members of the GONI subgroups that had been responsible for much of the illegal surveillance Calderón had reported. Others, including Caballero, were members of the counterintelligence department—but Calderón knew that they had collected information about the GONI members. Prosecutors had never taken their testimony, even though Calderón believed they were key witnesses. After the shootings, Calderón later reported, the first people to arrive on the scene were intelligence agents from the DAS. These agents insisted on conducting the initial crime scene investigation even though this was not their function, and they blocked judicial investigators from entering. One judicial investigator told Calderón that by the time he finally got in, it was clear that someone had tampered with the scene. After his arrest, Caballero—who had, according to Calderón, received a series of unusual promotions in the months before the shooting—admitted his guilt, which allowed prosecutors to close the case without investigating it. Unlike with many other cases, in this case Calderón found it very difficult to access case files, and Caballero refused to give interviews.

In November, Calderón learned of another suspicious death: a DAS agent who had worked in the agency's IT department, and who had been a good source for Calderón, had been shot in the head. The official explanation was that he had committed suicide after having a fight with his girlfriend. Calderón was sure that if prosecutors had interviewed him, he would have said what he knew. That was no longer an option.

In January 2010, a former DAS agent, Alexander Menjura, was teaching his teenage daughter how to play chess on the second floor of his house when the doorbell rang. It was around noon, and his wife had taken his two younger children to routine doctor's appointments. The children were on a school break. He was slow to answer, and as he reached the top of the staircase, he felt an enormous "boom" shake the house. He and his daughter were okay, but he ran down the stairs to find shattered glass everywhere.

At first, Menjura assumed the explosion had been caused by a gas leak, but when the firefighters and police came, they corrected him: someone had thrown a grenade at his house. Did he have any enemies, the police asked? Menjura could only think of one: the DAS.

Menjura had been a DAS agent for sixteen years, serving as chief of its counter-narcotics and then its money-laundering divisions. But he had left the agency in 2007, in the midst of a dispute with colleagues, and had been practicing law since then. Menjura had been upset about the circumstances surrounding his exit, and when a friend of his had introduced him to Calderón, he had been open about his grievances. He and Calderón had met regularly for a few months, and he had shared information about the issues he knew well—though he had not been a major source for the DAS surveillance stories. At one point, he learned from a friend, some other DAS agents had seen him with Calderón, and they had taken photos of them together. Ever since then, he had felt they had been persecuting him. His wife, who also worked at the DAS, had been transferred to a lower-ranking position. His brother, who had been working in the IT section of the DAS in Bogotá, had resigned after he was suddenly ordered to transfer to the remote region of La Guajira. His family's US visas were canceled out of the blue—he presumed because the DAS had sent bad information about him to the US embassy. Still, Menjura had never expected a physical attack: "Ricardo had many sources—good ones," said Menjura. "I think I was among the least important ones." Calderón confirmed that. But Menjura got the message. The day after the grenade attack, he and his family left Colombia for good.

Before the Halloween massacre, Calderón said, several DAS agents knowledgeable about the agency's illegal activities had been starting to come forward with what they knew, out of fear that they would be dismissed or unfairly transferred. But the murders put a stop to that. "After they killed two of the ones who were going to talk, who was going to dare to say anything about what was happening? The message was very clear," one DAS agent told Calderón. In fact, the killings fit into a broader pattern of threats against not only DAS agents but their family members as well, if they attempted to approach prosecutors. "Unjustified transfers and massive firings without explanation have become other types of warnings," wrote Calderón.

DAS AGENTS WERE not the only ones feeling the heat. The threats against Calderón had continued: from the start of the DAS scandal in early 2009 through 2010 he received six notices announcing his own death, three funeral wreaths, and multiple threatening phone calls.

Most went to his office, though one of the notices arrived at his home. Calderón was worried about the impact on Mónica, as well as on his father. His mother had passed away just a few months before the DAS scandal broke, and his father, who had served in the police in the 1970s, and then as a low-level DAS agent handling immigration (not intelligence) matters, before retiring in 1995, had generally stayed away from Calderón's work—Calderón tried not to talk to him about it, and neither he nor his father subscribed to his own magazine. But Calderón was not able to shield him from the threats: one of the funeral wreaths went directly to his father's house. It was especially worrisome because his father had already suffered a heart attack in 2006, probably due to stress, when Calderón had first reported on the paramilitaries' infiltration of the DAS under Jorge Noguera.

Calderón's wife, Mónica, had for years wanted him to quit his job and leave the country with her, though she also understood that he could not do that: being a journalist, being in the mix of everything in Colombia, was at the heart of who Calderón was. Still, the year or so since the DAS scandal had broken had been the most difficult yet for both of them. Calderón was working around the clock, so she rarely saw him. She didn't see or hear the threats, but she knew he must be in danger. And the work was taking a toll on his health: he barely slept, both because of the stress and because he was running out to appointments with his sources at all hours of the night. Calderón had never been very good about eating—his go-tos were coffee and cigarettes—but now he barely touched food. By 2010, he weighed around eighty pounds, about half of his normal weight, and he was suffering from painful bouts of gastritis, which repeatedly landed him in the hospital.

At least, Calderón felt, there was not much that his enemies could do to ruin him financially: he did not even own an apartment. He had a BMW from 1973 that was his first car, and a bulletproof truck that he got in an auction. Nor was there any legitimate way to discredit him: he didn't have affairs, didn't party, and other than his incessant smoking, didn't have any vices. All they could do was threaten him, and that—he thought—was just part of the job.

MEANWHILE, Velásquez was also under extreme stress. Even though the truth was starting to come out about the Tasmania story and the

DAS's surveillance of him, it felt like every time they took a step forward, they were then forced to take two steps back. One day, as Velásquez was in his car getting ready to go to work, he suddenly felt ill. He got back out and called María Victoria, and they rushed to the hospital. The doctors told him that the stress had caused an episode of tachycardia—rapid heart rate. In their words, he was like "a pressure cooker," Velásquez recalled.

CHAPTER 18

THE END OF AN ERA

PRESIDENT ÁLVARO URIBE SAT ATTENTIVELY on the White House stage, next to the prime ministers for Australia and the United Kingdom, John Howard and Tony Blair, respectively, as US president George W. Bush spoke. "Today the United States honors all Colombians by honoring the man they have chosen to lead them," said Bush. "By refusing to allow the land he loves to be destroyed by an enemy within, by proving that terror can be opposed and defeated, President Uribe has reawakened the hopes of his countrymen and shown a model of leadership to a watching world." In recognition of Uribe's courage, Bush said, he was awarding him the Presidential Medal of Freedom, the highest civilian honor awarded by the United States.

That January 13, 2009, Uribe seemed untouchable. He had consistently maintained popularity ratings at or above 70 percent, and much of the public credited him with not only bringing security to the country, but also improving their economic prospects. His image as a tireless worker who was sincere in his commitment to Colombia remained strong; it had not been diminished by his rages, or his cronies' involvement in criminal activity, or the questions swirling around the paramilitaries' demobilization. The president had eighteen months left in his term, and everyone expected him to run for office again—yet another constitutional amendment was making its way through Congress. If passed and then approved by the Constitutional Court, the bill would allow a referendum on whether Uribe could run for a third term. Given his popularity, its success seemed likely.

Colombians were tired of war, tired of the FARC, tired of the sense-lessness of it all. In November 2007, Colombian news media had pub-lished a photograph of a French-Colombian former presidential candidate, Íngrid Betancourt, who had been kidnapped in 2002; she was still a hostage, and in the photograph, she looked gaunt, ill, and broken. In an accompanying letter that the FARC had allowed her to send to her mother, as evidence that she was still alive, the once in-domitable Betancourt sounded defeated: "Here, we live dead. . . . I don't feel like anything. I think that's the only thing that is okay, I don't want anything because here in this jungle the only answer to everything is 'no.' It's better, then, not to want anything, to at least be free of desires." Earlier that year, Jhon Frank Pinchao, another FARC hostage, who had managed to escape after nine years in captivity, had publicly given chilling details of the conditions in which the FARC held the hostages—they tied them up with chains and used metal manacles on their hands, feet, and heads to punish them; several of the hostages had been ill. Betancourt and Pinchao were only two of the hundreds of people the FARC had kidnapped in previous years, for ransom or for political reasons, and held for years on end or killed. In January 2008, the FARC released two hostages, Consuelo Gonzales and Clara Rojas, as a result of negotiations by Venezuelan president Hugo Chavez. But the story of the dark-haired Rojas, a lawyer who had been Betancourt's campaign manager, had only made Colombians more aware of the FARC's brutality: Rojas had had a baby boy, Em-manuel, in captivity, delivering him through a C-section carried out by the guerrillas in the jungle, and the FARC seized him from her while he was still an infant. She was only reunited with him years later, after she was released and the government identified a three-year-old in the care of Colombia's Family Welfare Institute as her baby.

Uribe had not flinched in confronting the FARC—something new for the country. US military aid through Plan Colombia had allowed the Colombian military to purchase modern airplanes, surveillance technologies, and other equipment that had allowed the Uribe admin-istration to repel FARC efforts to take territory and to pinpoint their locations and target them. Early in his term, the government had ar-rested senior FARC commander Ricardo Palmera (aka "Simón Trini-dad"), who was extradited to the United States and sentenced to sixty years in prison in connection with FARC kidnappings of three US

Íngrid Betancourt in captivity. The image was published widely in the Colombian media in 2007.

contractors. Uribe and his defense minister, Juan Manuel Santos, could also claim credit for multiple military operations that had resulted in significant losses for the FARC: on March 1, 2008, for example, a joint military and police force conducted an airstrike and raid on a FARC camp across the Colombian border with Ecuador that killed senior FARC leader Raul Reyes. During the raid, they also recovered valuable computer files belonging to Reyes, some of which pointed to links between the FARC and officials in Ecuador and Venezuela. Later on, Uribe administration officials would also charge that some of the files indicated links between the FARC and the Colombian senator Piedad Córdoba, though she denied those claims; years later, one of Colombia's high courts would rule that Córdoba should not be barred from participating in politics based on the files, finding that the evidence collected from Reyes's computer had been manipulated. Although the strike caused a diplomatic rift with the government of President Rafael Correa in Ecuador, many Colombians viewed it as a huge and ground-breaking coup—a sign that the tide was truly shifting against the

FARC. A few days later, the Uribe administration claimed another success when a FARC fighter murdered guerrilla commander "Iván Ríos," hacked off his hand, and then brought it to the army as proof that Ríos was dead. A few weeks later, the FARC's top commander, "Manuel Marulanda," died of a heart attack.

Uribe's image as a hero shone even more brightly in July 2008, thanks to a spectacularly successful military operation (Operación Jaque, or Operation Checkmate) to rescue a group of fifteen high-profile hostages being held by the FARC, including Betancourt; three US contractors (Marc Gonsalves, Tom Howes, and Keith Stansell); and several members of the Colombian military and police. Following the successful operation, officials described how they had been able to infiltrate the FARC's First Front and deceive its leaders into believing that the FARC's high command had organized a hostages-for-prisoners swap. The First Front's command did not confirm the details, because of the dangers of communicating with the FARC leadership, and went ahead with the supposed plan. The government then sent in a military helicopter that it had painted white, with several soldiers on board pretending to be members of a nongovernmental organization. Thinking that this was, as promised, part of a humanitarian operation, and they were in no danger because they were headed for a meeting with a FARC leader, two FARC members got onto the helicopter along with the hostages. But as soon as they were in the air, the army immobilized the FARC members and told the hostages they were free.

In the past, the rescue of the hostages would have seemed inconceivable to most Colombians. But Uribe later wrote that he had declined Defense Minister Santos's invitation to go and greet the hostages when they landed in the capital, as it would be good for Santos's political future to handle it. "I wanted to signal to the nation that, in moments of great joy and moments of tragedy alike, our will to work would remain constant—our emotions would remain steady. We would proceed normally with the business of the Colombian nation, fulfilling our duty. So I kept the rest of my scheduled agenda for that day," he wrote. Later on, with the hostages at the presidential palace, he did deliver a message on television, reminding the country that many more Colombians were still in captivity. "This is our commitment," he said to those still being held by the FARC. "We won't forget you for a moment until you are *all* back in freedom."

In the midst of these military successes, the news about Tasmania's confession and Job's entry in the Casa de Nariño, which came out around the same time that Operation Checkmate took place, did little to dent Uribe's popularity.

Neither did the scandal over what became known as the "false-positives," when, in 2008, the media began to focus on long-standing allegations that the army had been killing civilians, and then dressing them up as guerrillas killed in combat, during Uribe's administration. Uribe and Defense Minister Santos responded by announcing a purge in military ranks, removing twenty-five members of the army. But the purges, which seemed to imply that the killings could be attributed to a few bad apples in the military, didn't even scratch the surface of the problem, in Calderón's opinion. Even while he was writing about the DAS, he published a story about a young man who admitted that, in exchange for money, he had repeatedly lured away young men in Bogotá—more than thirty in total—with false promises of jobs or membership in paramilitary groups, and then turned them over to members of the military. Several of the young men later turned up dead, with the military claiming they were guerrillas. Over time, it would become clear that there were thousands of similar cases around the country.

The false-positives and the DAS scandals did raise serious questions in Washington, however, where Congress was still holding up the US–Colombia free trade deal. The administration of Barack Obama also seemed to be keeping more of a distance from Uribe than Bush had—Obama's first budget request to Congress included significant money for Colombia, but reduced the proportion of the assistance that would go to the military. As a presidential candidate, Obama had opposed the trade deal, stating that Colombia needed to first deal with the unpunished killings of trade unionists, lest it make "a mockery" of the agreement.

But within Colombia, the Uribe administration largely managed to deflect criticism. "Uribe was God," Calderón later said. "It was impressive, the fanatical following he had." The journalist Daniel Coronell, who was very critical of Uribe, would later say that he thought that so many Colombians adored the president partly because the country was so frustrated by the failure of the earlier peace process with the FARC: "It is as if your house were on fire and the firefighter arrived. You don't care if the firefighter steals or beats his wife. It's the firefighter." Calderón offered a similar explanation: "The country was blind at that time. People settled for simple things, like being able to go out on the highways at night without being kidnapped. That, combined with his hardline rhetoric, made the bulk of the public see [Uribe] as some sort of savior of the country, of whom all things would be forgiven."

NONETHELESS, THE DAS criminal investigations were inching along. In the last week of January 2010, prosecutors from the attorney general's office indicted six midlevel DAS officials—plus José Miguel Narváez, the former deputy director, who had been removed in 2005— for some of the agency's illegal spying in 2004 and 2005 through the G-3. Among the targets of the spying, *Semana* reported later that week, were five justices of the Constitutional Court who were, at the time— in 2005—reviewing Uribe's first reelection amendment and eventually approved it.

Three weeks later, in February 2010, the Constitutional Court once again ruled on whether Uribe could run for reelection. But this time, it said no. The process by which the bill allowing the referendum had been approved, the court found, failed to meet several legal requirements. More importantly, allowing a president to serve a third term would irreparably damage the balance of powers set forth in the Constitution, and approving the amendment would mean undoing the Constitution itself. The message was unequivocal: no matter how strong, how popular, and how insistent President Uribe was, and no matter how corrupt or brutal the country had become, Colombia remained a country of laws—a constitutional democracy, with limits and rules that applied to everyone.

Uribe accepted the court's decision graciously, saying he would respect it; he hoped to "keep serving Colombia from whatever trench until the last day of my existence." The once untouchable president would step down in August.

SHORTLY BEFORE THE end of Uribe's term, Calderón published a story that would conclusively put an end to claims that the DAS had not engaged in illegal surveillance of the court, or that—as many officials had claimed—the surveillance was limited to the investigation of the justices' trip to Neiva that had supposedly been funded by

Ascencio Reyes. That would turn out to be simply a convenient cover for what they were really doing.

The DAS, it turned out, had assigned an agent specifically to spy on the Supreme Court. Calderón had known about the agent for several months, through sources who told him about what she was doing. But with the witch-hunt going on within the DAS, he had been unable to talk to her directly, and it had taken him a long time to finally assemble the story.

The agent, Alba Luz Flórez, whom *Semana* described as tall, with "cinnamon skin, green eyes, chestnut hair," and a voluptuous figure, and who soon became known as the "Mata Hari of the Supreme Court," spoke to prosecutors soon afterward. She explained that starting as early as March 2007—when the "parapolitics" scandal started to heat up, because of the Araújo indictment—her supervisor at the DAS, William Romero, had assigned her to spy on the court. Through a former boyfriend, she had met and recruited David García, who was then a bodyguard for one of the justices on the court. He eventually became a bodyguard for Velásquez. García, in turn, helped her to recruit another informant, Manuel Pinzón, a police officer who had been assigned to be Velásquez's driver. Pinzón was in financial straits, trying to support a large family, and so her promises of monetary rewards were a significant enticement. Flórez had also introduced herself as a representative of the presidency, and she had persuaded her sources that getting the information was a matter of national security. She cited the fights between the president and the court as the reason for the surveillance—in fact, this was how she understood the work as well: she believed "the president needed to find out what was happening inside the court so he could make decisions." Flórez said that Pinzón ended up being a key source, helping her to obtain photocopies of many of the classified case files for the parapolitics cases in the Supreme Court as well as information about planned arrests. At one point, she testified, Romero specifically asked her for copies of Mario Uribe's case file; when she said the file would be difficult to obtain because the case had already been transferred to the attorney general's office, he told her that didn't matter, and that she should go to impossible lengths to get it. She was ultimately unable to do so.

By March 2008, after the Tasmania scandal, and at a time of very high tension between the court and Uribe, Flórez said, Romero asked her to find out what the justices were discussing in their private meetings. So, through García, Flórez recruited Janeth Maldonado, one of the court's *señoras del tinto*—the women who, in what may be a uniquely Colombian profession, were charged with regularly walking around offices offering small cups of bitter coffee, along with clutches of long white sugar packets, to anyone who wanted them. Initially, Maldonado told Flórez little snippets of conversations that she was able to catch as she went in and out of meetings. But then, Flórez said, her supervisors gave her an audio recorder for Maldonado to hide in the court's conference rooms before their meetings. As a result, the DAS was soon receiving recordings of entire court deliberations on cases as well as meetings in which the justices discussed how to respond to the government's attacks on them.

Flórez confirmed that her work had continued until April 2009, two months after the DAS scandal first broke.

Calderón's publication of the story about Flórez, which other outlets then picked up, put an end to most of the doubts that other outlets were expressing about his reporting. It was now very hard to deny that the intelligence service had engaged in extensive illegal spying, including on the Supreme Court. And there was no way to explain that behavior other than as part of a plot to undermine, discredit, and sabotage the court's—and particularly Velásquez's—investigations. To Velásquez, Flórez's statements about his driver, Pinzón, were especially upsetting—he had liked Pinzón, and he felt betrayed and disappointed. But her testimony was also reaffirming, as he had been frustrated by the difficulty of getting to the truth about what the DAS had done to him.

In April 2010, the US ambassador to Colombia, Bill Brownfield, announced that all US assistance that had previously gone to the DAS would be redirected to the Colombian National Police.

Uribe left office, as promised, in August. He was the most popular president in Colombia's history.

CHAPTER 19

THE QUESTION STUCK IN THEIR THROATS

AT THE PODIUM IN DUBAI, Qatar, Iván Velásquez got ready to speak to the crowd. It was November 4, 2011, and he was standing before hundreds of lawyers to receive the International Bar Association's prestigious Human Rights Award, in recognition of his work on the parapolitics cases.

By then, the Supreme Court had convicted thirty-nine members of Colombia's Congress in connection with Velásquez's investigations. Velásquez was busily opening new lines of inquiry into events in the coastal state of Atlántico, into the activities of a still-active paramilitary group in the Casanare region, and into the little-known group known as the "Capital Block" of the AUC, which operated in the region of Cundinamarca, where Bogotá itself was located. In mid-2010, Velásquez had also finally been able to make arrangements to interview some of the extradited paramilitaries in the United States, including Salvatore Mancuso, the commander who had been involved in the El Aro massacre, and AUC Northern Block commander Jorge 40 (Rodrigo Tovar Pupo). But, despite the international acclaim Velásquez was getting, his job had grown much harder.

César Julio Valencia, the president of the Supreme Court, against whom President Uribe had pressed criminal defamation charges, and Álvaro Orlando Pérez, Velásquez's initial supervisor on the court, had both retired at the end of their terms, and the composition of the tribunal had gradually been changing. Several justices—some of whom Velásquez thought were close to Uribe or members of Congress— began to criticize Velásquez. Others, he sensed, were jealous of the media attention and praise he was receiving, considering that he was, as Velásquez put it, "merely an assistant." When he informed the jus- tices of the award the International Bar Association was giving him, he recalled later, none of them congratulated him or even asked him what the award was about. It was "as though it hadn't happened. . . . Not one word. That reveals what the situation is like."

Some of the justices and other officials seemed to be throwing road- blocks into Velásquez's path to make it harder for him to conduct the investigations. Velásquez recalled later that one justice, Leonidas Bus- tos, wanted to end the practice of conducting informational interviews in the early stages of an investigation—instead, Velásquez and his team would only be allowed to conduct interviews when they were formally collecting evidence as part of an open case. Velásquez argued that such restrictions would paralyze the investigations, and managed to fend off the initiative. But he was less successful in stopping another effort that he viewed as problematic: the new inspector general of Co- lombia, Alejandro Ordóñez, who was famous for his far-right-wing views, had said that Velásquez should include a representative from his office in all of the informational interviews he was conducting with the paramilitaries in the United States, and threatened to conduct a disciplinary investigation against him if he did not. Velásquez didn't want to do this; he did not believe it was an appropriate request—the informational interviews were not formal, and there was no need for someone from the inspector general's office to be present. Indeed, it was critical that investigators be able to build trust and a rapport with the paramilitaries to find out what they knew, and the presence of someone from the inspector general's office could change the dynamic and undermine that trust, making the paramilitaries less likely to speak. Justice Bustos supported Ordóñez's request, however, and the other justices agreed to the demand.

Velásquez had hoped at one point to be named a justice himself, and the court had considered him as a candidate, but had not selected him. According to Justice María del Rosario González, who had con- tinued to support Velásquez, it was his very success that prevented the other justices from supporting him: "Iván Velásquez has had a heroic role," she said. "He has put his life on the line for the cause of Colombia and for justice, with no recognition. On the contrary: when you mess with the political and economic classes, doors close. . . . Without him, nothing would have been done, and what little has been achieved has required fighting with everybody."

Meanwhile, the politicians who had been convicted by the court were continuing to charge that they had been treated unfairly. One of their main points of contention was that they had no way to appeal the Supreme Court's ruling. Velásquez, who believes in the right to an appeal, was sensitive to this issue, but it was a complicated matter. Though people convicted by ordinary criminal courts had the right to appeal, members of Congress in Colombia could only be investigated and tried by one of the four high courts, and in criminal matters, that was the criminal chamber of the Supreme Court. The arrangement was originally considered to be a privilege. But that meant that no appeal was possible, unless the defendant was claiming that his or her constitutional rights had been violated, which would involve the Constitutional Court. Eventually, the Constitutional Court would require that the code of criminal procedure be changed to establish an opportunity for defendants tried by the criminal chamber of the Supreme Court to appeal their rulings to the entire Supreme Court. That decision did not apply retroactively, however, so the politicians' convictions stood.

More broadly, some of the politicians and commentators sympathetic to them were continuing to sow confusion in the public by making vague claims that there was a "cartel of witnesses" being run by the court (or by Velásquez) to persecute them. A couple of years later, a group of politicians would go all the way to the Inter-American Commission on Human Rights alleging various due process violations. They argued that the "fight" between Uribe and the Supreme Court had politicized the investigations against them, rendering their convictions unfair and invalid. As of this writing, those petitions were apparently still pending.

In 2014, Luis Gustavo Moreno, a young lawyer who had represented several of the politicians accused of links to paramilitaries, would publish a book, El falso testimonio (False Testimony), in which he would make the case that there was a systematic problem with false witnesses in Colombia's criminal justice system. Pundits and commentators seized on the opportunity to argue that there had been a vast conspiracy to go after the "parapoliticians" with false witnesses. Whatever the broader situation in the country, however, Velásquez did not feel that the investigations he had led were tarnished: "Whenever you have evidence based on witnesses, it's easy to make arguments of this type, because it's a fact that witnesses can lie or be persuaded to lie," he said. "Naturally, there can be false witnesses, but not in the way they've presented it. . . . In the court we were always very careful not to use testimony unless we had strong reasons to believe it was credible. There were many witness statements against members of Congress that we never used because there was no way to corroborate them." In 2017, the author of *El falso testimonio*, who had by then become the anticorruption unit director at the Office of the Attorney General, would be arrested by Colombian authorities with the help of the US Drug Enforcement Administration. According to news reports, he allegedly solicited a bribe in Miami from a Colombian politician who was under investigation.

AT THE SAME TIME, more details were coming to light about the various plots against Velásquez and the court.

In October 2010, Ricardo Calderón published a story with additional details about what had happened with Ferney Suaza, the associate of Job's who had publicly claimed that someone was bribing him to accuse the president of crimes. On an audio recording from the day Suaza made his accusation (around the same date that Job had entered the Casa de Nariño with his videos), Job and Suaza could be heard discussing Suaza's statements: "Did you see the news? There's an interview, brother, and everything . . . on Caracol, RCN, Tele-antioquia [TV news stations], everything, brother," said Suaza. Job praised Suaza, and then asked: "When do you meet with Uribe?" President Uribe had announced that he wanted to talk to him directly. Suaza replied, "In the afternoon the high commissioner is coming . . . and later they say they'll do something to get me close to the president." Job then warned Suaza, "Don't tell the commissioner what you and I discussed, just the president, do you hear?" Later in the call, Suaza said he needed to see how he could get his family out of where they were. Job told him to go ahead and "look for a house, and tell me how much it costs." Suaza insisted that he needed to get them out right away, and he didn't know how to handle the cost of the plane tickets and other things, but Job told him not to worry, that he should go ahead and get them out and just tell him later how much it all cost.

Months later, Calderón wrote, Suaza ended up in "the worst of both worlds," as he was unable to back up the serious claims he had made. When he had finally gone before prosecutors, he had not identified any specific individuals as having been behind the supposed attempts to bribe him to testify against the president. According to Calderón, that bothered some administration officials, who had expected him to give a more "explosive" statement. Soon afterward, he lost the security detail the administration had been providing him. With Job now dead, Suaza had nobody to protect or speak for him, and he fled the country. *Semana* learned that Suaza had told other people that he had been part of a "strategy" organized by Job and government officials.

In February 2011, another dramatic scandal erupted when Ramón Ballesteros, an attorney representing some of the members of Congress accused of paramilitary links, was arrested in the middle of a Supreme Court hearing in the case of former senator Luis Alberto Gil. One of the witnesses in the hearing, David Hernández (also known as "Diego Rivera"), was a former paramilitary leader who had provided testimony against the defendant in the case. Hernández had gone to the United States a few years before and was apparently collaborating with the US Drug Enforcement Administration when—as he stated during the hearing—Ballesteros had contacted him to offer him US$100,000 to take back his accusations against Gil and other politicians, and instead claim that Iván Velásquez had improperly pressed him to make false statements. A US official present at the hearing submitted a video reportedly recorded at a restaurant in Dulles Airport, outside Washington, DC, in which Ballesteros appeared to seal the deal with Hernández. In the recording, according to news reports, Ballesteros could be heard saying to Hernández: "You're going to become the parapoliticians' 'star' and I'm going to charge whatever honoraria I want. Get money out of those sons of bitches." Ballesteros eventually pled guilty to bribery charges.

OVER THE COURSE of the following year or so, several DAS officials would also provide testimony about their involvement in surveillance of the court and other questionable activities. These included not only the "Mata Hari of the Supreme Court," Alba Luz Flórez, who confirmed what *Semana* had reported, but also William Romero, Flórez's supervisor, who provided detailed testimony about Flórez's mission, which he claimed started in May 2007. Romero corroborated much of Flórez's testimony about the sources she had developed within the court and around the justices, the pressure to get case files and recordings of the court's discussions, and the substantial sums of money that the DAS had paid their sources in the court. In October 2008, Romero said, a few months before Calderón broke the story, Intelligence Director Fernando Tabares had ordered him and others to get rid of all information they had collected about the court: somebody had "made a mistake," and they "should not leave a trace." Romero described an elaborate operation to disguise or destroy evidence.

Velásquez found a statement to prosecutors by Martha Leal, the deputy director for intelligence at the DAS, working directly under Tabares, to be particularly valuable, as it confirmed to him that he had been right to be raising questions about how the Tasmania letter got to the presidency, and when the letter was even written. Leal had said little to investigators when the scandal first broke. But after some of the agents working under her were arrested and started talking, Calderón later recalled, it became clear that she would have to disclose what she knew. Otherwise, she might end up facing serious charges, and lose the opportunity to get sentencing benefits in exchange for her testimony.

According to Leal, on Saturday, September 29, 2007, the DAS director, María del Pilar Hurtado, informed her that someone in the presidency had told her that Sergio González, Tasmania's lawyer, had some very sensitive information about a situation involving Tasmania and Velásquez. As a result, Hurtado needed Leal to travel to Medellín that very day to pick up a document from González. Leal flew to Medellín and met with González, who told her his version of the Tasmania events and gave her a photocopy of the Tasmania letter to Uribe, with Tasmania's signature and fingerprint on it. But two days later, on October 1, Hurtado sent her back to Medellín, because Mario Uribe had to deliver something to her. Leal said Mario Uribe's driver gave her a sealed envelope at the airport in Medellín. She then boarded the plane back to Bogotá and delivered the envelope to

Hurtado, without knowing the contents. Her boss, Fernando Taba-res, later told prosecutors that the document was the original copy of the Tasmania letter.

President Uribe had first called Velásquez about Tasmania on September 11—the day after Velásquez met with Tasmania, and the same day that the letter was supposedly written. So why was the presidency suddenly sending the DAS to get the letter more than two weeks later? The only intervening event was the September 26 decision to indict Mario Uribe. Velásquez had to wonder: Had the letter in fact only been written after the decision to indict, to allow the government to attack the court in retaliation? Was the president's call to Velásquez a way to lay the groundwork, taking advantage of Velásquez's meeting with Tasmania, and maybe to give the assistant justice an implicit warning not to mess with Mario Uribe? And was sending the DAS to get the letter a way to formalize and create an apparent independence in what had been a very intimate process? The fact that Tasmania's transfer to the much more comfortable Patio 1 of Itagüí prison was only ordered on October 1, after Mario Uribe's indictment, also suggested that the decision to use the Tasmania letter and reward the paramilitary had only been made after the indictment. There were still questions, and they would remain unanswered.

LEAL'S TESTIMONY ALSO pointed to an unusual level of collaboration between the DAS—and even the presidency—and two of the paramilitaries' lawyers, Sergio González and Diego Álvarez.

According to Leal, after she picked up the Tasmania letter, González called her again, but she ignored the calls, thinking they were unimportant. Hurtado confronted her about it soon after, saying the presidency had asked why Leal wasn't taking González's calls. Whenever he called, Hurtado impressed upon her, the deputy should pick up the call, and meet with him if necessary. So began a series of interactions between Leal and González—on several occasions, she had to travel to Medellín to meet with him and "receive messages that he was sending to the Casa de Nariño, and which were sent there through the director of the DAS." Among these messages, she recalled, was one where González asked her to tell Hurtado that he had learned that Francisco Villalba, the paramilitary who had accused President Uribe and his cousin Mario of involvement in El Aro, was receiving psychiatric treatment, which could be used to challenge the admissibility of his testimony in court. She also said that González suggested that Villalba be transferred to Itagüí prison, where the paramilitary leaders were staying, from the prison where he was at the time.

In December 2007, Leal said, Hurtado and Tabares ordered her to visit Diego Álvarez, the lawyer for Don Berna (Diego Murillo Bejarano, former head of the Envigado Office and the Cacique Nutibara Block of the AUC), who needed "technical support" to record Henry Anaya on video. According to Álvarez, Anaya was supposedly trying to extort money from Berna on behalf of the Supreme Court—Leal said she was later surprised to learn that Anaya didn't even work for the court. After the recording was completed, both Hurtado and Tabares were eager to get the video, apparently because the president's office was also following events closely. Leal also recalled having had to purchase a recorder for Don Berna to record his conversations in prison with Rafael García, after Álvarez requested it—though she didn't specify who instructed her to make that purchase.

Tabares, the intelligence director—and Leal's boss—was also a witness. He described a breakfast meeting that he and Hurtado had in early September 2007, when Hurtado had just taken over as DAS director, with Bernardo Moreno, President Uribe's chief of staff, at the upscale Metropolitan Club in Bogotá. At the meeting, Tabares said, Moreno told them that President Uribe was interested in having the DAS keep him informed about four subjects: the Supreme Court, Senator Piedad Córdoba, Senator Gustavo Petro, and journalist Daniel Coronell (who had broken the Yidis Medina story on the scandal involving Uribe's reelection bill, and had previously had to go into exile because of death threats against his family, which Coronell had attributed to a former congressman who was close to Uribe). Hurtado agreed, and, according to Tabares, instructed the various branches of the DAS to carry out work in accordance with Moreno's instructions, though Tabares claimed they did not monitor Coronell.

Both Leal and Tabares talked about being ordered to monitor the activities of the Supreme Court president, César Julio Valencia, and his lawyer, Ramiro Bejarano, after Valencia's falling-out with President Uribe. And both recalled that the DAS made payments to a journalist who—soon after the Yidis Medina scandal—claimed that Medina had links to the ELN guerrillas.

By October 2010, prosecutors were saying they had enough information to indict Hurtado, who had been replaced as DAS director in January 2009, when Felipe Muñoz had been named to the post. But within weeks, she had fled to Panama, which granted her asylum. On June 17, 2011, prosecutors charged Hurtado and Bernardo Moreno, the president's chief of staff, with "organizing, directing and promoting a conspiracy to commit crimes" against justices of the Supreme Court and some members of Congress, "who were categorized and treated as 'political targets,' as well as against one journalist [Daniel Coronell] and one lawyer [Ramiro Bejarano]." Specifically, the goal of the conspiracy, according to prosecutors, was to use the intelligence services to illegally obtain information that could be used to discredit these individuals, and handing this privileged information over to third parties and to the media. Prosecutors also charged Hurtado with ordering intelligence activities with no justification, among other offenses.

Another case that would come to an end soon afterward was the investigation of the slander and insult (known in Spanish as *injuria*) charges that President Uribe had started against Supreme Court president César Julio Valencia. The Accusations Committee closed the case in May 2012, after failing to find any merit to the president's charges. The president had brought in two key witnesses who he said could back him up, Claudia Blum and Carolina Barco, the Colombian ambassadors to the United Nations and the United States, respectively, but they had failed to do so. Blum's statement was full of gaps: she said she had overheard Uribe as he had made several calls that day, but didn't know who they were with; she recalled that he had mentioned Tasmania in one of the calls, but did not recall him mentioning Mario Uribe. Meanwhile, Barco said that she had been near Uribe when he was speaking to Valencia, but that she had arrived after the call had already started, and that out of "respect and good manners, I didn't pay attention to the conversation."

In August 2010, the attorney general's office charged Sergio González, Tasmania's attorney, with slander against Velásquez. The assistant justice had testified in the case, as had Tasmania and Iván Roberto Dugue, repeating the same facts that had been made public when Tasmania first confessed to Velásquez. In January 2012, González would be convicted and sentenced to nearly six years in prison.

But Velásquez was disappointed in the way the investigations had been conducted. González's sentence seemed disproportionately long for the crime for which he was convicted, and that offended Velásquez's notion of justice. Yet the charges against González only scratched the surface of what Velásquez felt he had done. More importantly, prosecutors had shown little interest in pursuing other people who might have been involved in plotting against him—for example, Tasmania had repeated his claims about Mario and Santiago Uribe, but prosecutors had not investigated that angle.

Velásquez and Calderón had similar concerns about the DAS case: yes, some important testimony had been brought to light, and there had been a number of convictions, but the early prosecutors handling the DAS investigation had paid little attention to the surveillance of the court. By the time new prosecutors took over, the government was starting to take the DAS apart, making it difficult to track down witnesses.

VELÁSQUEZ'S DIFFICULTIES with the Supreme Court finally came to a head in August 2012, when the criminal chamber asked him to give up his role as coordinator of the parapolitics investigations. The members of the chamber offered little explanation beyond stating that the coordinator role should rotate among various assistant justices. In the following days, the journalist Cecilia Orozco published an op-ed in El Espectador titled "Homage to a Brave and Decent Judge." She praised Velásquez, who, she wrote, "in his infinite solitude has borne the greatest threats and conspiracies against his life, good name, and honor." She criticized the majority of the members of the court, calling them corrupt bureaucrats who were primarily concerned with paying back other officials for getting them their jobs. That same day, Velásquez recalled, some of the justices called him to complain about the op-ed. They told him he was a loose cannon, that he didn't follow instructions, that he should have publicly made clear that he was not the "star justice" of parapolitics, and that it was unacceptable for him to be receiving international awards. They asked him to go to the media and publicly correct Orozco. The only one who didn't attack him, Velásquez recalled, was María del Rosario González. Velásquez did not do as they asked, and a few days later, after more pressure from the court, he tendered his resignation.

STILL, THE PANDORA'S BOX that Velásquez and Calderón had opened could no longer be shut. After years of near-total silence, some of the paramilitary leaders extradited to the United States completed their plea negotiations with US prosecutors or started serving out their sentences for drug trafficking. The United States had shown little obvious interest in pursuing the paramilitaries' allegations against their accomplices in the political system—though at least one source indicates that US prosecutors did attempt to do so—and none of the paramilitaries faced charges in the United States related to their human rights abuses. But some of the paramilitaries were beginning to talk more openly about their crimes, associates, and relationships with politicians. Their statements would slowly allow Velásquez to piece together a clearer picture of what lay behind the attacks against him in recent years—and even the murders of his friends and colleagues years before.

Juan Carlos "El Tuso" Sierra, Tasmania's protector in Itagüí, denied Tasmania's claims about how he (El Tuso) and the lawyer Sergio González had manufactured the letter that Tasmania sent to the president—he said the letter was genuine and reflected what Tasmania told him about his meeting with Velásquez and his colleague. However, El Tuso went on to say that the government gave the paramilitaries a number of benefits in exchange for their cooperation on the letter: they took Macaco (Carlos Mario Jiménez), from the AUC's Central Bolívar Block, off the ship where he was being held, moved Don Berna from the maximum-security prison in Cómbita to La Picota, and moved Tasmania to Patio 1 of Itagüí prison, where he could be with the paramilitary leaders. El Tuso went on to say that he and other paramilitary leaders had participated in plots with the government to smear Yidis Medina, the former congresswoman who claimed that Uribe administration officials had bought her vote for the amendment allowing for Uribe's reelection—in the smear campaign, they had tried to link her to the ELN. He also admitted that they had recorded Velásquez, in the hope of catching him doing something wrong. And he said that the government, at the peak of its confrontation with the Supreme Court, was desperately asking the paramilitaries for help in trying to discredit the court. The paramilitaries, he said, had helped to fabricate a letter from Francisco Villalba which had him withdrawing his claim that President Uribe and his brother Mario were involved in the El Aro massacre.

A 2015 court ruling noted that El Tuso also turned over a list, which has not yet been made public, of people who supposedly worked with the Envigado Office, including Mario Uribe and several other members of Congress and the military as well as businesspeople.

Setting aside El Tuso's claim that he hadn't pressed Tasmania to manufacture the letter, which Velásquez assumed was a lie because El Tuso didn't want to incriminate himself, Velásquez thought many of his statements were credible—they were consistent with other evidence Velásquez had seen. In 2014, El Tuso would be released from prison in the United States, after serving less than six years for drug trafficking; even though he was facing multiple serious charges in Colombia, he was never deported back to the country, apparently having successfully argued that he faced a risk of torture if he returned.

As early as November 2008, after his extradition to the United States, Mancuso had also begun to talk. He gave more details about the paramilitaries' entry into Ituango in 1996 and 1997, which he and Carlos Castaño had arranged in close collaboration with members of the military. In fact, Mancuso said, he met with Alfonso Manosalva, the head of the Fourth Brigade of the army, at least ten times to get information and coordinate the paramilitary incursion in the region. Mancuso said the paramilitaries had help from other parts of the government as well: they had coordinated directly with Pedro Juan Moreno, then chief of staff to Álvaro Uribe, who was governor of Antioquia at the time, to establish the "Convivirs" that the paramilitaries were using as cover for their activities. Mancuso said that at a meeting at a ranch in Córdoba, Carlos Castaño himself, in front of Mancuso, had given Moreno detailed information about their plans to go into El Aro, supposedly to reduce the guerrilla presence in the region and rescue some hostages the FARC was holding. For the massacre, Mancuso said, the paramilitaries had coordinated directly with army troops in the nearest town, Puerto Valdivia. "The army in the area knew everything that was happening, [and] the police knew everything that was happening," he said. Mancuso also provided more details about the helicopters he had mentioned before: There were four helicopters flying over the massacre site, he said. One belonged to the guerrillas, who used it to evacuate their leadership. Another belonged to the paramilitaries, and Mancuso flew in that one, taking in ammunition, removing bodies, and taking in wounded paramilitaries. The third, he said, was yellow and orange, and belonged to the Antioquia governor's office; he said he watched it fly over as the paramilitaries were conducting the operation. The fourth belonged to the army and flew over the site as the paramilitaries were leaving the town.

In 2012, Mancuso publicly stated that the paramilitaries had actively campaigned for Uribe's reelection in 2006. That same year, Mancuso stated before a Justice and Peace Tribunal that he had contributed financial support to Uribe's 2002 campaign. He also said that, at his request, the members of Congress Eleonora Pineda and Miguel de la Espriella (who were later convicted in the parapolitics cases) had met with Uribe at his ranch, El Ubérrimo, to tell him that the paramilitaries had contributed large sums of money to his campaign, and that if he won, the paramilitaries wanted to start peace negotiations. Pineda and De la Espriella backed Mancuso up in court.

Mancuso also stated that he had maintained a close working relationship since 1995 with Pedro Juan Moreno, and that this relationship continued until Moreno's death in a helicopter crash in 2006. He claimed that he had met with Álvaro Uribe himself when Uribe was governor of Antioquia, and that during the presidential campaign, he had continued to be in touch with the candidate through Moreno (in addition to Pineda and De la Espriella). At one point during the campaign, he said, Moreno had told him he was concerned about the damage that the paramilitaries' ongoing massacres might do to Uribe's image, and urged them to instead focus on more targeted operations. As a result, the paramilitaries agreed to hold off on massacres in the lead-up to the election.

In other statements, Mancuso said he had actually met Uribe in social settings before Mancuso joined the paramilitaries. But he said that he had formally met with Uribe once when Uribe was governor of Antioquia. Mancuso was already a paramilitary—"and the governor knew that as such." He said they met at Uribe's ranch, El Ubérrimo, in Córdoba, and that a police officer from Córdoba had introduced Mancuso as the man who was "helping" them with security in the state. Mancuso recalled that Uribe had said he was happy that Mancuso was helping them, and that they spoke specifically about an attack that the FARC was supposedly planning against Uribe and his ranch, and their efforts to figure out who exactly was involved in the plot.

Mancuso's statements didn't get as much public attention as they might have, in part because Calderón had already reported similar allegations in the past. In an interview with Fabio Ochoa Vasco, a major drug trafficker, that Calderón published in 2007, Ochoa claimed that he had witnessed Mancuso contributing substantial sums of money to Uribe's presidential campaign, as well as Mancuso organizing the paramilitaries to get out the vote for him, because he had been promised a favorable peace deal.

Uribe responded by issuing a statement strongly denying the claims of both the paramilitary leader and the former members of Congress, adding that he had contacted the US ambassador to Colombia because he had heard that Mancuso was improperly applying pressure on the former members of Congress to get them to make statements against him. He also announced, via Twitter, that he was planning to press criminal charges against them for making false statements. Eventually, Uribe sued Mancuso for slander and insult (*injuria*) and asked that he be removed from the Justice and Peace process for supposedly lying about him. Uribe's lawyer, Jaime Granados, told the media that Mancuso was making the statements out of a desire for revenge, because Uribe had arrested and extradited him.

DON BERNA, WHO in 2009 was convicted of drug trafficking and sentenced to thirty-one years in prison in Miami, also began talking in later years. He confirmed much of *Semana*'s reporting about his efforts with Job to smear the Supreme Court, as well as what he described as regular meetings between Job and representatives of the presidency and the intelligence service.

Berna also made disturbing new statements about the witness Francisco Villalba and the El Aro massacre. A little over a year after he first made his statements against Uribe, Villalba had suddenly received permission from a judge to serve his sentence under house arrest, supposedly on account of health concerns. In April 2009, twenty-three days after his release, as he was walking down the street with his wife and four-year-old daughter, three men came up to him and shot him to death.

According to Don Berna, Sergio González (the lawyer who represented Tasmania and El Tuso, and who was reportedly close to Mario Uribe) had approached him to see what could be done to keep Villalba from talking about El Aro. Berna said he later learned from a prosecutor that "the boss"—whom the prosecutor identified as President Uribe—was very concerned about Villalba's statements. So, Don Berna said, he met with Villalba in prison and tried to bribe him to stop talking. According to Berna, Villalba refused, because for him, talking about it was a form of "catharsis." So instead, Don Berna paid another paramilitary who had participated in the massacre, a man known as "Pilatos," to sign a statement disputing Villalba's claims. Berna said that he "had no doubt" that Villalba's murder was a "crime of state." He said that "powerful sectors of the country were involved in the death of Villalba because he was uncomfortable because of his knowledge of the El Aro massacre, because he was constantly talking about it, because he was insistent in continuing to implicate certain people of the establishment."

Prosecutors later ordered new investigations into Uribe's alleged role in the massacre and in Villalba's murder, but Uribe has strenuously denied any role in either, pointing to the many inconsistencies in Villalba's statements over time—such as his claim that General Manosalva was present at a meeting shortly before the massacre, even though Manosalva had been dead for months. In a letter to the newspaper *El Espectador* complaining about its coverage of the story, Uribe also noted that Mancuso at one point called Villalba a liar and said Uribe had nothing to do with El Aro. The ex-president emphasized that the national chief of police, General Óscar Naranjo, attributed Villalba's death to a dispute between criminals. Uribe also asserted that the prosecutor mentioned by Don Berna had contradicted the paramilitary leader and later sued him for defamation.

But to many investigators and victims of paramilitary crimes, several of Don Berna's revelations about their past seemed credible, and even confirmed their long-held suspicions. He spoke about the paramilitaries' involvement in a series of major assassinations that happened in the 1990s, for example, in some cases linking government officials to the crimes. These included the 1999 murder of beloved thirty-eight-year-old comedian Jaime Garzón, who had been involved in negotiations for the release of FARC hostages when he was gunned down by paramilitaries in his car in Bogotá. They also included the dramatic May 1997 killing of a married couple, Elsa Alvarado and Mario Calderón, who were investigators for the Center for Research and

Popular Education (Centro de Investigación y Educación Popular, or CINEP), a Jesuit foundation working for social change: in that case, the couple opened the door to their Bogotá apartment in the middle of the night to find armed men identifying themselves as CTI members. The men barged in and shot the couple, as well as Alvarado's father, Carlos, to death. Their baby, Iván, survived because he was hidden in a wardrobe.

Don Berna also shed light on the killings of the CTI investigators who had worked with Velásquez in Medellín in the late 1990s, explaining that, at the time, Castaño had viewed the investigators in the attorney general's office as enemies, because they were investigating the paramilitaries. Through Uber Duque, a member of the CTI whom the paramilitaries had put on their payroll, they were able to obtain detailed information about the investigations as well as the names and addresses of key investigators to target. Don Berna specifically highlighted the Padilla parking-lot investigation as the reason for some of the murders, explaining that the accounting information that Velásquez's team had found in the parking-lot shack was about "the sponsors of the self-defense forces," and that "it was very important." As a result, he said, Castaño had ordered the killings of the investigators who had participated in the Padilla search. The purpose of those killings was "to intimidate them and ensure that they would not continue with those investigations and end up identifying the people who worked with the AUC, since there were many businessmen, [and] ranchers."

Berna's statements about the Padilla parking-lot investigation were consistent with what other paramilitaries in prison would later say. One, Rodrigo Zapata, who had once been Vicente Castaño's right-hand man, stated in an interview for this book that the prosecutors' discovery of the paramilitaries' accounting records and the arrest of Jacinto Alberto Soto (aka "Lucas"), the accountant, in the parking-lot shack "hit the spot where all the investments of the groups in the area, all the financial backers, were. Everything was centralized. . . . Everything was left without a head, because Lucas kept all the accounts."

In another interview for this book, Raúl Hasbún, a wealthy banana businessman who had eventually run a paramilitary group in the Urabá region of Antioquia and Chocó, agreed about Lucas's importance as the accountant for Carlos and Vicente Castaño. He said the paramilitaries were surprised when the Padilla investigation did not end up having more of an impact on them or their supporters.

Éver Veloza, a paramilitary commander known as "HH" who was extradited to the United States in 2009, also talked about Lucas, confirming that he had been a key figure. Lucas had received all the contributions to the paramilitaries from banana growers and other businesspeople and had played a major role in managing the paramilitaries' relationships with military figures and politicians. HH recalled waiting for Lucas in a car while Lucas had meetings with commanders in the Fourth Brigade at the army's headquarters in Medellín. He said that Lucas had six separate beepers to manage his contacts with different officials, and that "he even had one for the governor, who in those days was Uribe." HH recalled accompanying Lucas to several meetings, including one with Pedro Juan Moreno, then Governor Uribe's chief of staff in Antioquia. After his escape from prison, Lucas participated in the demobilization process, but he had not been forced to go through the Justice and Peace process because there were no serious charges pending against him—he was now free. Given that Lucas had a wealth of information about the paramilitaries' accomplices, HH found it surprising that prosecutors weren't going after him to find out what he knew. It was easy for Uribe and others in power to argue that HH and other former paramilitaries were simply making up these statements out of a desire for revenge over their imprisonment or extradition. But as HH saw it, "it turns out we were extradited precisely to discredit our truths, the knowledge we have of the war. We were extradited to protect the interests of many people."

Hasbún, the former banana businessman who ran a paramilitary group, also claimed in an interview for this book that he had maintained a close relationship in the late 1990s with the governorship of Antioquia. At the time, Hasbún said, he personally set up fourteen Convivirs—the security cooperatives that then governor Uribe was promoting in the region. But, Hasbún made clear, "the Convivirs were the AUC—at least mine were, and I assume that Mancuso's and others were, too. It was a way to legalize the contributions of ranchers, businessmen, etc. to the AUC." At the beginning, he said, officials in the governor's office may not have had reason to know that the Convivir members belonged to the AUC. "But afterward, they did." According to Hasbún, Pedro Juan Moreno, would go to Hasbún's house, "where there was a guard standing outside holding an AK-47. We would meet with Lucas and speak openly about issues related to the AUC, to financing. He was happy about it. . . . Moreno never financed us directly, but through the Fourth Brigade he gave us weaponry, munitions for the self-defense forces—it was clear it was not for the Convivirs."

TO VELÁSQUEZ, much of what Don Berna said confirmed what he had already suspected for years. If in his early days as a lawyer and prosecutor Velásquez had been naive about the criminal networks operating around him, his experiences in Medellín and then Bogotá had cured him of that. Nevertheless, having one of the killers make these statements before prosecutors and judges vindicated his pursuit of justice through law. And in May 2012, Don Berna offered new evidence in the case that had, in a way, started Velásquez down this frustrating, endless search for the truth: the murder of Jesús María Valle.

In the intervening years, the Inter-American Court of Human Rights had found the state of Colombia liable for the death of Valle and its failure to adequately investigate his murder, and it recommended that the government conduct an exhaustive investigation in the case. In response, in 2011, the Supreme Court annulled the ruling acquitting the brothers Jaime Alberto and Francisco Antonio Angulo, the landowners whom Velásquez's team in Medellín had originally charged in connection with the killing. That cleared the way for prosecutors to reopen that investigation, though there were no public reports on the status of the case. It also remained unclear whether anyone within government had played a role in Valle's death. Don Berna's statements offered new evidence on that front.

According to Berna, AUC leader Carlos Castaño had ordered the Medellín-based gang "La Terraza," which answered to the paramilitaries and was run by a man known as "Elkin," to carry out the killing of Valle because Castaño believed that the human rights defender was helping the FARC. Berna said that he was part of the conversations about this, and that he was the person who had summoned Elkin to talk to Castaño about the planned murder. Elkin then sent a woman who worked for La Terraza to Valle's office to pose as a prospective client and collect intelligence on him. Based on that information, she and two other La Terraza members eventually went to his office and executed him.

But Berna also made another point: "I want to add that this action was a request by Dr. Pedro Juan Moreno, because he [Valle] was conducting an investigation of the events in El Aro." Specifically, he said, in early 1998 Pedro Juan Moreno had gone to a ranch where Carlos Castaño often met with officials, and told Castaño that Valle was conducting "an investigation" that was affecting members of the military and the government. "Carlos believed that whoever made that kind of accusation against the military was collaborating with the guerrillas." And so he agreed to have Valle assassinated. According to Berna, Castaño gave the assassination orders to Elkin, explaining that Valle was "uncomfortable" for members of the state because of his accusations over cases like the El Aro massacre.

AT THE PODIUM in Dubai, back in November 2011, Velásquez read a passage from Colombian novelist Gabriel García Márquez's *One Hundred Years of Solitude*. It described character José Arcadio Segundo's efforts to tell his disbelieving neighbors about a massacre that he had just witnessed, in which thousands were killed. Velásquez paused. He had known many José Arcadio Segundos in Colombia, he said, but he wanted to mention one of them: Jesús María Valle, who told the truth, and who paid for it with his life. "We didn't believe in José Arcadio Segundo," Velásquez went on: "We never believed him. Perhaps because the blood that was spilled by the assassins in the night was cleaned in the morning and the bodies thrown into the river." In giving him this award, Velásquez said, the International Bar Association was recognizing all the José Arcadio Segundos who were fighting for the truth, those who "even today, choke on the question—'why?'— stuck in their throats."

PEACE?

COLOMBIAN PRESIDENT JUAN MANUEL SANTOS walked with a small girl up to a giant door on an immaculate white stage, pulled out a large key, and opened it. Heads of state from around the region walked in, including the presidents of Venezuela, Ecuador, Peru, Chile, Mexico, and Argentina, as well as King Juan Carlos of Spain; the US secretary of state, John Kerry; and the UN secretary-general, Ban Ki-moon. A team of government peace negotiators, and then representatives of the FARC guerrillas, followed. All the people on stage, as well as the approximately 2,500 members of the audience, were clad in white. White flags joined the leaves of tall palm trees, waving in the breeze, and the late-afternoon sunlight glinted off the waters of the Caribbean Sea that were lapping the concrete edges of the convention center. It was September 26, 2016, and they were in the balmy, brightly colored, ancient port city of Cartagena. The audience and the dignitaries on stage had come to witness what they believed would be the end of the longest-running war in the Western Hemisphere.

For the past four years, the Santos government and the FARC, now under the leadership of the heavily bearded, round-faced Rodrigo Londoño Echeverri (aka "Timochenko"), had been engaged in peace talks in Havana, Cuba, and they had recently finished a final draft of a 297-page peace agreement.

On the stage in Cartagena, after performances of the national anthem and of a song commemorating the event, Timochenko walked up to a table, tripping once on the way, and, grabbing a pen made from recycled bullet pieces, signed the peace agreement on behalf of the FARC. He was then joined by Santos, who, after signing on behalf of the government, took a pin off his lapel—a white dove of peace that he had been wearing for years—and handed it to Timochenko, who affixed it to his own lapel. They then clasped each other's shoulders and shook hands.

Later on, they each gave speeches about their hope that the agreement would set the country on a path toward reconciliation. Near the end of Timochenko's speech, he added, to enormous cheers from the audience: "In the name of the FARC-EP, I offer sincerely our desire for forgiveness from all the victims of the conflict, for all the pain we may have caused in this war." Santos, for his part, stressed that "what we are signing today is a declaration of the Colombian people before the world that we are tired of war, that we do NOT accept violence as the means to defend ideas, that we are saying—strongly and clearly: No more war! No more war!"

By that time, Colombia's Center for Historical Memory had reported that more than 220,000 people had died in Colombia's fifty-two-year war with the FARC and other guerrillas, though some estimates were much higher. Millions had been forcibly displaced from their homes by war. Hundreds of thousands had been forcibly "disappeared." Countless more had had their lives ruined by kidnappings, extortion, torture, the loss of their limbs from antipersonnel landmines, the loss of their land, livestock, and livelihoods, and the loss of their loved ones. Could it finally be over? Millions hoped so.

Six days later, on October 2, their hopes were dashed when, surprisingly, around 6 million Colombians voted "No" in a national referendum on the peace agreement, just barely defeating the "Yes" vote and throwing the peace process into disarray. The overwhelming majority of voters—around two-thirds—didn't vote at all.

What had happened? In the days leading up to the plebiscite, polls suggested that the "Yes" vote would easily win. There were endless analyses in the aftermath: a hurricane on the Caribbean coast had dampened voter turnout in one of the strong "Yes" regions. Perhaps the Santos government had grown overconfident, had relied too much on campaigning for the "Yes" vote through major media, and had not done enough to campaign on the ground, talking to people. The "No" campaign, led primarily by the former president, Álvaro Uribe, had ably convinced evangelical Christians that language in the agreement about the rights of women and lesbian, gay, bisexual, and transgender people was bad for "families." Maybe the "Yes" campaign had underestimated the hatred that many Colombians felt toward the FARC, and their discomfort with parts of the agreement, including some of the concerns that Uribe was raising—in particular, that FARC leaders would serve no prison time, and that they were guaranteed to get some seats in Congress.

TO IVÁN VELÁSQUEZ, the outcome was a grave disappointment. He had felt conflicted about the agreement with the FARC; initially, in fact, he had been very critical of it, because essentially it gave the FARC a pass for its worst crimes—the massacres, the murders, the rapes, the massive use of children as soldiers. When Uribe had proposed a similar pass for the paramilitaries, Velásquez had opposed it, and he acknowledged that, in a way, it was "incoherent" for him to oppose such a deal for the paramilitaries and then accept one for the FARC, just as it was incoherent for Uribe to support a deal for the paramilitaries and oppose one for the FARC. After all, Velásquez believed in justice, including some form of punishment for serious crimes, and he thought it was deeply problematic to simply give that up in the name of peace. Plus, the peace agreement contained some provisions that were absolutely unjustifiable; they would let members of the Colombian military responsible for murders—the thousands of "false-positive" cases under investigation, in which members of the military killed civilians and then claimed them as guerrillas killed in combat—off the hook for their crimes.

But ultimately, Velásquez had supported the FARC agreement. Unlike Uribe's initial proposal for the demobilization of the paramilitaries, he reasoned, the FARC deal included mechanisms, such as a Truth Commission, that he felt could, if effectively implemented, finally contribute to uncovering many truths. "As a victim, I've come to the belief that truth has to come ahead of justice. As a victim of the DAS, it would have been more important for me to know who ordered [the persecution] than to have a captain sentenced to eight years in prison," he said. Plus, Velásquez felt that this agreement could actually lead to an end to the war—and, even more important, to an end to the war serving "as an excuse for the lack of social progress." If Colombia's government no longer had a war to justify pouring all its resources into the military, perhaps now it could finally address the country's millions of other injustices—the devastating poverty of many regions, the lack of education and health care, the hunger and social marginalization of so many of its people. The war had also served as an excuse for the harsh repression of all sorts of people—trade unionists, activists, community leaders—who had opposed the powerful in the country. If a peace agreement took away that excuse, then perhaps the country could finally put the persecution of dissidents behind it. Of course, there was no guarantee that the agreement would lead to any of these outcomes; but, in the end, perhaps, more than anything else, Velásquez's support of the agreement had more to do with his innate idealism.

RICARDO CALDERÓN saw things differently: "Obviously, the end of the war: everyone supports that," he said, "but not like this." In his view, the government had made many more concessions than it needed to; it was in too much of a rush to complete the agreement before the next presidential elections took place. The deal was going to lead to a "false peace," he said. Much as the paramilitary negotiations had left behind scores of "new" groups led by former midlevel paramilitaries, who were still threatening people, killing their foes, and running their drug businesses, he thought it was likely that many FARC members would return to criminal activity. "There's a lot that sounds good on paper, but I don't see how they'll implement it, or with what resources." The government had no way of ensuring sufficient resources to fulfill all the promises it had made to those who demobilized. Particularly in coca-producing areas, it was hard to imagine what incentives the government could possibly put in place that would keep demobilized guerrillas from returning to their profitable illicit activities. And the lack of prison terms for the worst crimes, he believed, almost guaranteed that there would be new outbursts of violence.

Calderón was also disturbed by the agreement's provisions allowing the military to evade justice for its atrocities. What would members of the military who had been under prosecution do once they got released? Their careers were over, so Calderón thought the likeliest scenario was that these men would simply join criminal groups.

THE FAILURE OF the peace deal was an enormous victory for former president Álvaro Uribe. Since leaving the presidency, the image of the former head of state had lost some of its luster. After backing Juan Manuel Santos's candidacy for the presidency in 2010, Uribe had quickly turned against the new president once Santos had started peace talks with the FARC. In the 2014 presidential elections, Uribe had backed another candidate, Óscar Iván Zuluaga, who was running against Santos, but Zuluaga had lost. Uribe himself had won a Senate seat in 2014, and from that perch, he had been vociferously criticizing the Santos government—but his stridency hadn't seemed to match the public's mood.

Uribe's image had also been tarnished by numerous scandals. His former chief of security, Mauricio Santoyo—with whom he had worked since the 1990s, when Santoyo was in the Medellín police force and Uribe was Antioquia's governor—pled guilty in the United States to providing material support for terrorism for having collaborated with paramilitary groups from 2001 to 2008. He was sentenced to thirteen years in prison. Moreover, the attorney general's office had charged Uribe's younger brother, Santiago, with homicide and conspiracy, partly on the basis of the testimony of a former police officer, Juan Carlos Meneses, who had testified that the younger Uribe had been one of the leaders of the paramilitary group known as the "Twelve Apostles," which was said to have committed numerous killings in the mid-1990s in Yarumal, Antioquia, where Santiago had a ranch known as "La Carolina." The Supreme Court had convicted Uribe's former minister of agriculture, Andrés Felipe Arias, on corruption charges. Former DAS chief María del Pilar Hurtado, who had sought asylum in Panama, was extradited back to Colombia in 2015; she was sentenced to fourteen years in prison in connection with offenses committed while she ran the DAS. Uribe's former chief of staff, Bernardo Moreno, was also convicted in connection with the DAS scandal; his sentence was eight years of house arrest. In its decision convicting Moreno and Hurtado, the Supreme Court formally communicated to the Accusations Committee of the Colombian Congress a request by the victims that Uribe be investigated in connection with the DAS scandal. Jorge Noguera, Uribe's first DAS chief, had already been convicted in 2011 and sentenced to twenty-five years in prison; José Miguel Narváez, who worked in the DAS under Noguera, would also be convicted in 2016 for his involvement in wiretapping. The Supreme Court also convicted the former president's cousin, Senator Mario Uribe, in 2011 for conspiring with the paramilitaries. In total, more than sixty members of Congress or candidates—nearly all of them from Uribe's coalition—had been convicted in connection with the Supreme Court's parapolitics investigations, and many other officials had been convicted in cases brought by the attorney general's office. On June 22, 2017, the Colombian attorney general's office announced that it had charged former presidential legal counsel Edmundo del Castillo; César Mauricio Velásquez, the former press secretary; and the lawyers Sergio González and Diego Álvarez with conspiracy. The charges were based on their alleged involvement in a plot to smear the Supreme Court, and particularly Iván Velásquez, in retaliation for the parapolitics investigations.

Former president Uribe himself was facing the possibility of new investigations, in addition to the one involving the DAS. These included an investigation into the death of his former right-hand man in Antioquia, Pedro Juan Moreno, in a 2006 helicopter crash. Moreno and Uribe had grown distant in the years before Moreno's death: according to one of Uribe's advisers, Moreno had expected Uribe to establish and allow him to control a new agency overseeing all of the government's intelligence services, and had felt betrayed when Uribe did not do so. During his presidential campaign, Uribe had also become closer to other advisers, such as the wealthy entrepreneur Fabio Echeverri, who disliked Moreno. Perhaps as a result, after Uribe's presidential election, Moreno had become harshly critical of people near the president, routinely lambasting Uribe's team through his magazine, La Otra Verdad (The Other Truth), and writing stories or bits of gossip that seemed designed to undermine the administration. When Moreno died, the official results of the investigation said there had been a technical malfunction in the helicopter, and that no evidence of foul play had been found. But rumors had swirled about Moreno's death ever since.

In 2010, General Rito Alejo del Río—whom Uribe had honored during a ceremony in 1999, after the Pastrana administration had cashiered the officer—stated to prosecutors that the helicopter crash that had led to Moreno's death had been no accident. Moreno, Del Río claimed, had been murdered (Del Río was later convicted of homicide in an unrelated matter, and as of this writing he remained under investigation for a paramilitary massacre in Mapiripán, Meta, in 1997). In February 2016, after a former paramilitary known as "Don Mario" claimed that Uribe had been involved in Moreno's death, the attorney general's office asked the Supreme Court and the Accusations Committee of the Colombian Congress to investigate.

In response to written questions for this book, Don Berna also stated that Pedro Juan Moreno had died as a result of "sabotage" to the helicopter he was riding in—"an action that was carried out on Uribe's orders." However, he offered no way to verify his claim or evidence to back it up. When pressed on the basis for his statement, Don Berna only said that "in the world of illegality, one knows many things, but because they are illegal they cannot be proven. It's like when a policeman ask[s] you for a bribe, he will never give you a receipt."

Uribe has forcefully denied these allegations. He stated that Moreno had never given any signs of closeness to paramilitary groups. "With the cowardice of criminals," Uribe said, people had started to accuse

Moreno of links to paramilitaries after his death, but not when he was alive. In a 2016 radio interview, Uribe expressed pain at the possibility that the new investigation might make Moreno's family wonder whether he was involved in his former chief of staff's death. He challenged the credibility of Don Mario, noting that during his administration he continually pressed for the former paramilitary's arrest until it was achieved. He didn't respond to written questions for this book about Don Berna's statements, though he has repeatedly questioned the credibility of the extradited paramilitary leaders.

In a February 2015 ruling by the Justice and Peace Tribunal of Medellín, the court instructed the attorney general's office to investigate Uribe in connection with the reports that a helicopter from the Antioquia governor's office had been seen flying overhead as the El Aro massacre happened.

And in a September 2015 ruling signed by a different judge from the same tribunal, the court ordered that Uribe be investigated for promoting, supporting, or conspiring with paramilitary groups and the Convivirs linked to them, either as governor or as president. The court mentioned the many examples of people around Uribe who had links to the paramilitaries, as well as situations and cases involving the paramilitaries or public officials—such as the El Aro massacre—that occurred when he was governor of Antioquia. "It can't be the case that he did not know everything that was happening in these cases, or that all of these actions were committed behind his back," said the court, noting that "it's not a matter of testimony. It's about logic and reasons. As the director of the newspaper El Espectador Fidel Cano Correa once said, it's not possible to be in a swimming pool and not get wet."

Uribe argued that many of these issues—such as the presence of a helicopter from the governor's office during the El Aro massacre—had been thoroughly investigated before. And he continued to insist that the charges were part of a political vendetta against him and his allies, now led by the pro-Santos camp, and that the paramilitaries' statements against him were in retaliation for their extradition.

While there have been many allegations against former president Uribe, and in some cases these may result in investigations, as of this writing he had not been indicted in connection with any offense, and he may never be. Uribe remained a very high-profile and influential politician and a polarizing figure who sparked intense feelings, both positive and negative. Many people close to him have been convicted of serious crimes, but it is up to Colombia's institutions of justice to determine what, if any, knowledge or role he may have had in them. So far, there have been no public reports about the Accusations Committee of the Colombian Congress or the attorney general's office moving forward on any of these investigations.

WITH THE VOTE against the peace deal in 2016, Uribe was once again in the thick of things, claiming to represent the opposition. Many of his critics were concerned that, now that his hand was strengthened, he would make any renegotiation of the peace deal impossible—or, at best, that he would do irreparable damage to some of the positive elements of the agreement, such as the provisions allowing for some measure of land reform. With new presidential elections only eighteen months away, Uribe might have another chance to put one of his close allies in office.

On November 24, 2016, President Santos—who was awarded the Nobel Peace Prize a few days after the plebiscite—and Timochenko signed a new peace deal, again using a pen made out of bullets, though this time, there was less fanfare. Santos claimed that they had made adjustments to the agreement that addressed the concerns of its critics: the new deal didn't allow foreigners to participate in special peace tribunals, limited the period during which investigations could be conducted, and required FARC members to disclose all the information they had about drug trafficking and reveal all their assets. However, as expected, Uribe dismissed the changes as cosmetic and demanded that the government hold another plebiscite. Santos refused, instead taking the deal directly to the Colombian Congress, which approved it on November 30. The Colombian Constitutional Court later ruled that Congress had been authorized to approve the deal; as a result, there was no longer any need to submit it to a plebiscite.

DESPITE THEIR DIFFERING positions on the original peace agreement, both Ricardo Calderón and Iván Velásquez agreed that the failure of the plebiscite had created a much more precarious situation than had previously existed in the country. Former president Uribe and his allies would continue to claim that the final version lacked legitimacy because the public had not approved it. The true outcome of the process would probably not be known for years: Would the FARC truly demobilize? If they followed through, would other groups and individuals fill their shoes? Would Colombia's war ever end?

Both men were also appalled by an adjustment to the deal that Santos made after the FARC signed off on it, apparently under pressure from the Colombian military. That change distorted the international concept of "command responsibility" as it applied to the military, meaning that in thousands of pending criminal cases involving military killings of civilians, troops might be held accountable, but their commanders could be completely off the hook.

In the first few weeks after the deal was finalized, the FARC announced that five of its commanders in the state of Guaviare had gone into "dissident" status: they were still at war. There was also a spike in reported killings of activists and community leaders, which appeared to be tied to their promotion of the peace process. Dozens were killed in 2016, and many local organizations were blaming groups calling themselves paramilitaries that were increasingly turning up in small towns.

It was not a surprise. As both Velásquez and Calderón knew from experience, whenever things looked like they might be improving, their country had a way of smacking people back into reality. But whatever the outcome of this particular negotiation, neither Velásquez nor Calderón had given up on the hope that through their work they could make a difference for others.

Since 2013, Velásquez had been serving as the new head of the United Nations Commission Against Impunity in Guatemala, where he had been leading groundbreaking investigations into organized crime linked to that Central American country's security forces and political establishment. In September 2015, one of his joint investigations with a special prosecutor's office into high-level corruption in the country's customs office contributed to massive nationwide protests, which ultimately led to the resignation and then jailing of the president of Guatemala at the time, Otto Pérez Molina. Pérez Molina's vice-president and dozens of other officials were also prosecuted and jailed. In the aftermath of Pérez Molina's downfall, Velásquez continued his investigations, although—as in Colombia—he was facing constant efforts by the targets of his investigations to smear, discredit, and remove him.

In August 2017, Guatemala's new president, Jimmy Morales, declared Velásquez *persona non grata* and ordered him to leave the

Iván Velásquez at his office in Bogotá in late August 2013.
© Rainer Huhle.

country after Velásquez's office and Guatemala's attorney general's office sought to have Morales's immunity lifted so they could investigate him for alleged campaign finance law violations. As of this writing, the country's Constitutional Court had invalidated Morales's decision, allowing Velásquez to remain in the country.

Life in Guatemala was difficult for Velásquez. He slept in the same dark bunker where he worked, 24/7, and he could not step outside of his offices without a heavy armed guard. He had to live far from his family, as María Victoria couldn't leave her job in Colombia, so he was lonely—though he made a point of flying back to Bogotá every few weeks and talking with his wife and children as often as he could. María Victoria hated the fact that he was away so much, but she knew that most doors in Colombia were closed to him, and she understood his need to continue doing work that was meaningful to him.

And so far, Velásquez felt that his work in Guatemala was producing results. He wanted to see how far he could take the investigations.

After that, he hoped to make it back to Colombia. He had many enemies waiting for him there, but that was, after all, home.

Calderón was still doing investigative work at *Semana* and continuing to uncover big scandals. He had done a series of stories about corruption in the military prison of Tolemaida, which he had labeled the
"Tolemaida Resort." He had found that many of the 269 members of
the military in prison there, who had been convicted of terrible crimes,
were enjoying extraordinary privileges: getting paid when they
shouldn't be, organizing parties, having their relatives spend the night,
and even being allowed to leave the prison to go on vacation or to
nightclubs in the area. One of the cases Calderón highlighted involved
a sergeant who had been sentenced to forty years for having killed four
people, including two children and a six-month-old baby. The sergeant, Calderón reported, had his family living on the military base
where he was imprisoned. He was also permitted to leave the base once
a month on "medical visits" to Bogotá that lasted for several days.
Calderón's stories had upset the military establishment and forced
some reforms within the prison, but he kept writing about how many
of the abuses continued.

On May 2, 2013, Calderón drove out of town to meet with a source
in connection with his ongoing Tolemaida investigation. He waited all
day, but, after receiving a number of strange phone calls, realized the
source was not going to show up. At dusk, Calderón started to head
home. It was a new road, with lots of traffic but few stores or rest stops.
So at one point, Calderón, who needed a bathroom, pulled over on the
side of the road and got out of his car. As he approached the front of his
car, he heard another car pull up next to him, and someone called his
name. Calderón turned around and saw only the two hands that started
to shoot at him. He ran and rolled into a grassy ditch, holding his breath.
Was this the end? After a while, he heard the other car drive off, but he
stayed in the ditch for several minutes, waiting. He had left his phones
in the car, so all he could do was lie there. Finally, he crawled up and
looked around. The driver's side window of his car was shattered.
Calderón got in and drove until he found the highway police. He
stopped, but he could barely get out of the car to talk to them—he had
not been hit but could not feel his legs from the shock of the attack. The
police officers pointed at his car: he had not even noticed the five bullet

holes in it. Subsequent investigations pointed at the involvement of members of the military, working with paramilitaries, in the attack.

After the attempt on his life, Calderón received several offers to leave the country and work elsewhere, but he didn't want to abandon his investigations. He continued publishing.

Later that year, at age forty-two, Calderón became perhaps the youngest journalist ever to receive the Simón Bolívar Award for Lifetime Achievement (Vida y Obra), Colombia's highest journalism honor. Calderón had received other awards in the past, and usually he had ignored them—throwing certificates into his fireplace and letting his secretary keep the little trophies—because he believed that one shouldn't do journalism for awards. "It's like being a priest: you don't go out there to say, 'Look at what I did.' You have to do your work in silence and not expect anything in exchange." But this time, he agreed to overcome his tremendous fear of public speaking to give a speech, mainly because he viewed this award as a way of recognizing other journalists around the country who have worked quietly, and anonymously, in the face of grave danger. "Many of them," he said, " . . . would not have been able to climb onto this stage to receive this award if they had won it. In this country, where the press is corralled by the pressure of criminal groups and local and national powers, I'm privileged to be able to be here. That's why this award is not mine. It belongs to all journalists."

As for the value of his own work, to Calderón it was all very simple: "It has helped to expose the bad guys." Even with all the problems, that fact, that he had ultimately been able to expose what was going on in the DAS, which in his opinion was "the darkest thing" that had happened in government, mattered.

Velásquez had a similar take on the parapolitics investigations: "It was like telling the people that despite all that power [against us], it was possible to confront crime." In a society where there were hardly any critical voices, "the fact that the court stayed firm, persistent, acting like it was supposed to, probably gave heart to many people." He acknowledged that "justice does not transform reality," but believed in what it could do: "help to create some different conditions in a country so that the government and people can work better, have greater participation and better construct democracy." Ultimately, the "fight against corruption" should not be fought for its own sake; instead, its value should be measured in "the extent to which it contributes to creating dignified social conditions for people." In that sense, the true impact of his work, both in Colombia and Guatemala, had yet to be seen.

Still, Colombians now know much more than in years past—not only about the horrors that paramilitaries perpetrated in the name of counterinsurgency, but also about the deals that many politicians were striking with killers. And even if, deep down, they suspected the truth, the efforts of Valle, Velásquez, and Calderón—as well as their closest colleagues, family, and friends, and so many anonymous, forgotten Colombians over the years—have made them begin confronting it. Colombia has not, as paramilitaries like Rodrigo Zapata warned, "fallen apart" as a result of these disclosures. Instead, its government has been forced, however imperfectly and partially, to begin a conversation about how it will address its worst crimes and injustices.

MEANWHILE, in Jesús María Valle's birthplace of La Granja, Ituango, in a school named after the activist, teachers regularly tell their students about the noble man who twenty years ago gave his life for their rights. Armed men calling themselves paramilitaries passed through the community of about 1,500 people again in early 2017. Nobody was hurt—this time. But the courage and commitment that Valle exemplifies might well be needed again. So may the conviction he shared with them: that even in the darkest of times, as long as some people insist on telling the truth, there will be a reason for hope.

Acknowledgments

This book belongs to the many Colombians who shared their stories with me.

Iván Velásquez and Ricardo Calderón spent countless hours talking to me, in person, on Skype, on the phone, going over events again and again, and digging up long-lost documents and materials. I owe them my deepest gratitude for their trust and time. Special thanks are also due to María Victoria, Catalina, Víctor, and Laura Velásquez; Calderón's wife, "Mónica"; Miladis and Maryori Restrepo; Amparo Areiza; and Nelly, Magdalena, and Darío Valle, as well as Gloria Manco, Patricia Fuenmayor, María Victoria Fallon, Amelia Pérez, Gregorio Oviedo, J. Guillermo Escobar, Beatriz Jaramillo, Carlos Elías Muñoz, Jorge Núñez, Rainer Huhle, Judge Rubén Darío Pinilla, Darío Arcila, Juan Diego Restrepo, Ramiro Bejarano, Daniel Coronell, and the survivors of the Antioquia CTI and Fiscalía of the late 1990s. I am also grateful to the many other people in Colombia who shared memories, photographs, documents, advice, and books. Many would not want to be named.

My agent, Larry Weissman, was an enthusiastic believer in the project, knew exactly how to help me shape and sell the book proposal while staying true to my vision, and was a fierce advocate on its behalf. My editors Katy O'Donnell and Alessandra Bastagli at Nation Books were thoughtful and wonderful partners in this project. Katy's suggestions and questions improved the book immensely. Kathy Streckfus did a terrific job copy editing it, and Sandra Beris, project editor, was a helpful guide through the production process.

My able and dedicated research assistant, Pamela van den Enden, did a tremendous amount of work chasing down news articles, cables, history books, and other sources and drafting summaries of her findings to help me verify or flesh out various parts of the book.

Human Rights Watch allowed me the time to write this book, despite the world's ever-increasing demands on the group's resources. I am especially grateful to Alison Leal Parker, with whom I codirected the US Program, who supported the project even when my repeated absences significantly added to her workload. Deputy Program Director Joe Saunders, my direct supervisor, and Executive Director Ken Roth were also both supportive of the project and of allowing me to take the necessary time to complete it. I am greatly indebted to José Miguel Vivanco, executive director of the Americas division, who introduced me to Colombia and taught me an enormous amount about the country and about human rights activism; and to Daniel Wilkinson, managing director of the Americas division, who in 2002 first mentioned to me that there was a job opening I might want to look into in the division.

The board and staff of the Drug Policy Alliance, my new professional home, embraced this project and gave me the space to finish it.

Photojournalist Stephen Ferry, who has taken some of the most powerful images of Colombia I know, contributed many of the photos in this book. Journalist and author Sibylla Brodzinsky offered sage advice and critical insights. Above all, I am grateful to both of them for their support and friendship.

Jairo and Ricardo were always helpful, reliable, and positive drivers and assistants as I conducted research in Colombia, though they did not know exactly what I was working on.

Many friends, colleagues, family members, and others read parts of the book, offered advice and encouragement, housed me at key moments, or were helpful in other ways. These include Kim Barker, Stephen McFarland, Max Schoening, Ana Arana, Amy Braunschweiger, Kathy Rose, Pierre Bairin, Nicole Martin, Laura Pitter, Joanne Mariner, José Miguel Vivanco, Daniel Wilkinson, Juan Pappier, Minky Worden, Dinah Pokempner, Patrick Ball, José Carlos Ugaz, Pamela Yates, Paco de Onís, Tim Rieser, John Biaggi, Bruce Rabb, Terry Christie, Andy Kaufman, Francisco Goldman, Jon Lee Anderson, Tico Almeida, Carlos Villalón, Andrea Lari, Juan Forero, John Otis, Adam Isacson, and Jim Moody Wyss. Leslie Sharpe and Jill Rothenberg at Mediabistro gave me valuable guidance when I was assembling the book proposal. The community of writers at Paragraph Writer's Space in New York offered companionship and advice as I figured out how to pitch the book to agents.

John, Ivonne, Anne, and Karin McFarland, Carla Saenz, John Tisdale, Patricia Foxen, David McNaught, Jackie Robb, Bill and Robin Robb, Patrick Pearce, and María del Carmen Vega consistently showed interest in this project, even after several years of hearing me talk about it.

My beloved parents, George McFarland and Rosario Sánchez-Moreno, taught me to appreciate challenging places and to value standing on principle. They never failed to encourage me, even when they were afraid for my well-being. I could not have asked for more enthusiastic readers and listeners, or for better role models.

Phelim, you, more than anyone else, believed in this book and accompanied me on this journey. Your love and joyful partnership have made the past five years of writing not only easy, but also the happiest chapter of my life so far.

Glossary

ACCU: Autodefensas Campesinas de Córdoba y Urabá (Peasant Self-Defense Forces of Córdoba and Urabá), a paramilitary group led by the Castaño brothers in the 1990s.

Attorney general's office (Fiscalía): Colombian government agency charged with investigating and prosecuting crime.

AUC: Autodefensas Unidas de Colombia (United Self-Defense Forces of Colombia), an umbrella group for all paramilitary groups in Colombia, formed in the late 1990s.

Constitutional Court: One of Colombia's four high courts, charged with hearing constitutional challenges to laws and constitutional appeals in cases.

CTI: Cuerpo Técnico de Investigación (Technical Investigation Team), a branch of the attorney general's office that conducts criminal investigations, working with prosecutors.

DAS: Departamento Administrativo de Seguridad (Administrative Department of Security), Colombia's national intelligence service until October 2011. The agency also had other functions, including handling migration matters.

ELN: Ejército de Liberación Nacional (National Liberation Army), a left-wing guerrilla group.

EPL: Ejército Popular de Liberación (Popular Liberation Army), a left-wing guerrilla group that demobilized in 1991.

FARC: Fuerzas Armadas Revolucionarias de Colombia (Revolutionary Armed Forces of Colombia), Colombia's oldest and largest left-wing guerrilla group, founded in 1964. It officially disarmed in 2017.

G-3: A group operating within the DAS in 2004 and 2005 that was allegedly involved in persecution of human rights groups and labor activists, among others.

GONI: Grupo de Observación Nacional e Internacional (National and International Observation Group), a group established within the DAS in 2005 after the dissolution of the G-3 and allegedly involved in conducting illegal surveillance.

Inspector general's office (Procuraduría): Colombian government agency charged with investigating misconduct and violations of administrative rules by government officials and representing civil society.

M-19: Movimiento 19 de Abril (19th of April Movement), a left-wing guerrilla group, more urban and middle class in composition than others, that demobilized in the late 1980s.

MAS: Muerte a Secuestradores (Death to Kidnappers), a death squad formed by members of the Medellín cartel in the early 1980s. Some members of MAS later became paramilitary leaders.

Los Pepes: Perseguidos por Pablo Escobar (Persecuted by Pablo Escobar), a group of former associates, rivals, and enemies of cocaine kingpin Pablo Escobar, who joined forces in the early 1990s to kill the drug lord and his associates.

Supreme Court: One of Colombia's four high courts, charged with hearing appeals from lower courts as well as investigating and trying cases against members of the Colombian Congress; it is also charged with trying (but not investigating) cases against the president and various other senior officials. It has twenty-three members, who are divided among three chambers covering civil, criminal, and labor matters, respectively.

UNASE: Unidad Anti-Secuestro y Extorsion (Anti-Kidnapping and Extortion Unit), an elite anti-kidnapping unit that was a joint squad of the military and police. It was established in 1990 in response to the rising number of abductions in the country.

UP: Union Patriótica (Patriotic Union), a left-wing political party formed in 1985 to be a civilian arm of the FARC. Many of its members were murdered soon after.

Main Characters

PROLOGUE
Rodrigo Zapata: Former paramilitary, close to Vicente Castaño, serving time in Itagüí prison.

PART I
Velásquez Family

Iván Velásquez: Chief prosecutor for Antioquia and other states in the late 1990s, and later assistant justice on the Colombian Supreme Court and lead investigator in the parapolitics cases.

María Victoria Velásquez: Iván Velásquez's wife, also a lawyer, from Medellín.

Catalina Velásquez: Iván and María Victoria's eldest child.

Laura Velásquez: Iván and María Victoria's youngest child.

Víctor Velásquez: Iván and María Victoria's second child.

Valle Family, Colleagues, and Friends

Jesús María Valle: A prominent human rights activist in Medellín, a member of the Permanent Human Rights Committee of Antioquia, and a councilman from Ituango, who was reporting collusion between paramilitaries and the military in Ituango in 1996 and 1997.

Magdalena Valle: One of Jesús María Valle's sisters.

Nelly Valle: Jesús María Valle's sister and receptionist.

María Victoria Fallon: A friend of Jesús María Valle, a fellow member of the Permanent Human Rights Committee of Antioquia, and a lawyer representing survivors from the El Aro massacre in a suit before the Inter-American Court of Human Rights.

Patricia Fuenmayor: A friend of Jesús María Valle and a fellow member of the Permanent Human Rights Committee of Antioquia.

Beatriz Jaramillo: A friend of Jesús María Valle and fellow member of the Permanent Human Rights Committee of Antioquia.

Gloria Manco: A close friend and colleague of Jesús María Valle.

FARC Leaders

Pedro Antonio Marín (aka "Manuel Marulanda" or "Tirofijo"): The FARC's most senior commander.

El Aro Massacre

Amparo Areiza: Daughter of shopkeeper Marco Aurelio Areiza, who was murdered in the El Aro massacre; a contact of Jesús María Valle.

Miladis Torres: A survivor of the El Aro massacre in Ituango, Antioquia, in 1997.

Wilmar Torres: Miladis's little brother.

Governor's Office

Álvaro Uribe: Governor of Antioquia (1995–1997); president of Colombia (2002–2010); senator in Colombia (since 2013).

Pedro Juan Moreno: Chief of staff to Álvaro Uribe in the Antioquia governor's office.

Military Officers

General Alfonso Manosalva: Commander of the Fourth Brigade of the Colombian Army until his death in April 1997.

General Carlos Alberto Ospina: Commander of the Fourth Brigade of the Colombian Army after Manosalva's death. He went on to become commander of Colombia's armed forces from 2004 to 2007.

PART II

Attorney General's Office and CTI

Diego Arcila: Investigator and wiretapping expert at the Antioquia CTI in the late 1990s.

J. Guillermo Escobar: A mentor to Iván Velásquez, friend to both Velásquez and Valle, and prosecutor working for Velásquez when the latter served as chief prosecutor in Antioquia in the late 1990s.

Jorge Fernández: Deputy to Gregorio Oviedo at the Antioquia CTI in 1998.

Pablo Elías González: Head of the national CTI in Colombia in the late 1990s.

Alfonso Gómez Méndez: Attorney general of Colombia in 1997–2001.

Gregorio Oviedo: Head of the CTI of Antioquia, working closely with Iván Velásquez, in 1997–1998. Led raid on Padilla parking lot. Married to Amelia Pérez.

Amelia Pérez: Prosecutor in the Human Rights Unit of Colombia's attorney general's office in the late 1990s. Married to Gregorio Oviedo.

Javier Tamayo: Prosecutor working in Velásquez's office in the late 1990s.

Members of the ACCU or the Envigado Office

Diego Murillo Bejarano (aka "Don Berna" or "El Ñato"): Longtime drug trafficker, former associate of Pablo Escobar and member of Los Pepes, head of the Envigado Office, and eventually member of the AUC leadership.

Carlos Castaño: Commander of the ACCU in the late 1990s, and then of the AUC. Former member of Los Pepes.

Jacinto Alberto Soto (aka "Lucas"): Paramilitary detained during the Padilla parking-lot raid. Later found to be the main accountant for Carlos Castaño.

Gustavo Upegui: Businessman believed by investigators to be a leader of the Envigado Office.

Members of the Medellín Cartel

Pablo Escobar: Colombia's most famous drug lord, head of the Medellín cartel in the 1980s, responsible for high-profile killings and bombings through the early 1990s. Killed in 1993.

Gonzalo Rodríguez Gacha (aka "El Mexicano" or "The Mexican"): A member of the Medellín cartel.

Jorge Luis, Fabio, and Juan David Ochoa: Brothers from Antioquia who became members of the Medellín cartel. Their father, also Fabio, was known for raising horses.

PART III

Calderón Family

Ricardo Calderón: Investigative journalist for *Semana* magazine.
Mónica: Ricardo Calderón's wife (pseudonym).

Former AUC Members

Vicente Castaño: A senior AUC commander. Carlos's brother.

Luis Eduardo Cifuentes (aka "El Águila" or "The Eagle"): AUC leader in the region of Cundinamarca, where Bogotá is located.

Iván Roberto Duque (aka "Ernesto Báez"): A senior commander of the AUC.

Edwin Guzmán: Former paramilitary in the United States who made allegations against Iván Velásquez in 2007.

Carlos Mario Jiménez (aka "Macaco"): Commander of the Central Bolívar Block of the AUC.

Antonio López (aka "Job"): Demobilized paramilitary, senior leader of the Democracy Corporation of Medellín, and close adviser to Don Berna.

Salvatore Mancuso: A senior commander of the AUC; involved in the El Aro massacre.

José Orlando Moncada (aka "Tasmania"): Former paramilitary serving time in prison. In 2007 he became the subject of a scandal after a letter he had supposedly sent to President Uribe was made public. In the letter, Tasmania accused Iván Velásquez, the Supreme Court assistant justice, of trying to get him to implicate Uribe in a murder attempt.

Rodrigo Mercado Peluffo (aka "Cadena" or "Chain"): A midlevel AUC commander who operated in Sucre.

Rodrigo Tovar Pupo (aka "Jorge 40"): Senior commander of the Northern Block of the AUC from Valledupar, Cesar.

Former Colombian Presidents

César Gaviria: President of Colombia from 1990 to 1994, later secretary-general of the Organization of American States.

Andrés Pastrana: President of Colombia from 1998 to 2002.

Ernesto Samper: President of Colombia from 1994 to 1998.

Government Officials or Advisers to the Uribe Administration

José Obdulio Gaviria: Adviser to Álvaro Uribe since the 1980s.

Mario Iguarán: Attorney general of Colombia from 2005 to 2009.

Members of Congress

Álvaro Araújo: Senator from Cesar; brother of Foreign Minister María Consuelo Araújo; investigated in the parapolitics cases.

Rocío Arias: Representative from Antioquia; investigated in the parapolitics cases.

Muriel Benito: Representative from Sucre; among the first investigated in the parapolitics cases.

Miguel de la Espriella: Senator from Córdoba; investigated in the parapolitics cases.

Álvaro García: Senator from Sucre; among the first investigated in the parapolitics cases.

Yidis Medina: Representative from Santander. Her allegations about why she voted for a bill allowing President Uribe to run for a second term led to a scandal in 2008.

Jairo Merlano: Senator from Sucre; among the first investigated in the parapolitics cases.

Eric Morris: Representative from Sucre; among the first investigated in the parapolitics cases.

Gustavo Petro: Senator from Cundinamarca; former member of the M-19 guerrilla group. In 2007 he led a congressional hearing about paramilitary activity in Antioquia.

Mauricio Pimiento: Senator and former governor of Cesar; investigated in the parapolitics cases.

Eleonora Pineda: Representative from Córdoba; investigated in the parapolitics cases.

Mario Uribe: Senator from Antioquia; second cousin and close political ally of President Álvaro Uribe; investigated in the parapolitics cases.

Supreme Court Justices

María del Rosario González: Justice in the Criminal Chamber of the Supreme Court.

Álvaro Pérez: Justice in the Criminal Chamber of the Supreme Court. Velásquez worked directly for him until becoming the coordinator of the parapolitics investigations.

César Julio Valencia: President of the Colombian Supreme Court from 2007 to 2008.

DAS Officials

José Miguel Narváez: Deputy director of the DAS during Noguera's directorship.

Jorge Noguera: Director of the DAS from 2002 to 2005. Investigated for conspiracy and other offenses related to paramilitary groups.

Witnesses in the Parapolitics Cases

Jairo Castillo Peralta (aka "Pitirri"): Former paramilitary who became a protected witness against paramilitaries and politicians in Sucre. He eventually fled to Canada. He became a witness in the Supreme Court's parapolitics investigations.

Rafael García: Former IT director for the DAS under Noguera; convicted of various offenses. Provided extensive statements about ties between senior DAS officials and paramilitaries and criminal activity within the DAS.

Claudia López: Political analyst whose work on voting patterns in the regions where paramilitary violence had been most acute fed into the parapolitics investigations.

PART IV
Former Paramilitaries

Juan Carlos Sierra (aka "El Tuso"): Colombian drug lord who managed to join the paramilitary demobilization process and was later extradited to the United States.

Ferney Suaza: Demobilized paramilitary close to Job, who claimed that someone was trying to bribe him to accuse President Uribe of criminal activity.

DAS Officials

Alba Luz Flórez: DAS detective who became known as the "Mata Hari of the DAS" due to her role in spying on the Supreme Court.

María del Pilar Hurtado: Director of the DAS in 2007 and 2008.

Jorge Lagos: Director of counterintelligence in the DAS at the time of the 2009 surveillance scandal.

Martha Leal: Deputy operations director of the DAS during the Tasmania and Job scandals of 2007 and 2008.

Felipe Muñoz: Director of the DAS in 2009.

Fernando Tabares: Director of intelligence in the DAS at the time of the 2009 surveillance scandal.

Other Officials

Bernardo Moreno: Chief of staff to President Uribe.

General Óscar Naranjo: Chief of the National Police of Colombia from 2007 to 2012; vice president of Colombia since March 2017.

Juan Manuel Santos: Minister of defense of Colombia in 2006 to 2009, in the Uribe administration; president of Colombia since 2010.

General Mauricio Santoyo: Security chief for President Uribe.

Characters Related to the "Tasmania" or "Casa de Nari" Incidents

Diego Álvarez: Lawyer for Don Berna.

Henry Anaya: A lawyer who was recorded on video talking to Diego Álvarez and appearing to hold himself out as close to the Supreme Court.

Sergio González: Lawyer for El Tuso and Tasmania.

Notes and Sources

This book is largely based on my interviews over the course of five years (in some cases, more) with characters in the book and witnesses of the events described therein. I got to know both Iván Velásquez and Ricardo Calderón through my work as a human rights activist in Colombia between 2004 and 2010, and was in communication with them as many of the events in the book were unfolding. I also interviewed them extensively in later years. I conducted additional interviews with their family members, including María Victoria Velásquez, Velásquez's children, and several of his siblings, as well as with Calderón's wife, whom I have given the pseudonym "Mónica" in this book. Many of their colleagues and friends provided valuable information; these include, among others, Velásquez's mentor and friend J. Guillermo Escobar; Gregorio Oviedo, the CTI chief in Medellín in the late 1990s; prosecutor Amelia Pérez; Supreme Court justices César Julio Valencia, María del Rosario González, Mauro Solarte, and Álvaro Pérez; several CTI investigators and prosecutors who worked with Velásquez in both Medellín and Bogotá, who would prefer to remain unnamed; Calderón's editor, Alfonso Cuéllar, his colleague Rodrigo Pardo, and his fellow journalists Félix de Bedout and Daniel Coronell.

Jesús María Valle had already been killed by the time I started working on Colombia, but he is still loved and dearly remembered by many friends, colleagues, and community members who are grateful for his help. Walking around Medellín, one sees constant reminders of the mark he left on the city, from murals depicting his image at the University of Antioquia to schools bearing his name and a plaque at the prosecutor's office—not to mention countless people who light up at the mention of his name. His sisters Nelly and Magdalena shared many of their memories about his life with me, as well as written records and photographs. So did Gloria Manco, his fellow activist, close friend, and lawyer. Patricia Fuenmayor, María Victoria Fallon, Beatriz Jaramillo, Amparo Areiza, Darío Arcila, Jesús Abad Colorado, Óscar Castaño, the late Carlos Gaviria, Jairo León Cano, and many others also shared details and stories that allowed me to reconstruct some of this remarkable character's life and his final months.

Former president Álvaro Uribe never responded to multiple interview requests that I sent by email and fax between 2014 and 2016. In 2017, one of his staff members at the Centro Democrático political party said that Uribe had received my requests, but was unable to take an interview because he was recovering from surgery. Uribe never responded to another meeting request that I sent a few weeks later, when he was once again appearing in the media. Nor did he send a response to a detailed questionnaire asking for his take on the various events described in this book. However, his close adviser, José Obdulio Gaviria, granted me two interviews, including one that lasted approximately four hours, in 2014. I obtained additional insights about Uribe's life and actions from some of his friends and from officials who worked with him in Antioquia and Bogotá, including Fabio Echeverri, Jaime Jaramillo Panesso, Alberto Rendón, General Óscar Naranjo, former attorney general Mario Iguarán, and others who asked not to be named. I have also relied on reports in the media and Uribe's autobiography, *No Lost Causes* (New York: Celebra, 2012), for the quotations attributed to him in the book.

Several former Colombian officials shared additional contextual information about the country's history and the events described in the book. These officials include former Colombian presidents César Gaviria and Ernesto Samper, former attorney general Alfonso Gómez Méndez, former deputy attorney general and then Constitutional Court justice Jaime Córdoba Trivino, former CTI chief Pablo Elías González, former inspector general Carlos Gustavo Arrieta, former senator Rafael Pardo, and others who asked not to be named.

I interviewed former paramilitary commanders Raúl Hasbún and Rodrigo Zapata at Itagüí prison, and exchanged emails with Diego Murillo Bejarano ("Don Berna"), who is in prison in Miami, Florida. As part of my Human Rights Watch work, I had in previous years interviewed Antonio López (aka "Job," now deceased) and several other paramilitaries who participated in the demobilization process.

Additional interviewees included the former IT director for the DAS, Rafael García, who became a witness in investigations of the DAS, and a former DAS member who was a source for Calderón, Alexander Menjura.

Miladis and Maryori Restrepo Torres shared their painful memories of the El Aro massacre.

Other interviewees, including a former US official, asked not to be named.

Ricardo Calderón shared a great deal of documentary material and audio and video recordings corroborating his reporting and allowing me to flesh out details for the book. The case files on the Parqueadero Padilla case, Jesús

María Valle's murder, and the El Aro massacre also contained critical documents backing up the statements of many of my sources. Other documentary sources included rulings by the Supreme Court and by the Justice and Peace Tribunal in Medellín; publicly available testimony in the parapolitics cases; the first CTI report and testimony given by multiple witnesses in the investigations of the DAS illegal surveillance scandal; and video recordings of testimony by several witnesses, including Iván Roberto Duque (aka "Ernesto Báez") and José Orlando Moncada (aka "Tasmania") in the case against attorney Sergio González over the Tasmania scandal.

The *Semana, El Colombiano, El Tiempo,* and *El Espectador* news archives, as well as the website VerdadAbierta.com, a nonprofit providing in-depth reporting on Colombia's conflict, offered a wealth of valuable information, as did reporting by several journalists for foreign media, including Sibylla Brodzinsky, Juan Forero, John Otis, Simón Romero, Steven Dudley, and Jeremy McDermott. The Colombian journalist Juan Diego Restrepo has also written extensively about the situation in the Medellín attorney general's office in the late 1990s. My own Human Rights Watch reporting in Colombia between 2004 and 2010, as well as that of my predecessor as Colombia researcher, Robin Kirk, and my successor, Max Schoening (all available on www.hrw.org/americas/colombia), were also references. US cables that have been declassified and are available through the National Security Archive at George Washington University, as well as cables leaked to the website Wikileaks, provided additional useful information.

Many public events described in the book, including press conferences, congressional hearings in Colombia, the ceremony in which US president George W. Bush awarded Uribe the Presidential Medal of Freedom, and the first signing of Colombia's peace agreement with the FARC, were recorded on videos that are available online.

I have used numbers sparingly in the book; where statistics do appear, their sources are noted in the text or in this section. Numbers concerning Colombia's conflict—homicide and kidnapping rates, total numbers of people killed or displaced, estimates of combatants—often vary wildly according to source. Numbers are often political tools in Colombia and used by different actors to support their versions of history. During the Uribe administration, the government used numbers particularly effectively to build a narrative according to which Colombia's conflict was largely becoming a thing of the past. More recent analysis by data expert Patrick Ball suggests that this analysis was at least partly incorrect. See Patrick Ball and Michael Reed Hurtado, "Cuentas y mediciones de la criminalidad y de la violencia," *Forensis* 16,

no. 1 (2014): 529, available at www.medicinalegal.gov.co/documents/88730
/1656998/Forensis+Interactivo+2014.24-JULpdf.pdf/9085ad79-d2a9-4c0d
-a17b-f845ab96534b (*Forensis* is the magazine for Colombia's Institute of
Forensic Medicine). See also P. Ball and M. Reed, "El registro y la medición
de la criminalidad: El problema de los datos faltantes y el uso de la ciencia
para producir estimaciones en relación con el homicidio en Colombia, dem-
ostrado a partir de un ejemplo, el departamento de Antioquia (2003–2011),"
Revista Criminalidad 58, no. 1 (2016): 9–23, https://hrdag.org/wp-content
/uploads/2013/01/criminality-registration-Colombia-PBall-2016.pdf.

According to Ball, official datasets on homicides remained pretty flat
from about 2003 to 2011. Yet in 2006, estimates—based on those datasets—of undocumented homicides in the regions of Antioquia and Valle
del Cauca (which were the focus of the analysis) skyrocketed. In subsequent
discussions of the study, Ball suggested that there could be multiple explanations for the fact that official figures did not capture these killings, including that official sources "overflowed" when homicides increased. In
other words, they covered what they could, but in times of increasing violence, they simply didn't have the capacity to document more than they
normally did. It was also possible that, for various reasons, officials chose
not to document the additional cases.

The following books cover some of the events described in this book and
offer additional information:

Abad Colorado, Jesús. *Mirar de la Vida Profunda*. Bogotá: Paralelo 10,
2015.

Abad Faciolince, Héctor. *Oblivion*. Translation of *El Olvido Que Seremos*. Anne McLean and Rosalind Harvey, translators. New York:
Farrar, Straus and Giroux, 2012.

Aranguren Molina, Mauricio. *Carlos Castaño: Mi Confesión*. Bogotá:
Editorial La Oveja Negra, 2001.

Betancourt, Ingrid. *No Hay Silencio Que No Termine*. Bogotá: Aguilar,
2010.

Bowden, Mark. *Killing Pablo: The Hunt for the World's Greatest Outlaw*.
New York: Atlantic Monthly Press, 2001.

Braun, Herbert. *The Assassination of Gaitán: Public Life and Urban Violence in Colombia*. Madison: University of Wisconsin Press, 1985.

Brodzinsky, Sibylla, and Max Schoening. *Throwing Stones at the Moon:
Narratives from Colombians Displaced by Violence*. San Francisco:
McSweeney's and Voice of Witness, 2012.

Bushnell, David. *The Making of Modern Colombia: A Nation in Spite of Itself*. Berkeley: University of California Press, 1993.

Comisión Nacional de Réparación y Reconciliación, Grupo de Memoria Histórica. *Bojayá: La Guerra Sin Límites*. Bogotá: Aguilar, Altea, Taurus, Alfaguara, 2010.

Coronell, Daniel. *Recordar es Morir*. Bogotá: Aguilar, 2016.

Dudley, Steven. *Walking Ghosts: Murder and Guerrilla Politics in Colombia*. New York: Routledge, 2004.

Duzán, María Jimena. *Así Gobierna Uribe*. Bogotá: Planeta, 2004.

Ferry, Stephen. *Violentology: A Manual of the Colombian Conflict*. New York: Umbrage Editions, 2012.

Instituto Popular de Capacitación and Corporación Jurídica Libertad. *Memoria de la Impunidad en Antioquia: Lo Que La Justicia No Quiso Ver Frente Al Paramilitarismo*. Medellín: Pregón, 2010.

Kirk, Robin. *More Terrible Than Death: Massacres, Drugs, and America's War in Colombia*. New York: Public Affairs, 2003.

Otis, John. *Law of the Jungle: The Hunt for Colombian Guerrillas, American Hostages, and Buried Treasure*. New York: William Morrow, 2010.

Palacios, Marco. *Between Legitimacy and Violence: A History of Colombia, 1875–2002*. Durham, NC: Duke University Press, 2006.

Roldán, Mary. *Blood and Fire: La Violencia in Antioquia, Colombia, 1946–1953*. Durham, NC: Duke University Press, 2002.

Ronderos, María Teresa. *Guerras Recicladas: Una Historia Periodística del Paramilitarismo en Colombia*. Bogotá: Aguilar, 2014.

Safford, Frank, and Marco Palacios. *Colombia: Fragmented Land, Divided Society*. New York: Oxford University Press, 2002.

Salazar, Alonso. *La Parábola de Pablo: Auge y Caída de un Gran Capo del Narcotráfico*. Bogotá: Planeta, 2012.

Soto, Martha. *Velásquez: El Retador del Poder*. Bogotá: Intermedio Editores, 2016.

Uribe Vélez, Álvaro. *No Lost Causes*. New York: Celebra, 2012.

PROLOGUE

Part of the prologue is based on notes from my interview with Rodrigo Zapata. Additional information came from the January 30, 2017, ruling in his case by the Justice and Peace Tribunal of Medellín, which convicted him of various offenses, including homicide. The ruling is available at Tribunal Superior de Distrito, Sala de Conocimiento de Justicia y Paz, January 30, 2017, https://www.ramajudicial.gov.co/documents/6342975/6634902/30.01.2017 -sentencia-bloque-pacifico-frente-suroeste-rodrigo-zapata-sierra-y-otros.pdf /286792b7–084b-415a-89f3-e664b5bd8af0. As of this writing, Zapata has appealed.

PART I: DEATH

A copy of Jesús María Valle's November 20, 1996, letter to Governor Álvaro Uribe was among the papers his family kept.

The account of the assassination of Jorge Eliecer Gaitán is largely drawn from Herbert Braun's *The Assassination of Gaitán: Public Life and Urban Violence in Colombia* (Madison: University of Wisconsin Press, 1985). Some of the details about La Violencia's impact in Antioquia are drawn from Mary Roldán, *Blood and Fire: La Violencia in Antioquia, Colombia, 1946–1953* (Durham, NC: Duke University Press, 2002).

The quotation about the state of siege during La Violencia came from Marco Palacios, *Between Legitimacy and Violence: A History of Colombia, 1875–2002* (Durham, NC: Duke University Press, 2006).

The stories from Valle's childhood came primarily from his sister Magdalena.

The account of the assassination of Dr. Héctor Abad Gómez is drawn from *Oblivion*, the English translation of the memoir written by his son, Héctor Abad Faciolince, titled *El Olvido Que Seremos*, translated by Anne McLean and Rosalind Harvey (New York: Farrar, Straus and Giroux, 2012), though additional details were provided by other witnesses. The quotation from the kill list including Abad's name also comes from *Oblivion*.

Details about the 1996 La Granja massacre are drawn from the ruling by the Inter-American Court on Human Rights on the La Granja and El Aro massacres.

The quotations from Valle are drawn from video recordings and the case file of his homicide.

The account of Valle's meeting with Uribe on December 9, 1996, is based largely on the account of a witness who asked not to be named. That account is partly corroborated by a statement that Valle gave on February 6, 1998, to a prosecutor in Medellín. In that statement, Valle described a meeting he had with Uribe and others to inform the governor of the deaths in Ituango. At the meeting, Valle said that Uribe "sent us to talk to General Manosalva (r.i.p.). After the visit, the governor did nothing, and . . . in the commission to

Ituango . . . he cleverly took me off the commission so I could not go, and the bloodshed continued."

Former President Uribe did not respond to a March 15, 2017, set of written questions for this book. These included questions about his version of events of the December 9, 1996, meeting, such as whether Uribe recalled the meeting, whether Valle had told him about having evidence about collusion between the military and paramilitaries in Ituango, whether Uribe called General Manosalva and told him that Valle was falsely accusing the military of collusion and should be sued, whether Uribe told Valle that he should present his allegations to Manosalva, whether Valle told him he had evidence of mass graves in Ituango, whether Uribe organized a committee to visit Ituango—with Valle—by helicopter the following Saturday, and whether Valle was informed at the last minute that he could not join the group by helicopter. The same questionnaire also included questions about, among other issues, Uribe's views on the Convivirs, his knowledge of paramilitary activity in Antioquia when he was governor, his response to the massacre of La Granja, Ituango, in July 1996, his recollection of Valle's reports of paramilitary abuses and military collusion, the El Aro massacre, and his alleged statement accusing Valle of being an enemy of the armed forces.

Uribe's quotation, cited in Chapter 1, in which he backs the Fourth Brigade commander's account of an alleged FARC attack in Ituango, which Valle challenged, was reported in "Connivencia en Antioquia entre Fuerza Pública y Paramilitares No Fue una Ficción" (Collusion in Antioquia Between Public Security Forces and Paramilitaries Was Not Fiction), *Semana*, February 25, 2008. It is unclear whether it was previously reported elsewhere.

The unclassified US cable calling Governor Álvaro Uribe a "bright star in the Liberal Party firmament" is Cable Bogota 003714, March 1995, available through the National Security Archive.

The quotation from Uribe about witnessing Liberal guerrillas coming to his house as a child comes from the English translation of his autobiography, *No Lost Causes* (New York: Celebra, 2012), 54.

Some of the history about Pablo Escobar is drawn from Alonso Salazar's *La Parábola de Pablo: Auge y Caída de un Gran Capo del Narcotráfico* (Bogotá: Planeta, 2012) and Mark Bowden's *Killing Pablo: The Hunt for the World's Greatest Outlaw* (New York: Atlantic Monthly Press, 2001), among other sources.

The account of Velásquez's early effort, with Uribe and Álvaro Villegas, to get Pablo Escobar to turn himself in came from interviews with Velásquez.

Álvaro Villegas also confirmed it to journalist Martha Soto, according to her book, *Velásquez: El Retador del Poder* (Bogotá: Intermedio Editores, 2016). Pablo Escobar's letter to the Colombian government can also be found in an appendix to that book. The March 15, 2017, questionnaire sent to Uribe asked for his account of these events.

The decree authorizing the establishment of the Convivir program was Decree 356 of February 11, 1994.

Then governor Uribe's quotations about the Convivir program in Chapter 2 come from "Las Convivir Apoyan a la Fuerza Pública" (The Convivirs Support the Public Security Forces), *El Tiempo*, November 11, 1997.

The account of the El Aro massacre is based primarily on interviews with Miladis and Maryori Restrepo, as well as a review of excerpts of the El Aro case file; the Inter-American Court of Human Rights ruling in the El Aro and La Granja massacres; rulings of the Justice and Peace Tribunal in Medellín in the cases of Jesús Ignacio Roldan ("Monoleche"), Ramiro ("Cuco") Vanoy, and Juan Fernando Chica; and interviews with prosecutor Amelia Pérez, attorney María Victoria Fallon, and Amparo Areiza, among others. In the years since the massacre, several women have told investigators that they were raped during the massacre, but in the immediate aftermath of the slaughter, most remained silent out of fear or shame. Miladis's exchange with "Junior" is based on her account. Junior has admitted to having participated in the El Aro incursion and is in prison for various paramilitary crimes.

Carlos Castaño's comment about the El Aro massacre was quoted in an article in *Semana* titled "Las Cicatrices de El Aro" on October 21, 2008, available at www.semana.com/nacion/conflicto-armado/articulo/las-cicatrices-el-aro/96472-3.

The account of Valle's murder is based on the statements of Nelly Valle as well as the case file on his homicide. In 2014, the Angulo brothers, mentioned in Chapters 4 and 8, were ordered detained in connection with the El Aro massacre; the Supreme Court also approved a prosecutor's motion that the investigation against them in connection with Valle's murder be reopened. It is unclear, based on publicly available information, where these investigations stand. It does not appear that they have ever been charged in connection with the drug-trafficking allegations made by witness Carlos Jaramillo and mentioned by others.

PART II: THE HUNT

Relatively little has been written about this chapter of Colombian history. As a result, this section is overwhelmingly based on my own reporting.

One exception is *Memoria de la Impunidad en Antioquia: Lo Que La Justicia No Quiso Ver Frente Al Paramilitarismo* (Medellín: Pregón, 2010), a lengthy book written jointly by the Medellín-based organizations Instituto Popular de Capacitación and Corporacion Jurídica Libertad. It contains a great deal of detailed information about many of the cases that the chief prosecutor's office for Antioquia was handling at the end of the 1980s. It also includes accounts of several of the killings of CTI investigators, as well as analysis of possible explanations.

Carlos Mario Aguilar, the former CTI agent who was mentioned in Chapter 5 as having been involved in recruiting other CTI agents to work with the Envigado Office, was years later reported to have become the head of the Envigado Office. In 2008, he turned himself in to US authorities and served several years in prison in New York pursuant to a plea bargain. News reports indicate that he completed his sentence in 2015 and that he may have remained free in the United States.

"Junior" and "Cobra," both of whom Francisco Villalba identified, in Chapter 6, as participants in the El Aro massacre, are also mentioned as commanders of troops who participated in the massacre in a February 2, 2015, ruling by the Justice and Peace Tribunal of Medellín in the case of paramilitary leader Ramiro Vanoy. That ruling, which discusses the El Aro massacre at length, is available at República de Colombia, Rama Judicial del Poder Público, Tribunal Superior de Medellín, Sala de Justicia y Paz, February 2, 2015, https://www.ramajudicial.gov.co/documents/6342975/66 34902/1.+2015.02.02+Sent_Bl_Mineros-ramiro-vanoy-murillo.pdf. Junior is in prison for various paramilitary crimes. There is no recent public information about Cobra's whereabouts.

PART III: HOPE

On September 1, 2014, the Justice and Peace Chamber of the Court of Bogotá convicted Luis Eduardo Cifuentes, aka "The Eagle," of several crimes related to his involvement in the paramilitaries, including multiple homicides. The ruling is available at Tribunal Superior de Bogotá, Sala de Justicia y Paz, September 1, 2014, www.fiscalia.gov.co/jyp/wp-content/uploads /2014/12/2014-09-01-SENTENCIA-BLOQUE-CUNDINAMARCA -1-sep-2014.pdf. The charges did not include drug trafficking, though prosecutors told the court that several of the defendants in the case had confessed that they had obtained resources for the group from drug trafficking.

The numbers of victims in the Bojayá massacre of 2002, when the FARC lobbed a gas cylinder bomb into the town of Bellavista, comes from Comisión

Nacional de Reparación y Reconciliación, Grupo de Memoria Histórica, *Bojayá: La Guerra Sin Límites* (Bogotá: Aguilar, Altea, Taurus, Alfaguara, 2010).

The quotations from Uribe in Chapter 9, about being in the bullring, come from his *No Lost Causes* (New York: Celebra, 2012), 45–46.

Some of the allegations about Uribe's father's connections with the Ochoa family and about Uribe's actions at the Civil Aviation Agency appear in Joseph Contreras's book, *El Señor de las Sombras: Biografía No Autorizada de Álvaro Uribe Vélez* (Bogotá: Oveja Negra, 2002). Other journalists, including Fabio Castillo, in the book *Los Jinetes de la Cocaína* (Bogotá: Editorial Documentos Periodísticos, 1987), had already published about some of them. According to the newspaper *El Tiempo*, Contreras's book received some harsh criticism when it was published during the 2002 presidential campaign, with one editor stating that the book had been written "lightly," though Contreras said it was the result of a serious investigation.

A February 24, 2007, letter from Jaime Bermúdez, then the Colombian ambassador to Argentina, to the newspaper *Clarín*, includes quotations from Uribe responding to the allegations made against him in the 2002 campaign. A copy of the letter can be found at http://web.archive.org/web/2011070 6084412/http://www.embajadacolombia.int.ar/site/indexnb.asp?IdSeccion =389&IdSector=1.

Ministry of Defense estimates of the number of paramilitary troops were cited in a 2004 US cable available at https://www.scribd.com/document /84833997/Cable-914-US-Assessment-of-Size-and-Organization-of -Armed-Paramilitary-and-Insurgent-Groups-in-Colombia.

Attorney General John Ashcroft's statement is available at the US Department of State Archive, http://2001-2009.state.gov/p/inl/rls/rm/13663.htm.

Carlos Castaño's emails were obtained by Ricardo Calderón through his reporting.

The US cable cited in Chapter 10 is US Cable 06BOGOTÁ010596, November 17, 2006, available at http://cables.mrkva.eu/cable.php?id=86233& show=original.

The members of Congress from Sucre mentioned in Chapter 10, Jairo Merlano, Eric Morris, Muriel Benito, and Álvaro García, were all convicted at various times of offenses related to their involvement with paramilitary groups. García was also convicted of involvement in the homicide of Georgina Narváez and the massacre of Macayepo. While the politicians challenged the credibility of the testimony by Jairo Castillo (aka "Pitirri"), in its rulings the Supreme Court cited corroborating evidence and other factors that supported Castillo's version of events. With regard to Morris, the court did not find that he had been directly involved in diverting public resources as governor, as suggested by Castillo, but it did find that he had conspired with paramilitaries. Prosecutors also pressed charges against landowner Joaquín García in connection with the Macayepo massacre; in rulings in some of the other cases, the court talks about him as a well-known promoter of the paramilitaries. However, according to news reports, Joaquín García disappeared in September 2010 after unknown men reportedly took him from his apartment, and the investigation against him was closed on the grounds that García was presumed dead. The former governor of Sucre Salvador Arana was convicted of the murder of the mayor of El Roble, Eudaldo "Tito" Díaz.

In May 2008, the Supreme Court convicted Senator Mauricio Pimiento, who is mentioned in Chapter 11, of conspiring with paramilitaries and of voter "constraint." In March 2010, the court convicted Senator Álvaro Araújo, also mentioned in Chapter 11, of the same offenses.

Details of the Chivolo and Pivijay pacts cited in Chapter 10 are available in Supreme Court ruling 35227 against José María Imbeth and Feris Chadid. Additional information is available in ruling 26585, involving Rubén Dario Quintero.

Colombian journalist Juanita León analyzed Mancuso's statements about Juan Manuel Santos, as well as the responses by Santos and various witnesses, in an article in *La Silla Vacía* on April 13, 2010, available at http://lasillavacia.com/historia/9420.

The description in Chapter 12 of the meeting that Ricardo Calderón had with then minister of defense Juan Manuel Santos is based on Calderón's account. Santos, who later became president, did not respond to a request for his account of the meeting sent via a July 7, 2017, letter to his adviser Enrique Riveira.

The US cable cited in Chapter 13, which indicates that Colombian officials expressed concern that the Supreme Court would permanently block extraditions, is US Cable 05BOGOTÁ5310_a, June 2, 2005, available at https://wikileaks.org/plusd/cables/05BOGOTÁ5310_a.html.

Don Berna's claim that his brother killed Pablo Escobar is recorded in Don Berna's book *Así Matamos al Patrón: La Cacería de Pablo Escobar*, by Diego Murillo Bejarano (Bogotá: Ícono, 2014).

The US chargé d'affaires's statements to the Colombian government about the handling of Don Berna's case in 2005 are recorded in US Cable 05BOGOTÁ5753_a, June 16, 2005, available at https://wikileaks.org/plusd/cables/05BOGOTÁ5753_a.html.

Official information about the demobilization of each paramilitary block, including the date, the number of members demobilizing, and the number of weapons turned over, is listed in the Final Report on the Peace Process with the Self-Defense Forces, produced by the Colombian government (undated). See "Proceso de Paz con las Autodefensas," available at www.cooperacion internacional.com/descargas/informefinaldesmovilizaciones.pdf.

"Mónica" is a pseudonym for Calderón's wife.

The *Noticias Uno* video of Yidis Medina's statements about her vote in favor of Uribe's reelection is available on YouTube at https://www.youtube .com/watch?v=1NbO8O-ZN34. The events around it are also summarized in Daniel Coronell's book *Recordar es Morir* (Bogotá: Aguilar, 2016).

The quotation from Uribe in Chapter 14 about why he extradited the paramilitary commanders comes from the English version of his autobiography, *No Lost Causes*, 287.

Mancuso's allegations about the involvement of "General Ospina" in the El Aro massacre have not been confirmed. According to news reports, prosecutors instructed that an investigation be conducted into the possible involvement of General Carlos Alberto Ospina, who at the time was the commander of the army's Fourth Brigade, in the El Aro massacre. But as of this writing, it was unclear whether such an investigation was moving forward. Years earlier, before Mancuso's statements, the inspector general's office had reportedly closed a disciplinary investigation of Ospina in connection with the massacre.

Former president Uribe never responded to the questionnaire sent to him in connection with this book in March 2017, which asked him for his version of events concerning his meeting with then attorney general Mario Iguarán, mentioned in Chapter 14. The same questionnaire included numerous detailed questions about, among other issues, the Tasmania scandal, Yidis Medina's allegations against him, the parapolitics investigations, the paramilitary demobilization process, Rafael García's allegations of electoral fraud in Magdalena during the 2002 presidential elections, his public falling-out with the Supreme Court, Calderón's reports about ongoing paramilitary crimes after the demobilization, and his decision to extradite most of the paramilitary leadership.

PART IV: TRUTH

The Supreme Court eventually issued an order (an *auto inhibitorio*) closing the investigation into Senator Nancy Patricia Gutiérrez, mentioned in Chapter 15, for lack of sufficient evidence.

In a TV interview with *Noticias Uno*, Henry Anaya, the man who appeared in the Job video, apparently trying to ask Don Berna's lawyer for a bribe, denied that that had ever happened. He said he had no connection to the court and that he had only met with attorney Diego Álvarez because he admired him.

The reference in Chapter 17 to DAS chief Felipe Muñoz's inaccurate claims that there were no recordings of illegal surveillance, and that Attorney General Mario Iguarán had said he had found no evidence against anyone in the presidency, came from US Cable 09BOGOTÁ1618_a, May 22, 2009, available at https://wikileaks.org/plusd/cables/09BOGOTÁ1618_a.html.

Additional information came from US Cable 09BOGOTÁ2921_a, September 10, 2009, available at https://wikileaks.org/plusd/cables/09BOGOTÁ 2921_a.html, and US Cable 09BOGOTÁ2963_a, September 16, 2009, in which the ambassador and Vice President Santos discuss the response to the DAS scandals, available at https://wikileaks.org/plusd/cables/09BOGOTÁ 2963_a.html.

The quotation in Chapter 17 from presidential adviser José Obdulio Gaviria in response to Jorge Lagos's allegations against him appeared in a newspaper interview, "Oposición pudo haberse infiltrado en el DAS para provocar escándalo," *El Tiempo*, May 14, 2009, www.eltiempo.com/archivo/documento /CMS-5188254.

The quotation from US State Department spokesman Ian Kelly comes from "Determination and Certification of Colombian Government and Armed Forces with Respect to Human Rights Related Conditions," a press statement dated September 11, 2009, available at US Department of State, https://2009-2017.state.gov/r/pa/prs/ps/2009/sept/129135.htm.

Accounts of Operation Checkmate, which is described in Chapter 18, are available in John Otis, *The Law of the Jungle: The Hunt for Colombian Guerrillas, American Hostages, and Buried Treasure* (New York: William Morrow, 2010), as well as Íngrid Betancourt's *No Hay Silencio Que No Termine* (Bogotá: Aguilar, 2010), among many other accounts. The quotations from Uribe about his decision to keep his regular schedule during Operation Checkmate, and about his comments to the rescued hostages, come from the English version of his autobiography, *No Lost Causes* (New York: Celebra, 2012), 300–301.

The quotations from Alba Luz Flórez in Chapter 18 are drawn from her statement to the attorney general's office on May 24, 2010.

The court ruling referenced in Chapter 19, which mentions a list of Envigado Office collaborators turned over by Juan Carlos Sierra, aka El Tuso, is a

September 24, 2015 decision by the Tribunal Superior de Medellín, Sala de Conocimiento de Justicia y Paz, in the case of Edilberto de Jesús Cañas Chavarriaga et al., for conspiracy and other offenses, para. 161.

The 2016 letter mentioned in Chapter 19, in which former president Uribe asked *El Espectador* to correct its reporting about the allegations against him related to El Aro, is available at "Álvaro Uribe Vélez se refiere a la massacre de El Aro, *El Espectador*, June 3, 2016, www.elespectador.com/noticias /judicial/alvaro-uribe-velez-se-refiere-masacre-de-el-aro-articulo-635870.

As Pedro Juan Moreno is dead, he cannot respond to the allegations against him by paramilitary leaders Don Berna, Mancuso, and Hasbún. Former president Uribe has questioned the credibility of Don Berna and other paramilitary leaders and defended the record of his former chief of staff.

The questionnaire sent to former president Uribe in March 2017 in connection with this book, to which he never responded, included detailed questions about the allegations that have been made against him and his associates, the scandal over "Job" and his entry into the Casa de Nariño, and the DAS scandal.

AFTERWORD: PEACE?

Numbers of people killed in the Colombian conflict are drawn from the Center for Historical Memory of Colombia, which estimated that 218,094 people were killed between 1958 and 2012. See "Estadísticas del conflicto armado en Colombia," Centro Nacional de Memoria Histórica, www.centrodememoria-historica.gov.co/micrositios/informeGeneral/estadisticas.html.

The Supreme Court ruling convicting María del Pilar Hurtado and Bernardo Moreno came in Case No. 36784, dated April 28, 2015. The press release from the attorney general's office announcing charges against César Mauricio Velásquez, Edmundo del Castillo, Sergio González, and Diego Álvarez is available at "Fiscalía acusó al ex secretario jurídico y al exjefe de prensa de la Casa de Nariño por planear supuestamente desprestigio a la Corte Suprema de Justicia," Fiscalía General de La Nación, June 22, 2017, www.fiscalia.gov.co/colombia/noticias/fiscalia-acuso-al-ex-secretario-juridico -y-al-exjefe-de-prensa-de-la-casa-de-narino-por-planear-desprestigio-a-la -corte-suprema-de-justicia.

The February 2015 ruling from the Justice and Peace Tribunal of Medellín in the case of Ramiro Vanoy, in which the court ordered Uribe's investigation in connection with the El Aro massacre, is available at República de Colombia, Rama Judicial del Poder Público, Tribunal Superior de Medellín, Sala de Justicia y Paz, February 2, 2015, https://www.ramajudicial.gov.co/documents

/6342975/6634902/1.+2015.02.02+Sent_Bl_Mineros-ramiro-vanoy-murillo. pdf. The quotations from the second ruling are drawn from the same court's September 24, 2015, decision in the case of Edilberto de Jesús Cañas Chavarriaga et al., for conspiracy and other offenses. According to a legal expert interviewed for this book, the status of that ruling is currently uncertain, as, on appeal, the Supreme Court held that the ruling was unnecessary, as the Medellín court had already issued instructions for Uribe to be investigated on the same grounds in a ruling in 2013. But the Supreme Court had previously overturned the 2013 ruling on other grounds, leading to confusion about whether the instructions to investigate Uribe still stood. The Supreme Court's decision on the appeal from the 2015 ruling should, in theory, mean that the 2013 order still stands.

Former president Uribe never responded to a March 15, 2017, set of written questions for this book, which referenced Don Berna's claim that Uribe had ordered that Pedro Juan Moreno's helicopter be sabotaged, leading to his death. The same questionnaire included questions about the allegations of Mancuso and others against Uribe and against Pedro Juan Moreno, as well as about the ruling by the Justice and Peace Tribunal in Medellín, in which the court requested that Uribe be investigated for promoting paramilitary groups.

The information included in this book about the status of potential investigations against Uribe and of Uribe's lawsuits against others is based on public reports and conversations with knowledgeable people and is current to the best of the author's knowledge as of the writing of this book.

Part Opener Image Captions and Credits

Prologue, p. 1 A young woman practices juggling at the headquarters of the Youth Network of Medellín (Red Juvenil de Medellín), a pacifist organization that encourages young people to stay away from all the armed groups in the conflict. Because of their pacifist ideology, the leaders of Red Juvenil have been subject to death threats. Medellín, August 22, 2009. © Stephen Ferry.

Part I, p. 7 Paula Lance sits on the remains of the house that she and her husband were building on land that was taken from them by paramilitaries and then returned to her by court order. The day before this photograph was taken, an armed group, descended from the original paramilitaries who displaced her, knocked the frame of the house down in order to intimidate her. Curvaradó, Chocó, June 7, 2011. © Stephen Ferry.

Part II, p. 65 Hands of the bodyguard of Medellín's human rights ombudsman, Jorge Ceballos. Ceballos was the target of numerous death threats by right-wing armed groups due to his work as a human rights defender. Medellín, May 9, 2009. © Stephen Ferry.

Part III, p. 105 Salvatore Mancuso addresses paramilitary troops on a video screen during the demobilization ceremony of the Cacique Nutibara Block of the United Self-Defense Forces of Colombia, Medellín, November 25, 2003. © Stephen Ferry.

Part IV, p. 195 Juan David Díaz looks out onto the street below. He keeps the curtains drawn in his house because he and his family have been subject to threats and attacks ever since he denounced the murder of his father at the hands of paramilitaries, June 6, 2009. © Stephen Ferry.

Afterword, p. 267 A fifteen-year-old FARC combatant guards a jungle camp. Caquetá, February 6, 2000. © Stephen Ferry.

Index

Maria McFarland Sánchez-Moreno is the executive director of the Drug Policy Alliance, the leading organization in the United States advocating for an end to the war on drugs. Previously, she held several positions at the international organization Human Rights Watch, including as its senior Americas researcher, covering Colombia from 2004 to 2010, and as codirector of its US program. McFarland grew up mostly in Lima, Peru, during that country's internal war. She has written widely on drug policy and human rights issues, and is a frequent voice in the media. She lives in Brooklyn.

Photograph © 2017 George Baier IV

The Nation Institute

NATION
BOOKS

Founded in 2000, **Nation Books** has become a leading voice in American independent publishing. The imprint's mission is to tell stories that inform and empower just as they inspire or entertain readers. We publish award-winning and bestselling journalists, thought leaders, whistle-blowers, and truthtellers, and we are also committed to seeking out a new generation of emerging writers, particularly voices from under-represented communities and writers from diverse backgrounds. As a publisher with a focused list, we work closely with all our authors to ensure that their books have broad and lasting impact. With each of our books we aim to constructively affect and amplify cultural and political discourse and to engender positive social change.

Nation Books is a project of The Nation Institute, a nonprofit media center established to extend the reach of democratic ideals and strengthen the independent press. The Nation Institute is home to a dynamic range of programs: the award-winning Investigative Fund, which supports groundbreaking investigative journalism; the widely read and syndicated website TomDispatch; journalism fellowships that support and cultivate over twenty-five emerging and high-profile reporters each year; and the Victor S. Navasky Internship Program.

For more information on Nation Books and The Nation Institute, please visit:

www.nationbooks.org
www.nationinstitute.org
www.facebook.com/nationbooks.ny
Twitter: @nationbooks